A GUIDE TO
Birds

A GUIDE TO
Birds

by Karel Hudec

TREASURE PRESS

Translated by Olga and Ivan Kuthan
Illustrations by Jan Dungel and Miloš Váňa
Maps by Zdeněk Hedánek
Graphic design by Pavel Helísek
Designed and produced by Aventinum in 1990
for Treasure Press,
Michelin House, 81 Fulham Road
London SW3 6RB

Reprinted 1992

ISBN 1 85051 621 9

Printed in Czechoslovakia

3/07/19/51-02

Contents

Identifying birds in the wild

The repeated publication of new guides and atlases on European birds may seem superfluous, but such books continue to be good sellers and the best of them are regularly reprinted. This indicates not only a permanent interest in such literature on the part of readers, but also the diversity of their viewpoints or reasons for acquiring these books. One very substantial reason is the illustrations, for these capture the reader's attention and are often in line with man's aesthetic interest in birds. At all events, however, it is the text that plays the main role in determining the value and usability of such books. Ornithological literature has hitherto paid little attention to ecology and to methods of finding birds. Information of this sort is very incomplete and often even unavailable. In the endeavour to compensate to some degree for this lack, this book includes, in addition to more or less standard information, also a body of knowledge about when and how to find individual species of birds in the wild. This is of primary importance to nature lovers and novice ornithologists. It is likewise extremely important with an eye to the ever increasing scope of the systematic determination and in particular the mapping of the distribution of bird species. Every experienced field ornithologist knows that some species may be found in the wild at any time and with relative ease, others readily during the nesting period but with difficulty at other times and vice versa, and that in the case of certain species it is quite impossible to tell with certainty when they may be sighted. It is also common knowledge that information which is useful for locating a nest or a bird in central Europe need not necessarily be useful elsewhere.

For the correct and quick identification of a bird in the field, the selection of identification characters and their degree of importance is decisive. Both may naturally vary during the course of the year. The voice, for example, is a decisive identification character throughout the year for some species, but for others only during the nesting season. The same is true of coloration, be it general coloration or that of individual parts of the body, and like changes may occur also in morphological features (for example, the presence or size of a crest), even though these are the most constant.

Naturally, the selection and order of the identification characters depend on the knowledge and experience of the observer. With increasing experience the selection becomes progressively simpler, and two other factors, often decisive ones, enter the picture: habitat and period of occurrence. Whereas the period of occurrence during the course of the year is determined primarily by the geographic location of the place of observation, it is useful to take the biotope into account automatically during every observation for it greatly limits the selection of species that come into consideration for this purpose.

Size

The absolute size of each species is generally given in terms of the body length in centimetres; for some species the wingspan is also included. These are average values and it is necessary to take into account differences between individual birds, between males and females, and between adult birds and juveniles. As a rule, these differences are immaterial for observation in the field.

Far more useful than absolute values for judging the size of a bird in the field, however, are relative relationships based on comparison of the size of the given bird with that of a commonly known species.

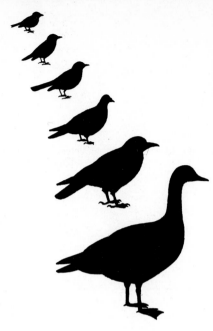

the tail, its size and the shape of the tip — whether it is forked, straight, rounded, wedge-shaped, or graduated (when the feathers are increasingly and markedly shorter from the centre towards the sides); added to this for some species is the shape of important feathers, mainly the outer feathers such as the long tail feathers of the Swallow or the lyre-shaped feathers of the Black Grouse. The shape of the wings is generally discernible only in flight. The length and width of the wing and the shape of the wing tip (pointed, rounded) should be known, sometimes also the location of the wing on the body (at the front, in the middle, farther back). As for the legs, important and well discernible in the field is first and foremost their relative length, and sometimes also whether they extend

Sizes of common species of birds. From top to bottom:
sparrow (14.5 cm), Starling (21.5 cm),
Blackbird (25 cm), pigeon (33 cm),
Rook (46 cm), goose (85 cm).

Morphology

Morphological features are frequently the best identification characters. These include the shape of the various parts of the body and their size, including their proportions in relation to the other parts of the body. Often, however, the bird's general appearance suffices for purposes of identification, or at least for determining the group to which it belongs — whether it is a duck, raptor, etc.

An important identification character is the bill, its shape and size and sometimes also its positioning in relation to the forehead, which is discernible mainly in profile. Another important character is

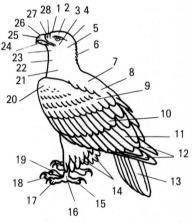

Topography of a raptor:
1 — forehead, 2 — crown, 3 — cheek,
4 — nape, 5 — ear region, 6 — hind neck,
7 — shoulders, 8 — back, 9 — median
wing-coverts, 10 — greater wing-coverts,
11 — secondaries, 12 — primaries, 13 — tail
quills, 14 — tibial feathers, 15 — hind or first
toe, 16 — tarsus, 17 — outer or fourth toe,
18 — middle or third toe, 19 — inner or second
toe, 20 — bend of the wing, 21 — fore neck,
22 — throat, 23 — chin, 24 — lower mandible,
25 — upper mandible, 26 — culmen,
27 — nostrils, 28 — cere.

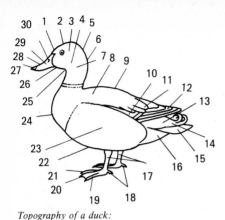

Topography of a duck:
1 — forehead, 2 — crown, 3 — ear region,
4 — cheeks, 5 — nape, 6 — hind neck,
7 — fore neck, 8 — shoulders, 9 — back,
10 — secondaries, 11 — scapulars,
12 — primaries, 13 — rump,
14 — uppertail-coverts, 15 — tail quills,
16 — undertail-coverts, 17 — tarsus, 18 — hind
toe, 19 — outer toe, 20 — middle toe, 21 — inner
toe, 22 — belly, 23 — flank, 24 — breast,
25 — throat, 26 — chin, 27 — nail, 28 — culmen,
29 — upper mandible, 30 — nostrils.

wing-coverts, etc. Other species have entirely bare patches on the body, generally covered with thicker skin or also skin lesions or protuberances.

Morphological features may differ between males and females (this is known as sexual dimorphism) as well as between adult and juvenile birds, and some even differ during the course of the year. For instance, the knob at the base of the upper mandible on the male Mute Swan is markedly enlarged only prior to and during the nesting period; at other times it is also evident but far less prominent.

For the precise identification of some species that are difficult to tell apart in the field, it is necessary to catch the bird and examine its wing formula, i. e. the relative length of the individual primaries, plus in some cases also the location of the notch in the web of a wing feather. The wing formula is best evident in the pictures alongside, for example, the individual species of warblers in this book.

beyond the tail in flight; also important is any feathering on the legs, for on some species the legs are completely feathered, on others entirely bare, while on still others the feathers form 'trousers' etc. Some species have characteristic feather ornaments on the body such as a crest, ear tufts or 'horns' on the head, extended

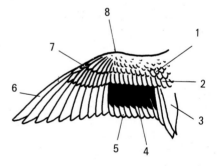

Wing of a duck:
1 — median wing-coverts, 2 — greater
wing-coverts, 3 — scapulars, 4 — speculum,
5 — secondaries, 6 — primaries, 7 — bastard
wing, 8 — bend of the wing.

Head of a raptor:
1 — forehead, 2 — crown, 3 — nape, 4 — ear
region, 5 — hind neck, 6 — cheek. 7 — gape,
8 — edges of the bill, 9 — lower mandible,
10 — tooth, 11 — upper mandible,
12 — culmen, 13 — nostrils, 14 — cere.

Coloration

The general coloration of birds is extremely varied and in only few bird species do all its members have the same external appearance. Frequently contributing to differentiation, particularly on males, is the striking coloration of some part of the body, e. g. a cap on top of the head, the chin, 'whiskers', the eye-ring, etc. Some colour feature is common to all species of certain bird groups, e. g. the speculum on the wings of dabbling ducks; another may be specific only for members of a given species, e. g. the bands on the wings of the Bohemian Waxwing. Sexual dichroism, in which generally the female is more soberly coloured than the male, is also very common among birds.

Regardless of the existence or non-existence of sexual dichroism, there is a regular change in the coloration of a bird's plumage during its lifetime. This is due to the wear and abrasion of the feathers and to their regular shedding and replacement by new ones during the process known as moulting. The moult may be either complete, when the bird changes its whole plumage, or partial, when only part of the feathering is replaced. Moult generally takes place twice a year: following nesting and prior to nesting again. The change in the colour of the plumage after moulting, however, need not be caused by the replacement of feathers but, as sometimes happens, it can come about through the gradual rubbing off of the margins, which differ in colour from the remainder of the feathers: examples are the blackening of the head in the Brambling and the loss of speckles in Starlings. A bird's plumage changes during its lifetime in a specific sequence. If the various plumages are visibly different, they also have various names and follow one another in a given order.

The coat of down is what covers the young birds when they hatch. Some are only sparsely covered with a light down, whereas others — mostly nidifugous species that are capable of feeding themselves shortly after birth — have a thick, fine, furry coat; some young birds are completely naked on hatching. The down feather (plumule) has only a very short soft tube (the quill) bearing a tuft of soft

barbs. In shape and function it is more similar to fur and has excellent insulating properties. It grows directly next to the skin. The young of divers, owls, tube-nosed swimmers and waterfowl have one and then a second coat of down, which may be (but need not necessarily be) different. The down may be species-specific, but it may also be the same in various species and groups (e. g. white, light down). In most cases it is the same in nestlings of both sexes. It lasts only a very short time and is not referred to again in this book. The juvenile plumage, that of young birds, is the first full plumage, which generally lasts until the onset of or throughout the first winter. It is usually simply coloured and resembles the plumage of the female; only in a smaller number of species does it differ according to sex. In small birds, which attain maturity in the year immediately after hatching, this juvenile plumage is replaced by the adult plumage. In large species of birds that attain full maturity only after several years (e. g. swans and eagles, which are mature only after four years), the plumage of the young increasingly resembles that of the adult after each moult. The plumage of juveniles, until they become mature, is often called immature or subadult plumage.

The adult plumage has the full specific coloration of the given species, even though it may exhibit permanent changes during the bird's lifetime (e. g. the colour grey changes almost to white in old age). There are regularly two different adult plumages a year. The nuptial (or breeding) plumage is acquired by some birds (e. g. ducks) during the pre-nesting period from autumn till spring, by others (many songbirds) not until prior to or after their arrival at the nesting grounds. The nuptial dress is typical for the given species and usually more brightly coloured, especially in males; it is acquired by a partial moult. After the nesting season the bird undergoes a complete moult and acquires the duller, winter plumage, which generally resembles the plumage of the females and juveniles. During this period, when the birds are in their winter plumage, it is sometimes difficult, or even impossible, to determine the sex and often even the age of the bird in the field.

Between the two basic moults there may sometimes be yet another moult and thus, along with transitory colouring and differences owing to age and sex, there may be great differences in the coloration of one and the same species (e. g. in the Long-tailed Duck). In a small number of species (e. g. Common Buzzard and male Ruff) there is also marked variation in the coloration of individual birds, and some species even occur in various colour forms, or phases — grey and brown as a rule, or light and dark (e. g. the Common Cuckoo, Tawny Owl, Booted Eagle); to this may be added rare colour aberrations (black — melanism, white — albinism, etc.), either complete (e. g. pure albinos) or partial (e. g. a normally coloured bird with white patches).

Most bird species form mutually discrete subspecies in the various parts of their range. These are designated in the nomenclature by a third name, e. g. *Aegithalos caudatus europaeus*. Some species have only a small number of subspecies, e. g. the Mallard has seven, the Common Pintail only two, whereas others have many, e. g. the Crested Lark has roughly 30. The subspecies differ mainly in size and/or coloration; sometimes the differences are great, but at other times only slight and indiscernible without direct comparison with a greater number of birds. In some cases a species is divided into two or more groups of subspecies; there may be a marked difference between groups, but within each group the subspecies are similar. The differences between such groups may be evident even in the field, as, for instance, in the case of the ash-grey Hooded Crows and the black Carrion Crows. These instances are mentioned in the book and the characteristics of the group are designated by the basic type. For example, the white-headed group of subspecies of the Long-tailed Tit is referred to as *caudatus,* for it includes the subspecies *Aegithalos caudatus*; and the other group with dark stripes on the head is designated as *europaeus,* for it includes the subspecies *A. c. europaeus.*

The so-called sibling species pose a problem in identification. These are birds so alike morphologically as to be practically indistinguishable, differing only in details, and in the case of some specimens making it impossible even to decide what species they belong to. Examples of such sibling species among European birds are the Treecreeper and the Short-toed Treecreeper, and the Reed Warbler and the Marsh Warbler. Identifying these species in the field, however, is often simpler than identifying them according to their morphological characteristics, for their behaviour and above all their voices are markedly different as a rule.

Voice

A bird's voice is extremely important, sometimes even crucial, for identifying it in the field. This is true in particular of the song of the largest order of birds, the perching birds or songbirds. The song is associated with the preparation by birds for nesting; above all it is intended to mark the nesting territory staked out by a given bird, and thus is heard primarily prior to and during the nesting period, from February to July. Some species sing throughout the year, even during their stay in their winter quarters. Also characteristic are various other calls or sounds, e. g. the hooting of owls, the White Stork's clapping of the bill, the alarm cries of herons, mechanical noises such as the whizzing or whistling sound made by the wings of the Common Goldeneye in flight or the 'bleating' sound caused by the vibration of the tail feathers of the Common Snipe.

Recording and describing or interpreting bird voices is difficult. Sonagrams, i. e. graphic analyses of tape recordings, are the means most often used for objective depiction. This method, however, requires a certain knowledge of how to interpret these graphic analyses and therefore it is simpler and more useful to express the sounds in concocted words. Tape recordings of these voices, now available for all species of European birds, are useful in learning to recognize bird voices. In general, however, in order to remember the voices of the individual birds it is best to see and study carefully the bird to which the unknown voice belongs.

Locomotion

Their power of flight is the most distinctive characteristic of birds, and only a few groups (e. g. penguins) have secondarily lost the ability to fly. The types of flight are many, active as well as passive. Of the active forms the most common is flapping, effected by the repeated beating of the wings in roughly the same, constant rhythm. This form of flight is generally in a direct line, though in some species it may follow a zigzag path or in others the birds rock from side to side. In gliding flight, regular beats of the wings alternate with periods when they are kept motionless and the bird is carried forward by momentum. An extreme example of this form of flight is the undulating flight of woodpeckers: with several wingbeats the bird flies upward, and in the gliding phase drifts downward along a curving path. A special kind of flight is hovering in one spot, made possible by the rapid whirring motion of the wings, usually used to aid birds in sighting prey below them; hovering is often interrupted by a rapid descent to the ground. Passive flight is flight without any motion of the spread wings, in other words gliding: the wings are outstretched and the bird regulates the direction and height of its flight by turning the primaries, bastard wing (alula), or tail. In gliding flight the birds avail themselves of rising air currents for

Types of flight and flight formations:
1 — regular flight, 2 — gliding flight,
3 — hovering flight, 4 — V-shaped flight
formation of geese, 5 — haphazard formation
of ducks, 6 — line of Eiders.

soaring, or changes in the direction and speed of the wind.

Some birds are distinctly solitary, even in flight, whereas others — generally outside the nesting season — occur in larger or even huge numbers. Their flight may be in groups with greater distances between the individual birds, or in flocks of various types. The latter are either irregular, sometimes with typical shifting of the density and sudden synchronous changes of direction (starlings), or arranged in various formations, chief of these being lines or V-formations (geese, cranes).

In some species characteristic flights form part of the courtship display. Waders, for instance, fly in circles around their nesting territory, generally to the accompaniment of wild calls, occasionally executing somersaults and abruptly lowering the elevation of their flight, giving the impression of falling, plummeting in headlong flight, etc. Some species of warblers (*Acrocephalus, Sylvia*) and pipits fly up in the air, singing as they wing their way upwards, and then return again to cover. The Serin and Greenfinch sing in a characteristic flight typified by swooping turns like those of a bat, holding their wings outstretched and changing the direction of flight with a rocking motion.

On dry land some birds (e. g. divers) move very awkwardly and with difficulty, others nimbly and adroitly, be it by walking, running or hopping. Some species are adept in all three methods, others only in walking and running, still others in only one of the three. The manner of locomotion sometimes differs even between closely related forms: the House Sparrow hops, whereas the Rock Sparrow walks.

For waterbirds, movement in water is particularly important. The usual method is swimming on the surface with the feet moving alternately backward and forward. Only in exceptional instances, e. g. during the imposing passage of the male Mute Swan, does the bird move both legs simultaneously, resulting in its gliding along the surface with a jerky motion. Running along the surface of the water accompanied by flapping of the wings generally serves as a preliminary to takeoff. This is typical of the Eurasian Coot. A common action is diving and swimming underwater, sometimes for quite a long time and distance. Movement typical of swans, dabbling ducks and even the coot when foraging for food is upending, i. e. submerging the forward part of the body and raising the rear end straight up above the surface.

In some environments birds must travel by specific means. On trees they jump between branches, climb branches, sometimes with back or head downward, hang from branches and cones, and climb tree trunks — some species (treecreepers, woodpeckers) only from the bottom up, others (the Nuthatch) from top to bottom. Birds also climb in reedbeds and similar dense vegetation, generally foot over foot up a single stem (reed warblers), but less often also by straddling between two stems (Bearded Tit).

The bird's posture at rest, the way it holds its body (upright or horizontally), the way it holds its feet or tail, all these may also be important characters in identifying the various species. The silhouettes of birds perched on poles or wires alongside roads enable one to identify the species from a distance. The silhouettes of herons are also typical, while storks may be identified in flight from afar by the way they hold their necks (below or level with the body's axis) and eagles by the wing profile viewed from the front (straight or curved).

Nesting

Nesting is a very important part of a bird's life and is also important from the viewpoint of ornithological research. A bird's range is sometimes considered to be only the regions in which the given species breeds, and that is why great attention is focused on its occurrence during the nesting period. In view of the fact that many birds are to be found in a given biotope during the nesting period but do not nest there, it is necessary to show proof of nesting by locating the nest or young nestlings that are definitely of local origin. In this case it is of utmost importance to be particularly careful not to disturb the nesting birds or destroy the habitat or the nest itself.

Nesting is accompanied by a great many manifestations that facilitate the identification of birds, though, on the other hand, the wariness of birds at this time sometimes makes it practically impossible to prove their presence. A great many species acquire a brightly coloured nuptial dress in the pre-nesting period, and pairing and the beginning of nesting are often accompanied by a striking courtship display. The construction of the nest is a process that is usually easily observed. Most birds are territorial nesters: in other words they have a specifically delimited area around the nest — the nesting territory — advertising their ownership of this area by conspicuous behaviour, mainly by various sounds, and defending it against other birds of the same species. Sometimes the territory is limited just to the immediate vicinity of the nest: for instance, in colonies of terns or gulls only as far as the female sitting on the nest can reach with the bill. From the beginning of nesting until the young leave the nest the birds are tied to the nest site; colonial nesting sites are then very conspicuous and can hardly be overlooked. The young of many species are fed all day long, and the nestlings maintain vocal communication with the parents which sometimes continues even after they have fledged.

Some species are characterised by a fixed period for nesting: large raptors and Ravens nest very early in spring. A greater number of species, however, do not begin nesting until much later, depending on the time of their arrival at the breeding grounds. Also associated with the beginning of nesting is the number of broods the birds have in a year; in the case of smaller species there may be several, e.g. the House Sparrow often has as many as five broods a year. As a rule, however, only some pairs of a species have several broods in one year. In species that do not form permanent pairs, one partner may incubate the clutch while the other begins nesting with another partner. It is necessary to distinguish, however, between multiple nesting and supplementary nesting, i.e. when the first attempt is unsuccessful and the pair nests again. Supplementary nesting often takes place even in species that normally breed only once in a year. Some species, however, do not nest again when the first clutch does not hatch, while others do so only when the first clutch has been destroyed in the early stages, e.g. at the time when the eggs are being laid.

In birds of the same species, the beginning of nesting and the number of broods they have in a year also depends on the geographic latitude and the altitude above sea level of the given locality: the higher up in the mountains and the farther north it is, the later the birds begin nesting and the fewer number of broods they have in a year.

The location of the nest is often typical for a given species, e.g. the nest holes of the Sand Martin in steep sand or clay banks, the nest of the White Stork on poles, chimneys, solitary trees and rooftops, etc. The same is true of the size, shape and material of which the nest is made. For example, the presence of the Penduline Tit in a given locality may sometimes be determined only from its characteristic nests visible in trees after the leaves have been shed. Various species, e.g. thrushes, however, build nests that are very much alike and are placed in similar sites so that they cannot be identified easily. If one comes across such a nest during the breeding season, it is usually necessary to check on the species nesting there.

Some birds use the same nest over and over again — it is permanent. Usually these are large birds such as storks and large raptors. Sometimes only the nesting grounds are permanent but the nest itself is located in a different spot every year; this applies to both larger territories (e.g. cliffs, forests) and smaller areas (e.g. the Penduline Tit often builds a new nest every year in the same tree).

A very specific identification character for the majority of species is the shape, size and coloration of the eggs. The precise identification of the eggs of many species, however, requires their comparison with similar eggs, which generally cannot be done in the wild. Furthermore, in a great many species there may be marked differences in the coloration of the eggs, be it in the ground colour or in the colour and size as well as the density of the spots. There is likewise a certain variability in the size of the eggs of all species. Therefore, when it is not possible reliably to identify a clutch and nest, then it is necessary to await the arrival of the adult bird at the nest. This holds true also when a bird sitting on a nest suddenly takes fright and flies away: first it is necessary to identify the flying bird, and only then turn to an examination of the nest.

In certain instances the entire clutch, i.e. the number of eggs, serves as a good means of identification. The number laid by some species is nearly always constant: auks regularly lay a single egg, pigeons two, gulls three, waders four. In many species, however, the number of eggs in the clutch is very variable. It must also be borne in mind that any clutch discovered need not be complete; and in the case of an exceptionally large number of eggs the possibility that several females of the same species laid their eggs in the same nest, as is common, for example, in ducks, must be considered. A further complication is mixed clutches. Apart from the social parasitism of the Cuckoo, which regularly lays its eggs in the nests of other birds, other species also sometimes do the same. This often happens on the colonial nesting grounds of ducks, or when waterfowl are restricted to the small areas suitable for breeding on islands or in narrow belts of shoreline vegetation.

The length of incubation varies, approximately from 10 to 60 days, depending on the size of the bird. Some species start incubating after the first egg is laid or during the course of laying, and others not until the clutch is complete. The young hatch accordingly, either all at one time or successively. Hatching of the young at one and the same time is the general rule in the case of nidifugous or semi-nidicolous birds, whose offspring leave the nest in the company of their parents as soon as they are dry. These nestlings sometimes remain in the vicinity of the nest, returning there every now and then (young coots), or else they are guided by the parents elsewhere, either nearby or to a more distant place (goslings and ducklings). The young of nidicolous birds, which are helpless at birth and require their parents' care, usually remain in the nest until they fledge. Sometimes they leave the nest while still unable to fly but remain in the vicinity, where they are fed by the parents

(e.g. raptors). Occasionally some disturbance may force them to abandon the nest prematurely. In quite a few species, however, the young are cared for by the parents for a certain time even after they are able to fly, until they gradually become fully independent.

Parental care may take many forms. Where birds live in pairs, both parents as a rule share the duties of both incubation and care of the young. These tasks, however, are usually not divided equally between the two. Sometimes it is only the female that incubates, either feeding herself or being fed by the male. At other times the birds take turns incubating at varying intervals. In some raptors the male hunts food and brings it to the nest, where the female portions it out to the young. When the birds have two broods, the female sometimes incubates the second clutch while the male takes over the care of the first brood (e.g. rails). Parents may also be helped in caring for the young by older offspring (e.g. Bearded Tit). Phalaropes have the roles reversed: the eggs are incubated and the young cared for only by the male, who is also more soberly coloured. In many, generally nidifugous species, however, only one partner incubates and tends the young: with ducks, for example, the males leave the nesting grounds altogether once the initial phase of the nesting period is over; in the case of geese, only the female incubates, but the male remains close by and returns to the family circle again when the young hatch. Families sometimes live quite openly (e.g. swans, diving ducks), but most live a very secluded life so that they are hard to find.

Diet

Diet, though of little importance in identifying birds, is very important in terms of bird behaviour; it directly influences a number of morphological adaptations, and is the principle indicator of the requirements of each bird species in terms of type of habitat, where the respective species can then be looked for. In the case of tree-dwelling birds, for example, it is reflected in their manner of foraging for food on branches (Great Tit on thicker branches, Blue Tit on weaker branches, Coal Tit on the underside of branches), on cones (Siskin, Redpoll), in bark and the layer of wood beneath it (treecreepers, Nuthatch), in wood inside the trunk (woodpeckers), or on the ground beneath trees (thrushes). In waterfowl it is reflected in diving (divers, diving ducks), upending (swans, dabbling ducks), climbing through reeds (rails), foraging on dry ground (plovers), plunging the bill into mud (Redshank, Curlew), hunting prey in one spot (herons), etc. These manifestations are often species-specific or characteristic for a given group, and are thus a very important aid in identifying birds.

Diurnal activity

When looking for and sometimes also identifying individual species or groups of birds, the diurnal activity of the given species may be a determining factor. Most birds are active during the daylight hours, the maximum activity being early in the morning and late in the afternoon, with the night spent resting and with a period of lowered activity at noon. A certain rhythm of this type is observed also in the lengthy summer days of northern Europe. Some species are almost solely nocturnal (owls), and their activity at night exhibits a similar rhythm. Activity changes during the course of the year, particularly in connection with the migration period. Small insectivorous birds, which are otherwise very active during the daytime, migrate by night; the same is true of waders, whose calls may be heard at dusk as they prepare to take off from their communal daytime resting places. Diurnal birds may also be active by night in the pre-nesting period — especially

when singing (nightingales, reed warblers, grasshopper warblers), or their activity extends into the evening hours. Biologically uncongenial factors, such as cold, rain, wind, or cloudy and foggy weather, have an inhibiting effect on diurnal activity. Diurnal activity is also reflected in conspicuous social behaviour, particularly in connection with common nocturnal roosting sites where birds converge in large numbers for the night, arriving very conspicuously one after another, often from far and wide (Starlings, Rooks). Some birds (sparrows, Blackbirds) are very raucous at such times.

Habitat

Habitat is an extremely important aid to identification and must be taken into consideration under all circumstances. Firstly, it is the basic type of habitat — forest, water, human habitations, etc. — that helps narrow down the selection of species to which the observed bird belongs. The ecological niches of individual species, i.e. the habitat supplying the factors necessary for the existence of a species, are, however, delimited much more closely. For example, birds that live on water may make use of the water's surface, or the muddy shoreline and bottom, or marsh vegetation, woodland birds will inhabit treetops or tree trunks, others thickets, and so on. Some species are more versatile in their use of the environment, e.g. the Great Tit, others are often restricted to a very definite type of environment, e.g. the Great Reed Warbler and Bearded Tit to reedbeds. Individual species may thus be looked for accordingly either in several types or only in a certain type of habitat. Very important in determining the presence of individual species in a given place are various changes in the environment, mainly seasonal climatic changes that govern changes in the vegetation, but also changes of a lesser degree such as the freezing of water, fall-

ing of snow, harvesting and the plough-
ing up of fields, etc.

Population density

The population density of a species is ex-
pressed by the number of individuals per
area unit. It is not constant and depends
on many factors, though first and foremost
on the quantity, distribution, and availability of food. A large quantity of food in
a limited space enables the occurrence of
a large number of individuals and their
concentration into flocks or nesting in
colonies. By contrast, a smaller quantity of
food and its wide dispersion force birds
to occupy sufficiently large territories,
primarily during the nesting season,
thereby also causing them to be widely
dispersed. The population density is likewise regulated by the character of the locality and the availability of suitable nesting sites, places of concealment, climatic
conditions, and direct persecution of
a species. The total number of individuals
belonging to a species may be mere tens
or hundreds, e.g. some cranes and large
raptors, or hundreds of thousands or mil-
lions, e.g. some small songbirds.

The total number need not be directly
evident in the wild. The chief reason is
the manner of dispersion: the species
may be characterised as being numerous
only in several places where a whole population gathers, or it may be present
everywhere, but not in large numbers.
The manner of dispersal generally
changes during the course of the year:
birds that nest in colonies may be dispersed throughout a large area and live
by themselves in the non-breeding period
(e.g. seabirds) and, by contrast, birds that
nest singly may congregate in a small
number of places outside the nesting period (e. g. geese). A lot also depends on the
character of the land and the birds' way
of life: some species keep to environments where they are difficult to see, or
they are very shy, or else they lead a secretive way of life, do not call, and therefore can be located in the field only with
great difficulty.

Annual periodicity of occurrence

As a result of Europe's geographical location, there are annual changes in the occurrence of birds throughout the entire
continent. Some species are resident, but
most are migratory and journey for the
winter to regions with a more congenial
climate. A third group is the dispersive
birds which outside the nesting season
roam the countryside but usually not far
from the nesting grounds. Some migratory species travel only a short distance
for the winter; the region along the Baltic
coast, for example, serves as winter quarters for some species that nest farther
north. The regular wintering grounds of
a greater number of species, however, are
located in western and southern Europe,
and many species leave Europe altogether for the winter. Besides nesting resident species that are found there throughout the year, and nesting migratory species that depart for the winter, everywhere one will also find, to a greater or
lesser degree, non-nesting species, either
wintering, passing through, or occurring
during the nesting period but without
nesting. The nature of their presence is
extraordinarily diverse, from regular annual, more or less numerous occurrence
to the rare occurrence of an individual
bird discovered after decades. Every district may simultaneously contain birds of
various categories, e.g. in Great Britain
the resident population of Starlings is
augmented in winter by migratory Starlings from northeastern Europe; or populations of one and the same species may
interchange, as in the case of Rooks in
central Europe, whence birds that nest
there depart for the winter and are replaced by wintering populations from
northeastern Europe. If a species is resident in one region and migratory in another, then it is a partially migratory spe-

cies. The circumstances of a species being migratory or resident in various parts of Europe are thus very complex and differ from place to place.

Similarly, in smaller territorial units there are also differences in the time of the arrival and departure of species not present there throughout the year. The times depend on the location of the site and vary according to the particular conditions in any given year. This book gives the average times for each species. The general range of the arrival and departure periods is very broad: from February until June in the first instance, and from July until November in the case of departures. For species that arrive in early spring and depart late in the autumn, the specific dates of arrival and departure vary much more markedly each year than for species that arrive late and depart early.

How, where and when to look for birds

The way to go about locating birds depends on a person's experience and on the purpose of his or her quest. For the beginner, it is best gradually to become acquainted with the birds found in the immediate neighbourhood. Necessary equipment consists of suitable binoculars (ones with 7—10× magnification will suffice), a basic bird guide and a notebook. Listening to tape recordings of bird voices is a good idea, but identifying the voice by one's own observation of a bird is a much better way of remembering it. The company of an experienced ornithologist is also excellent. The first step in getting to know birds is to become acquainted with the species that are most common in each type of habitat and throughout the year. This will make it possible to acquire knowledge about the basic species, including their bionomy (way of life), and about the average local conditions, including seasonal changes.

The next step is the deliberate looking up of ornithologically interesting localities noted for the concentrated occurrence of various species. Here it is advisable to join forces with another person. Unless birdwatching is to remain a mere hobby, then it is recommended to contact and become a member of an ornithological society and successively participate in local or regional research programmes. Systematic observation and determination of the occurrence of birds will make it possible not only to perfect one's knowledge of the environment and its bird population, but also gradually to become acquainted with most local species. Recording the occurrence of birds and then after a time working up this material will not only give a picture of the birds' presence in a given territory, but will furthermore become valuable material primarily from the viewpoint of the protection of the environment. The ultimate stages of these investigations are systematic large-scale projects such as the all-European mapping of bird distribution during the nesting period, regular quantitative research, mapping of bird distribution in winter, etc. Naturally it is not at all difficult then to find other suitable problems for one's own work, but a good knowledge of birds and their reliable identification are a necessary prerequisite.

To be able to apply and deepen one's acquired knowledge it is most useful to participate in the mapping of nesting birds, done nowadays by most European countries. Each country is imaginarily divided into squares of a certain area and in each a detailed study is made of the species occurring there during the breeding season. This grid map may be obtained from the organisers of the project, along with instructions mainly on how to proceed in determining the occurrence of nesting birds — i.e. from merely observing a certain species during the nesting period to locating the nest containing the nestlings, or finding young newly fledged birds nearby. In mapping the breeding distribution of birds it is important not only to determine the birds' presence during the nesting period but also to prove that they have nested. For one's own work it is best to become acquainted in detail with the mapped square. It is necessary to determine what types of habitats, with different avifauna, are to be found within the given area: e.g. the various vegetation zones, the extent of woodlands and the various types of woodland, farm country (pastureland, fields, meadows), human habitations of varied size, water courses and bodies of water, various different elements in the environment such as cliffs, quarries or brickworks, and so on. A useful additional aid is geobotanical maps, vegetation maps, etc. Organisers will probably also be able to provide a list of species on which the presence of a species and degree of proof of nesting can then be recorded. The more experienced observer may preliminarily mark those species on the list that he or she can expect to find and plan the course and extent of the necessary field work accordingly.

Optimum knowledge of the nesting avifauna of a given square will require about ten field trips between the end of winter and end of summer (February — September), most of them of course during the main nesting period (April — June). At least two field trips should be devoted to nocturnal birds.

The best time for field observation is from sunrise until noon, when the majority of birds are most active and are also most vocal. Nocturnal species must naturally be observed at night. During such nocturnal observations one may sometimes also hear the voices of diurnal species that are otherwise less conspicuous in the daytime, e.g. the night song of the Nightingale, which can be heard for miles, the song of the Grasshopper Warbler, or the voice of the Stone-curlew. Outside the nesting season it is also useful to make observations in the evening, when birds gather at roosting sites and when they also call more often. It is necessary to observe the occurrence of birds over a longer period, even if one is on the lookout only for nesting species. Most conspicuous behaviour connected with nesting, such as song, flights above the bird's territory, and courtship displays, takes place shortly after the birds' arrival or at the beginning of nesting; during nesting itself the birds' behaviour is often less conspicuous. It should also be remembered that some species nest early in spring, and for that reason one should keep an eye out for the voices of owls and the territorial flights of raptors as early as the end of winter. Other bird species, though these are fewer in number, nest in the autumn or even in winter (e.g. crossbills when cones are ripe), in other words completely outside the main nesting period of the majority of species. Some species arrive at the nesting grounds very late; either such a late arrival is the rule for them, or else they have come from a region or locality where their earlier attempt to nest was unsuccessful. Locating young newly fledged birds is usually easiest at the end of the nesting period, when they fly about in the neighbourhood and communicate vocally with their parents.

The above information is the result of many years of observing a wide variety of bird species. Naturally it by no means covers all the aspects of field work, but for a start it will serve quite well as a guide and a basis for one's own observations and conclusions.

Importance and protection of birds

Birds are a permanent and important part of man's environment, and man's attitude to these fellow inhabitants has been and continues to be varied and diverse. The original attitude was naturally one that viewed birds as a source of food, which continues to this day in the economic utilisation of some species and their products. Another economic aspect is the damage caused by birds in certain spheres of human activity. The number of economically important bird species is limited. Most bird species are of growing cultural importance to man, mainly in terms of aesthetics, in the pleasure derived from watching them and listening to their songs. For many people interest in birds gradually shifts to the scientific sphere, where a mere enjoyable hobby turns into the collecting of scientifically valuable material. That is why ornithology has become an important part of biology, especially in the branches of ecology and ethology.

The results of these studies are nowadays used to a great degree in bioindication, i.e. the evaluation of the effect of current changes in the landscape on living organisms, and in the study of the ways organisms react to these changes. Regional studies of birds, above all in connection with quantitative indicators, are therefore used nowadays to determine the degree of disruption of the natural environment and the importance of individual sites from the viewpoint of the conservation of nature's biodiversity and genetic fund.

It is a well-known fact that the present deterioration of the total natural environment the world over brings with it also a deterioration in the conditions for the existence of many bird species. The International Union for Conservation of Nature and Natural Resources (IUCN) therefore compiled the Red Data Book of endangered organisms, including birds. The present book uses the 1981 evaluations made by the British ornithologists John Parslow and Michael Everett, who divide birds according to degree of endangerment into the following categories:

Endangered species — species in danger of extinction in Europe whose survival is unlikely if the causal factors continue to operate.

Vulnerable species — species which are likely to move into the endangered category if the causal factors continue to operate.

Rare species — species with small, often very localised populations, possibly at risk, but not at present considered endangered or vulnerable.

Red Lists and Red Data Books are continually put together and elaborated for smaller areas. Whereas the Red List contains merely a list of endangered species, the Red Data Book contains more detailed information, mainly concerning ways and means of protecting these birds. Besides Red Lists and Red Data Books, the protection and possible economic utilisation of birds is governed by game law and relevant decrees of every nation. The study of the conditions and possibilities of protecting endangered species is one of the basic tasks of contemporary ornithology, and applying this information in practice is the fundamental task for the protection of birds. The possibilities for the individual in bird protection are often restricted only to the minimum (putting out nestboxes, feeding birds in winter, educating the public). More effective habitat protection depends in greater part or entirely on state or private organisations, and it is necessary to support their efforts in every possible way. Information about these organisations may generally be obtained from the national sections of the International Council for Bird Protection (ICBP).

For active protection, particularly when putting out nestboxes and feeding birds in winter, it is necessary to consider the purpose and results of the measures taken. There is no point in excessively fostering species whose numbers increase by natural means and which, when there are too many of them, cause various different problems (pigeons in cities, etc.). Far more important, therefore, even from the viewpoint of the protection of birds, is ecologically based regional protection and general efforts to improve the environment, e.g. development of greenery in housing estates, and similar schemes.

System used in this book

The information contained in the following four sections will help the reader in looking for and identifying birds in all of Europe, from Iceland in the north to the

Urals and Caspian Sea in the east, and to Asia Minor and northern Africa in the south. It is deliberately designed and arranged as explicitly and comprehensibly as possible so as to serve the birdwatcher rapidly and reliably in the field. These sections contain detailed information on 241 bird species, accompanied by colour photographs and small illustrations. The first section deals with birds whose way of life is tied to water; the second with birds of prey that possess a downcurved beak and talons — raptors and owls; the third is devoted to songbirds — small and medium-sized birds with like structure of the vocal apparatus; and the fourth section includes birds specifically adapted to living on cliffs, in forests and on steppes.

At the beginning of each section the various groups of birds are briefly characterised by comparison with a commonly known species, which in appearance, behaviour and way of life is the embodiment of the type of birds in the respective group. Information on each individual species is then arranged in a particular sequence in subject areas, with abbreviations for facilitating orientation in the text.

As the word identification itself indicates, the section thus headed contains information from which it is possible to identify the species to which the observed bird belongs, as well as its age and sex. The various identification characters are arranged in order of their importance, starting with the most important. The habitat is mentioned only when it is narrowly limited, explicitly specific, and the given species is hardly ever to be found in another type of habitat. Heading the list of basic characters ($*$) is size. Absolute size is given by the length of the body in centimetres, in some cases also by the wingspan, and relative size by comparison with a common known species or in general terms such as small, large or medium-sized; the difference between male and female is given only when it is very pronounced. Information pertaining to appearance and coloration is limited to general appearance, characters apparent

in flight, and the most important features of the various plumages, with the months when the birds occur in the respective plumage given in parentheses. Where no specific note is made of sexual differences, the description applies to both sexes. Information on behaviour ($\leftarrow$) takes note of the most important, typical and most frequent observable forms of behaviour. The paragraph on vocal expressions ($\odot$) notes the typical sounds that are most often heard. Bird voices are described by verbal transcription and in some cases by comparison with common sounds. Great attention should be paid to the similarity of a given species to other species ($\circledcirc$).

Information on the ecology and bionomy of the respective birds serves to supplement that on the identification characters also contributing to the determination of a species' occurrence with regard to time and place. The section devoted to ecology is immensely important because it includes essential information on the environment of each bird species and on the possibilities or ways of orientation in the field when looking for the birds. Specified under $\diamondsuit$ is the habitat of the given species during the breeding and the non-breeding seasons. The terms used to describe the various elevations are lowland (up to 200 m above sea level), hilly country (ca 200—600 m above sea level), submontane (from ca 600 m to the lower mountain forest limit), mountain forest belt, mountain dwarf pine belt, subalpine belt (alpine grasslands), alpine belt (rocks above the forest limit), and high alpine belt (region of permanent snow and ice). The type of environment they inhabit is of necessity the starting point in looking for and observing adult birds, nests, or newly fledged young birds, and the information to this end may be found under the symbol ∞.

The section on bionomy contains basic information on the way of life of the respective species. Under $\leftrightarrow$ it tells whether the species is resident, migratory or dispersive, and when it can be found at its nesting grounds. The wintering grounds can be readily found on the respective map, where they are demarcated by a thin line. Often the wintering grounds are located outside the boundaries of the map (mainly in a southerly direction), and sometimes so are the nesting grounds in part: in both instances their location is indicated by arrows. The nesting grounds of the respective species are marked black on the maps. Under ω the reader will find information on where the nest is sited, its shape and size, and the material of which it is made, the number of eggs in the clutch and their size and coloration, the time of nesting and number of broods in a year, and which of the pair incubates and for how long. If only one of the sexes incubates this is noted; otherwise the birds take turns. Also stated is the manner in which the parents tend their young and how long it takes for the young to be fully grown (to fledge) or to be fully independent. All the values are to be taken as a guide, since there is often marked variation. The information on ◑ lists only the most important food items and describes the manner in which they are obtained.

The concluding paragraph deals with the most important aspects pertaining to the conservation, where necessary, of the respective species; its degree of endangerment, and its economic utilization.

Key to abbreviations and symbols

* ∗ — basic identification characters
* ✚ — behaviour
* ⊙ — voice and other sounds made
* ℗ — similar species
* ∞ — how to look for and find the birds
* ↔ — migration
* ◆ — habitat
* ⋈ — nesting
* ◑ — diet, feeding
* **Adult** — adult bird
* **Juv.** — juvenile bird
* ♂ — male
* ♀ — female
* **ssp.** — subspecies
* > — bigger than
* < — smaller than

Waterbirds

Water is a very diverse environment with plentiful supply and wide variety of food, and thus one will find here a large number of birds with various adaptations of body structure enabling them to make the most of the wide variety of foods available.

Diving birds that dive to hunt their food underwater are typified by the Black-throated Diver (1). They are generally to be seen swimming about with body sitting low in the water. Sometimes they remain underwater for a long time, coming up again far from the spot where they submerged.

Birds that forage for food while swimming are characterised by the Mallard (2). They can be seen well on the water, feeding on the surface or obtaining food by upending, some species also by diving.

Many waterbirds keep a lookout for food in or on the water while flying above the surface. These are typified by the Black-headed Gull (3). They can be observed well in flight, alighting on the water's surface to take their prey or else plunging headlong into the water in plummeting flight.

Birds that forage for food by waiting motionless or wading in shallow water are typified by the Little Egret (4). They are generally larger birds, with long legs, long neck and long bill. As a rule they keep to open water and can be seen well; some species spend much of their time hidden from view by the edge of reedbeds or in thickets.

Birds that forage for food on muddy shores are characterised by the Greenshank (5). They generally walk, run or patter about on the mud or in shallow water, often in flocks, and frequently fly from one spot to another. Species that keep mainly to dry land usually have short legs and a short bill. As a rule they frequent open shores and can be seen from afar; but they may also, though less frequently, move about hidden from sight amidst dense reedbeds (rails).

1

Black-throated Diver
Gavia arctica

Identification Appearance — behaviour — voice — coloration
∗: Bigger than the Mallard (65 cm). When swimming, the long body is held very low. It has a long neck, small head, and rather long straight bill (3). Adult birds in nuptial plumage (Mar.—July) have the front of the neck and the back coloured black with white spots and stripes; ♂ = ♀. Juv. and adult birds in non-breeding plumage (July—Mar.) are a rather uniform dark grey, with white underparts. Fig. 1 shows intermediate plumage. ✦: It generally swims on the water's surface, dives often and remains submerged for a long time. When taking off, it first patters along the water; the flight is rapid and straight (2). ☉: Outside nesting grounds it occasionally utters a deep, plaintive call; during the courtship display it also makes laughing and barking sounds. ♋: Mainly the Red-throated Diver (*G. stellata* — 5), which nests fairly commonly in northern Europe and winters in western, central and southern Europe. The Great Northern Diver (*G. immer* — 4) is scarce and winters in the north of Europe. The White-billed Diver (*G. adamsii* — 6) winters sporadically in the more northerly parts of Europe.
Ecology ◈: Remote deep lakes; in the non-breeding period sea coasts, less often inland bodies of water. ∞: Scan the water's surface at the nesting grounds; listen for the voice. The nest may be located by spotting incubating birds or by examining the shoreline. The young are guided about and fed by the parents on the water.

Bionomy ↔: It is migratory and is found at the nesting grounds in Apr.—Sept. In the non-breeding period it occurs singly or in smaller, loose groups. ♥: The nest, a haphazard cluster of leaves, grasses, etc., is sited right on the water's edge, mostly on islets. The two brown eggs (84.2×51.6 mm), sparsely speckled black-brown, are laid in Apr.—June. It has one brood a year, nests solitarily, and incubates for 28 days. The young soon leave the nest and are guided about on the water by both parents; they fledge after 60 days. ◐: Mainly small fish, caught underwater.
Conservation It is numerous and not imminently endangered. It is, however, very vulnerable to disturbance at the breeding grounds, and under no circumstances should the nests of any diver species be approached.

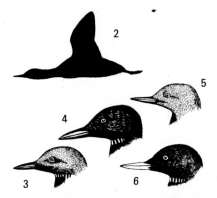

2

5

4

3   6

1

Little Grebe
Tachybaptus ruficollis

Identification Habitat — voice — appearance
— behaviour
∗: The smallest grebe (27 cm). The body is
rounded, with narrow neck and small head. In
breeding plumage (Mar.—Sept.) the birds are
dark brown-black with reddish-brown head; the
corners of the bill are yellow-green (1). ♂ = ♀.
The non-breeding and juvenile plumages
(June—Mar.) are brown and greyish-white. ✦:
It swims on water, diving continually; often
hides in vegetation. It flies only rarely. ☉: At
the nesting grounds it often utters a conspicuous piercing trill, *bibibibi* . . . ✆: In non-breeding plumage it slightly resembles the Black-
necked Grebe (2), which, however, is bigger,
with longer neck and more contrasting coloration.
Ecology ◈: At lower elevations it inhabits water of various kinds, including small ponds in
parks. ∞: At the nesting grounds listen for the
voice (Apr.—Aug.) and scan the water for quite
some time during the period when the young
are fed on the water (May—Aug.). In winter
the birds may be found on ice-free lakes and
water courses. The nest may be located by
searching from a distance through the vegetation at the nesting grounds (the similar nest of
the Black-necked Grebe has larger eggs).
Bionomy ↔: It is partly migratory and is found
at the nesting grounds in Mar.—Oct. In the
non-breeding period it occurs singly, as well as
in groups. ✿: The nest is usually located amidst
vegetation close to the water's surface. It is
a cone-shaped floating structure of rotting
plants with a shallow hollow. The four to six

white eggs (37.1×25.9 mm), which gradually
turn brown, are laid in Apr.—Aug. It has one
to three broods a year, nests solitarily and incubates for 19 days. Both parents tend the young,
which swim immediately; they fledge after 56
days. ◑: Aquatic insects and their larvae,
caught underwater.
Conservation It is declining in some areas, but
special protection is not necessary.

2

Great Crested Grebe
Podiceps cristatus

Identification Habitat — appearance — voice — behaviour

✳: The largest grebe (48 cm, wingspan 88 cm). In breeding plumage (1) there are two pointed feather 'horns' on the head, and the cheeks are strikingly patterned in white, reddish-brown and black. In non-breeding plumage there is merely an indication of the 'horns' and the head is dark grey and white. Adults are brownish-black above, with gleaming white underparts. ♀ < ♂ and duller in colour. The nestlings in their downy plumage have a striking contrasting pattern on the head (3 — Great Crested Grebe, 4 — Black-necked Grebe, 5 — Red-necked Grebe, 6 — Little Grebe). Juv. birds (May—Oct.) have the cheeks and sides of the neck longitudinally striped greyish-brown. ✦: It swims on open water, diving frequently. The body sits very low in the water, with the neck often erect. In flight the body is fully extended; the wings are pointed (2). It sleeps on the water, with head laid on the back and pointing forward. It flies infrequently, at a low height, with rapid, regular wingbeats. ☉: At the nesting grounds its loud trumpeting call, *irr kurrr-arr*, is often heard, even at night; during courtship a repeated *kök-kök*... During the feeding period the nestlings make loud piping sounds almost without cease. ♋: The Red-necked Grebe (p. 30) is slightly smaller but has a shorter and thicker neck, and in all plumages has a darker neck and breast.

Ecology ◆: Larger, shallow bodies of water with marsh vegetation; in the non-breeding period also rivers and the sea coasts. ∞: Scan the surface of water; during the nesting period may also be located by its voice. The nest may be located by scanning the vegetation at the nesting grounds; sometimes the nest is sited on open water. The young are fed on the water, uttering their cries incessantly.

Bionomy ↔: It is mostly migratory and is found at the nesting grounds in Feb.—Oct.; in the non-breeding period it occurs singly, as well as in groups. ᴥ: The nest is generally sited by the edge of vegetation on the water, either solitarily or in colonies numbering a greater number of pairs. It is a floating mass of rotting vegetation with a shallow hollow. The three to six eggs (55.3×37.3 mm), coloured white but gradually turning brownish and thick-shelled, are laid in Apr.—Aug. The birds have one to two broods a year and incubate for 27 days. The young swim on hatching. They are cared for by both parents, even being carried about on their backs for six weeks, and fledge after 70 days. ◖: Small fish, aquatic insects and their larvae, caught by the birds underwater.

Conservation It may cause damage in fish hatchery ponds. No special protection is required. It is a numerous species whose numbers are on the increase in some areas.

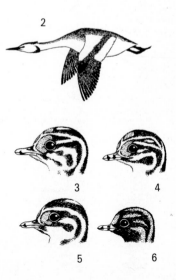

1

2

3　　4

5　　6

29

1

Red-necked Grebe
Podiceps grisegena

Identification Habitat — appearance — coloration — voice

✳: The same size as the Great Crested Grebe (48 cm). The head is large, with a slight crest on the hindneck; the neck is short and thick. In breeding plumage (1) (Mar.—Sept.) the cheeks are white and the foreneck and breast reddish-brown; in non-breeding plumage the foreneck and breast are pale greyish-white. ♂ = ♀. In juv. plumage (June—Oct.) the neck is pale reddish and the sides of the head are striped reddish-brown. The base of the bill is always yellow. ✦: It swims mostly on the surface, often diving. It flies infrequently, in a straight line and rapidly, with rapid wingbeats. ☉: During the nesting period it often utters a loud, neighing *ööö*. The young incessantly make piping *bibibi*... calls. ☜: The Great Crested Grebe (p. 29) has a longer and more slender neck, a gleaming white breast and a pink bill.

Ecology ◈: Large shallow bodies of water thickly overgrown with vegetation; in the non-breeding season also larger rivers and the sea coast. ∞: Scan the water's surface; during the nesting period (May—July) it may also be located by its voice. The young are fed on the water and utter their cries continually. NB: Young newly fledged birds that have not yet acquired adult plumage leave the nesting site and roam widely (from July); therefore their presence does not necessarily mean that the birds have nested in the given spot. The nest may be found by scanning through the vegetation at the nesting grounds.

Bionomy ↔: It is migratory and is found at the nesting grounds in Mar.—Sept. In the non-breeding period it generally occurs singly. ☙: The nest is generally sited in vegetation, close to the water's surface; it is a pile of rotting vegetation with a shallow hollow. The four to five white eggs (51.0×34.2 mm), which gradually turn brownish, are laid in May—July. It has one to two broods a year and incubates solitarily for 22 days. The young are cared for by both parents. They can swim on hatching and are carried about on the parents' backs and fed by them for 60 days. ◖: Small fish, large insects and their larvae, caught underwater.

Conservation A declining species. We do not know the reasons for its decline or how it should be protected; in any case it is necessary to protect the nests.

1

Black-necked Grebe
Podiceps nigricollis

Identification Appearance — size — coloration — behaviour

⚹: A smaller grebe (31 cm). The head is large, the neck long, the body short and rounded. In breeding plumage (1) (Mar.—Sept.) the upperparts are almost black, the belly white, the eyes red, and behind the eyes there are golden-yellow ear tufts; ♂ = ♀. In non-breeding and juvenile plumages the upperparts are blackish-brown, and the underparts, including the throat, white. ✦: It generally swims on the surface, diving frequently; its movements are very quick, jerky. It flies infrequently, in a straight line and rapidly. ⊙: Infrequent soft whistling notes. ♋: Mainly the Slavonian Grebe (*P. auritus*), in non-breeding plumage (2), which nests in northern Europe, winters in western and southern Europe and is not very numerous.

Ecology ◈: Shallow larger bodies of water with marsh vegetation; in the non-breeding season it is also found on open water and along the coast. ∞: Scan the water's surface alongside vegetation; in the non-breeding season also away from vegetation. Look for the nest in shoreline vegetation. The young may be seen being guided about and fed by the parents on open water close to the nesting site.

Bionomy ↔: It is migratory and is found at the nesting grounds in Apr.—Aug. In the non-breeding season it generally occurs in groups. ♒: It usually nests in colonies, less often also solitarily. The nest is a floating, cone-shaped pile of rotting vegetation, often in colonies of Black-headed Gulls. The three to five white eggs (43.7×30.0 mm), which gradually turn brownish, are laid in Apr.—July. It has one, sometimes two broods a year and incubates for 21 days. The young can swim on hatching and are cared for by both parents, often being carried about on their backs; they probably become independent after 21 days. ◕: Small aquatic invertebrates.

Conservation It is currently on the decline. Realistic means of conservation other than protection of the nesting grounds are not known.

2

1

Fulmar
Fulmarus glacialis

Identification Appearance — behaviour — coloration

✻: Slightly larger than the Black-headed Gull (46 cm, wingspan 1.1 m). It has a stocky body, short strong bill, thick neck, short straight tail and long, broad wings located in the middle of the body. The pale form, which is the more common (1, 2), is white, with back and upperwings light brown; the dark form is uniformly grey, including the head. ♂ = ♀ = juv.

✦: When swimming, the bird rides high in the water. It is continually on the wing, in gliding flight with wings held stiff and motionless, close above the water, often in the wake of ships. It occurs on dry land only during the nesting season. ☉: In flocks it often utters a hoarse *ög ög ög orrrr*, a muffled *crau* or *kar*. ☞: Large albatrosses that rarely visit Europe's shores, chiefly the Black-browed Albatross (*Diomedea melanophris*). Other common species of the Procellariidae family are dark, mainly on the upperside (e. g. the Manx Shearwater, *Puffinus puffinus* — 3).

Ecology ◈: High seas; the nesting grounds are on islands and coastal cliffs. ∞: Investigate concentrations of birds at sea; visually scan cliffs. In the non-breeding season keep a lookout for birds close to the surface of the sea.

Bionomy ↔: In the non-breeding season the birds are dispersed over the Atlantic Ocean. It occurs at the nesting grounds in May—Sept. ♒: The nest is on bare rock. The one to two eggs, white but gradually turning yellowish or speckled (74.0×50.5 mm), are laid in May—June. The Fulmar has one brood a year, nests in colonies that are sometimes enormous, and incubates for 50 days. Both parents tend the young, which remain in the nest 55 days. ◑: Pelagic animals, food remnants and offal gathered from the surface in flight or while swimming.

Conservation Assuring that the birds remain undisturbed at their nesting grounds is protection enough. Their number is on the increase and their range is expanding.

2

3

1

Storm Petrel
Hydrobates pelagicus

Identification Size — behaviour — appearance — coloration
∗: A small bird (15 cm, wingspan 35 cm) with round head, small bill, slender wings that are angled in flight, and a short, straight-tipped tail. Adults (1) are uniformly black-brown, with a white band in the middle of the inner under-wing adjoining the body and a white rump; the legs are black; ♂ = ♀. Juv. birds have a variable pale bar on upperwing (2). ✦: When swimming, it rides high in the water with head held upright and wings extending beyond the tail. In flight, it hovers close above the water with legs dangling as if walking upon the water (2). It often flies behind ships. ⊙: At sea it is silent; at the nesting grounds it makes a purring sound that ends with a resounding *hikav*. ➰: Other similarly coloured but larger Hydrobatidae are Leach's Petrel (*Oceanodroma leucorhoa*), occurring regularly in west Europe in Apr.—Oct.; and Wilson's Petrel (*Oceanites oceanicus*), which may be seen in Europe very occasionally in Aug.—Dec.

Ecology ◈: High seas; during the nesting period islands and sea coasts. ∞: Observations at sea; nesting sites may be located by the birds' nocturnal activity (they fly to the nesting sites by night and utter loud cries).

Bionomy ↔: In the non-breeding season the birds are dispersed over the high seas. It occurs at the nesting grounds in Apr.—Oct. ♡: The nest is in rock crevices or in burrows. The single white egg (27.7×21.3 mm) with ring of dark brown spots is laid in May—July. It nests once a year in colonies and incubates for 38 days. The nestling is cared for by both parents and remains in the nest 60 days. ●: Small pelagic animals, gathered from the surface in flight.

Conservation No special protection is required other than protecting the nesting grounds.

2

1

Northern Gannet
Sula bassana

Identification Habitat — size — appearance — behaviour
∗: The same size as the Greylag Goose (91 cm, wingspan 1.7 m). It has a large head with a long, strong bill, a long body with shorter wedge-shaped tail, long pointed wings, and short legs. The adult (2) is white, with a yelowish head and neck and black-tipped wings; ♂ = ♀. Juv. birds (from June) are dark brown, gradually (2nd—4th year) turning white. (1) ✦: It swims with head and tail held upright and dives well. It flies with slow wingbeats interspersed with gliding flight, close above the water, with bill pointing towards the surface when hunting prey; to catch food, it plummets headlong into the water with wings pressed close to the body (3). It hunts prey by itself, but there is always a great number of birds at the hunting grounds. ☉: At the nesting site it often utters barking and deep growling sounds such as *ärrah, kirra kirra*, and the like. ☞: It is unmistakable.
Ecology ◈: High seas; nesting colonies are located on rocky sea coasts, primarily on uninhabited rocky islands. Stray birds may occur inland after storms. ∞: Scan the space above water's surface. Observe the nesting sites from the water: they are readily located by the regular occurrence of large numbers of birds in the vicinity which fly to the colony from various directions.
Bionomy ↔: It winters on the high seas in the Atlantic, less often in the Mediterranean. It occurs at the nesting grounds in Jan.—Oct. ᴗ: The nests are located on island slopes and

on the ledges of steep cliffs. The one (two) bluish, thick-shelled egg (78.5×49.8 mm) is laid in Mar.—June. It breeds once a year and incubates for 44 days. The nestlings are tended by both parents and remain in the nest for 56 days. ◐: Sea fish caught by diving underwater.
Conservation Until recently this was a declining species, but currently its numbers are on the increase. Protection of the nesting grounds is apparently sufficient.

2

3

1

Eurasian White Pelican
Pelecanus onocrotalus

Identification Size — appearance — coloration — behaviour

⚹: One of the largest European birds (160 cm, wingspan 3.5 m). It has a huge bill with a leathery pouch, long neck, and short body, tail and legs. The feathers on the forehead extend into a point at the base of the bill (4). Adults (1) are white, tinged with pink; ♂ = ♀. Juv. birds are brown, gradually (2nd—3rd year) becoming white. ✦: It swims riding high in the water (2) with head drawn back. It flies with slow, regular wingbeats, its head laid on the back (3), and from time to time glides. ☉: At the nesting grounds it makes low, grumbling sounds. ☙: The same localities are inhabited by the very similar Dalmatian Pelican (*P. crispus*); its plumage is tinged with grey and the feathers on the forehead join the bill in a straight line (5).

Ecology ◈: Large lowland swamps and lakes with plentiful supply of fish; in the non-breeding season also the sea coast. ∞: The nesting site may be pinpointed by the permanent presence of birds, by their regular flights over the given spot, and by searching the area. In the non-breeding season the birds may be found by scanning the water or when they fly from place to place.

Bionomy ↔: It is migratory and is found at the nesting grounds in Mar.—Sept. In the non-breeding season it generally occurs in groups, less often alone. ☺: The nest is a floating pile of old vegetation. The two white eggs (94.0×59.0 mm) are laid in Apr.—June. It nests in colonies, has one brood a year, and incubates for 33 days. The young soon swim around the nest, are cared for by both parents, and fledge after 75 days. ●: Fish, which it scoops up into the pouch. When hunting, the birds form a long line that slowly advances, forcing the fish into the shallows.

Conservation This is an endangered, declining species; locally it causes damage in fish farms. It is essential to preserve sufficiently extensive wetlands and provide protection so that the birds are not disturbed at the nesting grounds.

4

5

2

3

Cormorant
Phalacrocorax carbo

Identification Size — appearance — coloration — behaviour
∗: The size of the Greylag Goose (91 cm, wingspan 1.3 m). The head is small and narrows into a long, thick bill. In breeding plumage (Oct.—July), birds of the ssp. *P.c. carbo* (found on the Atlantic coast) have a dark-coloured head except for the white chin and cheeks, and birds of the ssp. *P.c. sinensis* (from central, southern and eastern Europe) have the feathers on the crown, hindneck and sides of the neck mostly white (some adults of the ssp. *carbo*, however, are sometimes similarly coloured). In non-breeding plumage the head of both subspecies is dark. Juv. birds (1) are brown above, white below; some individuals have a brown belly. ✦: When swimming, it rides low in the water with neck outstretched and bill slanting upward (2). It dives frequently. It rests upright on rocks, stumps and trees in water and on muddy shores, often drying its partly spread wings (3). It frequently hunts fish in groups, but often solitarily. At night it roosts gregariously on trees. ☉: At the nesting grounds it utters its guttural *gok*, when returning to the nest a repeated *gok gok go gogogok* and other sounds. ♋: The Shag (*P. aristotelis* — 4) is very similar.
Ecology ◈: Large bodies of water rich in fish. ∞: Observe birds that are swimming, resting and drying their feathers or flying overhead. The nesting sites may be located by the regular occurrence of birds and the direction in which they fly to their nests. (NB: In the evening the birds fly to their roosting sites.) The nests, birds incubating on the nests as well as larger juvenile birds are readily visible at the site. Throughout the nesting period, non-breeding birds may be encountered outside the nesting grounds.
Bionomy ↔: It is migratory in the north and dispersive elsewhere, and is found at the nesting grounds in Mar.—Sept. In the non-breeding season it occurs in groups as a rule, but often solitarily. ☙: It generally nests in colonies. Birds of the ssp. *sinensis* nest in trees, occasionally also in reedbeds; birds of the ssp. *carbo* nest on rocks or cliffs. The nests are large (50—60 cm across) and made of strong twigs. The one to four eggs (63.0×39.4 mm), pale blue and thick-shelled, are laid in Mar.—May. It has one brood a year and incubates for 23 days. The young are tended by both parents and after a short time clamber around the nest. They fledge after 50 days but are fed for a further 50 days. ◗: Smaller fish caught underwater.
Conservation Where local populations are declining in number, consistent protection of the nesting grounds is a must.

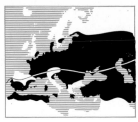

1

Eurasian Bittern
Botaurus stellaris

Identification Habitat — voice — appearance — behaviour

✻: This medium-sized member of the heron family (75 cm) has a long straight bill, rather short stout neck, short tail and legs, and broad, rounded wings. The adult (1) is streaked yellow-brown, paler on the underside; ♂ = ♀. Juv. birds are paler, with darker brown streaks and less conspicuous whiskers. ✦: It lives a solitary life concealed in reedbeds, occasionally flying close above the reeds with slow regular wing-beats to another site. It stands motionless in shallow water or amidst vegetation. When alarmed, it stretches its neck vertically and sways slowly in time with the reeds. ⊙: Heard often during the nesting period, mainly at night; ♂ utters a loud, booming *oop-woomp*, repeated at intervals of several seconds. ♋: The very similar American Bittern (*B. lentiginosus*) of North America occurs very rarely in western Europe.

Ecology ◀▶: Throughout the year it inhabits large old reedbeds. ∞: During the nesting season it may be identified by its voice, but this does not necessarily mean that the bird nests in the given spot. In the non-breeding season it may be located by chance sighting or by flushing.

Bionomy ↔: It is partially migratory and dispersive, and is found at the nesting grounds mainly in Mar.—Sept. ϖ: The nest of dry reeds is located in reedbeds close to the water's surface in a thick clump of vegetation. The four to six olive-brown eggs (53.0×38.5 mm) are laid in Apr.—July. It has one brood a year and usually one mate, though sometimes it is polygamous; ♀ incubates for 24 days. The young are cared for only by ♀; they soon disperse in the vicinity of the nest and fledge after 56 days. ◐: Smaller aquatic animals, caught, by waiting motionless, in shallow water or on the surface.

Conservation It has greatly decreased in number in recent years. The reasons for the decline and realistic means of protection are not clarified; total protection is necessary, as also is preservation of wetlands and protection from disturbance at nesting grounds.

1

Little Bittern
Ixobrychus minutus

Identification Habitat — size — appearance — voice — behaviour

✳: This smallest member of the heron family (35 cm) is smaller than a crow. It has a large head, with a long, straight bill, and a thick neck. The adult ♂ (2) is buff and black with a large pale wing patch; the ♀ is a duller, darker brown. Juv. birds (Jul.—Oct.) are buff-brown with dark longitudinal streaks (1). ✦: It lives hidden in marsh vegetation, quite often flying about close above it. It perches on reed stalks or branches close to the water's surface. ☉: During the nesting period its muffled but far-reaching croaking cry *vup*, uttered at regular brief intervals, is often heard, both day and night. ♋: It is unmistakable.

Ecology ◈: Marsh vegetation, mainly reedbeds and shrubby willows. ∞: During the nesting period it can be located by its voice and by lengthier observation of the vegetation from a good vantage point. When looking for nests, search the vegetation thoroughly: the sitting bird will fly up when you come near. The nest is characterised by its size, appearance, as well as the clutch. In the non-breeding season, the birds can be located only by chance.

Bionomy ↔: It is migratory and is found at the nesting grounds in Apr.—Sept. In the non-breeding season it is a solitary bird. ♡: The nest, located close above the water in reeds or thickets, is about 20 cm across and made of old reed stalks laid from the centre outward. The four to seven white eggs (35.2×25.9 mm) are laid in May—July. It has one brood a year, nests solitarily, though sometimes there may be several nests close together, and incubates for 18 days. The young are tended by both parents, dispersing in the vicinity from the seventh day and fledging after 22 days. ◐: Aquatic insects and their larvae, caught, by waiting motionless, at the water's surface.

Conservation The reasons for its decline are not known, and realistic means of protection other than preserving old reedbeds are not clear.

2 ♂

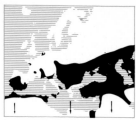

1

Black-crowned Night Heron
Nycticorax nycticorax

Identification Habitat — appearance — voice — behaviour

✳: This is a small heron (61 cm) with a short neck and legs. The adult ♂ (1) is black, grey and white, with long white nape plumes; the ♀ is duller, with shorter plumes. Juv. birds (June—Jan.) are very different: brown spotted with white, and streaked dark below. ✦: It perches on low branches closest to the water or at the edge of reedbeds. It flies at a low height, slowly and with slow, leisurely wingbeats. It roams the countryside in the vicinity of the nesting site, chiefly at twilight and daybreak. ☉: In flight and at the nesting grounds it often utters a loud, muffled *kvak, kvak-kvak,* and similar calls. ♋: It is unmistakable.

Ecology ◈: Wetlands at lower elevations. ∞: Nesting grounds can probably be located by the birds' regular occurrence and their flights out into the neighbourhood and back, mainly in the evening and morning. The presence of the birds during the nesting period need not be proof of their nesting. During the non-breeding season, the Night Heron may be observed and heard also by smaller bodies of water or as it flies from place to place.

Bionomy ↔: It is migratory and is found at the nesting grounds in Mar.—Sept. In the non-breeding season it occurs singly or in small groups. ౿: The nest is located in colonies in sites surrounded by water — on trees, in thickets or in reedbeds; it is a haphazard structure of twigs and stalks. The two pale blue eggs (49.7×35.6 mm) are laid in Apr.—July. It has one brood a year; the birds in the colony do not nest all at the same time but at staggered intervals. Incubation takes 22 days. The young are tended by both parents, disperse in the vicinity from the 20th day and become independent after 42 days. ◑: Smaller fish and aquatic invertebrates, caught, by waiting motionless, at the water's surface.

Conservation It is locally numerous, though its numbers fluctuate. It is necessary to protect the nesting grounds.

1

Little Egret
Egretta garzetta

Identification Appearance — size — behaviour ✳: This is a small member of the heron family (60 cm). It has a long, straight bill, long slender neck, short tail, and relatively long legs. Adults are snow-white, the bill and legs are black, and in the breeding plumage (Nov.—July) have elongated plumes on the hindneck (1); ♂ = ♀. Juv. birds lack the elongated plumes. ✦: It stands at or in the water in mud, on shrubs, in reeds, and walks slowly in shallow water. It flies slowly with regular wingbeats, interspersed with brief glides, with the head drawn backward and the legs extending beyond the tail. It often occurs in the company of other herons. ☉: Its call, a croaking *rrä* or *karrk*, etc., is heard fairly often but only at the nesting grounds. ♋: Mainly the Great White Heron (*E. alba*), regularly found locally in southern and central Europe. Also found in these parts are similar smaller species: the Squacco Heron (*Ardeola ralloides*) and the Cattle Egret (*Bubulcus ibis*).

Ecology ◈: Large swamps at lower elevations. ∞: The nesting grounds may be pinpointed by the regular occurrence of the birds; individual pairs often nest together with other herons. It is necessary to scan the colony and locate the birds. In the non-breeding season this egret may be found by water of various types.

Bionomy ↔: It is migratory and is found at the nesting grounds in Apr.—Sept. In the non-breeding season it is frequently solitary. When fully grown (July—Sept.), the young roam the neighbourhood in all directions. ♡: The nest is located in trees, shrubs, occasionally reeds, meas-

ures about 33 cm across, and is constructed of long, thin stalks. The four to five greenish-blue eggs (46.4×33.56 mm) are laid in Apr.—July. It has one brood a year and incubates for 22 days. The young are tended by both parents and climb out of the nest at the age of 30 days; they fledge when 40 days old. ◖: Smaller aquatic animals, caught by waiting motionless, near the surface.

Conservation It is essential to ensure that nesting grounds and wetland habitats are protected.

Grey Heron
Ardea cinerea

Identification Appearance — size — voice
✻: The largest European heron (91 cm, wingspan 1.4 m), bigger than a goose. It has a long, slender head and bill, long neck, and long legs. The plumage of adults (1) is grey, white and black, with a conspicuous black band above the eye extending into elongated feathers on the nape. ♂ = ♀. Juv. birds (June—Jan.) are more uniformly grey, with the nape feathers shorter. ✦: It stands motionless (2) at the edge of water, in shallow water, as well as in mowed fields, occasionally walking about slowly. It also perches on the branches of trees. Its flight is leisurely, with regular slow wingbeats; it also glides occasionally, mainly when landing. In flight the neck is drawn back on to the back in an S shape, and the legs extend far beyond the tail (3). ☉: It frequently utters a loud, deep, harsh *krau*. In the presence of the adults the young birds in the nest continually cry *kakaka....* ♋: It is unmistakable.
Ecology ◆: Wetland habitats and wooded districts with water, from lowland to submontane elevations. In the non-breeding season it also flies over areas without water. ∞: The birds do not hide and can be readily observed in the appropriate habitats. Nesting colonies may be pinpointed by the regular occurrence of the birds and the direction of their flights throughout the day during the nesting period (Mar.—July). Large colonies are permanent and the nests conspicuous (4). Solitary nests are difficult to find, the best clues being the cries of the young when they are being fed. NB: Non-breeding birds are often present during the nesting period.
Bionomy ↔: It is resident or migratory and is found at the nesting grounds in Feb.—Aug. It may be seen throughout the year both singly and in groups. Fully grown young birds disperse over the countryside in all directions in July—Sept. ♡: It nests in colonies sometimes numbering hundreds of pairs, but some pairs also nest solitarily. The nest is located in treetops, occasionally in reeds; it is made of twigs and measures about 75 cm across. The nests in

colonies are permanent and are refurbished each year by the birds before nesting. The two to five pale blue-green eggs (60.5×43.1 mm) are laid in Mar.—July. It has one brood a year and incubates for 26 days. The young are tended by both parents. From the 20th day they clamber over the branches around the nest; they remain in the nest for 50 days. ◉: Small fish, larger insects, frogs, voles. The birds hunt by waiting motionless, watching the water's surface, or in fields beside mammal holes and in other suitable spots.
Conservation This is a very numerous species locally, but its numbers often fluctuate. Occasionally it causes damage in small fish hatchery pools. In areas where its numbers are declining, legislative protection and effective protection of the nesting grounds are required.

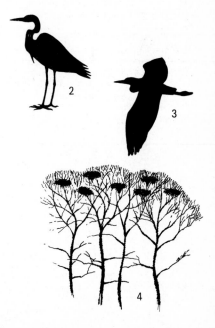

1

1

Purple Heron
Ardea purpurea

Identification Appearance — coloration — size
✳: This is a large (85 cm, wingspan 1.3 m),
slender heron with a long straight bill, long
neck and long legs. Adults (1) are dark reddish-
brown with grey upperparts; ♂ = ♀. Juv. birds
(June—Jan.) are a dull brown, without contrasting black markings on the head. ✦: It skulks in
reeds or stands at the edge of shallow water, occasionally walking about leisurely; rarely it
perches on trees. The flight is slow, with regular wingbeats; occasionally it glides briefly.
☉: In flight it utters a short hoarse *kreek*, and
when landing on the nest *korr*; the begging call
of the young in the nest is *kekeke*... ☺: The
Grey Heron (p. 43) has broader wings in flight,
with more widely spread primaries.
Ecology ◈: Swamps and larger shallow bodies
of water with extensive reedbeds, at lower elevations. ∞: The nesting grounds may be pinpointed by the frequent flights of the adult
birds over the site and their dropping down out
of sight at the given spot; when disturbed, the
adults fly up and circle above the nests. Away
from the nesting grounds, the birds may be
found by chance observations.
Bionomy ↔: It is migratory and is found at the
nesting grounds in Mar.—Aug.; in the non-
breeding season it leads a solitary existence. ♡:
It generally nests in smaller colonies; occasionally individual pairs nest solitarily. The location
of the nesting sites changes. The relatively large
nest, built of reed stalks, is placed amidst reeds
or in bushes close above the water. The four to
six pale greenish-blue eggs (56.3×40.7 mm) are
laid in Apr.—June. It has one brood a year and

incubates for 26 days. The young are cared for
by both parents. After 10 days they leave the
nest, and fledge after 50 days. When they have
fledged (July—Sept.), they disperse in all directions. ◖: Small fish, aquatic insects and their
larvae, which it catches, by waiting motionless,
at the water's surface.
Conservation A rather scarce species, apparently declining in numbers. It is essential to enact legislation for year-round protection, ensure
that the birds are not disturbed at the nesting
grounds, and preserve old reedbeds and vegetation.

1

Black Stork
Ciconia nigra

Identification Size — appearance — coloration — behaviour

∗: Slightly smaller than the White Stork (97 cm, wingspan 1.5 m), to which it exhibits a marked resemblance in shape. Adults (1) are glossy black with white belly; the bill and legs are red. ♂ = ♀. Juv. birds (July—Jan.) are dull blackish-brown, with pale markings on head and breast, white below and with green bill and legs. ✦: It stands in or by the edge of shallow water, walks about slowly, and often perches on branches and in treetops. It flies with outstretched neck and regulaɪ wingbeats, gliding often and for long stretches; the neck and head are held below the level of the back (3). ☉: Very occasionally it makes hissing and other sounds at the nesting grounds. ☯: In flight and from a distance the White Stork (2), which is, however, entirely white except for the rear and outer parts of the wings and in flight holds the head and neck level with the back.

Ecology ◆: Old forest stands near water, from lowland to mountain districts. ∞: It may be located at the nesting grounds by its regular occurrence there, but it often roams far from the nest and, furthermore, individual birds as well as pairs that have not nested may be found in the given locality. Finding a new nest is difficult: as a rule it is located by accidentally passing by and flushing the adult birds; if you find a nest in winter on a leafless tree, check the nest in the summer. In the non-breeding season, the Black Stork is usually seen only when encountered by chance.

Bionomy ↔: It is migratory and is found at the nesting grounds in Mar.—Sept. Away from the nesting grounds, it occurs singly or in small groups. ♡: The nest, located in an old tree, sometimes also on a cliff, is a permanent structure; it is made of twigs and measures about 1 m across. The three to five white eggs (65.4×48.8 mm) are laid in Apr.—May. It has one brood a year, nests solitarily and incubates for 36 days. ◑: Smaller fish, frogs and larger insects, which it watches for and catches in the water.

Conservation A vulnerable species, but one which is increasing in number and expanding its range. Locally it causes damage in trout streams. It is necessary to provide it with total protection and to ensure freedom from disturbance around the nests.

2

3

1

White Stork
Ciconia ciconia

Identification Size — appearance — coloration — behaviour

∗: A large bird (110 cm, wingspan 1.6 m) with a small head, long straight bill, long neck and legs, and long, broad wings. Adults (1) are white with black-tipped wings, the bill and legs being red; ♂ = ♀. Juv. birds (June—Jan.) are black, tinged with brown, and have a blackish-brown bill. ✦: It stands by water, in meadows and in fields, walks slowly, and perches on trees, rooftops, haystacks, chimneys. It flies slowly with outstretched neck, alternating wing-beats with lengthy gliding, and soars in circles. ⊙: At the nest it often claps its bill continually. ☺: In flight it resembles the Black Stork (p. 45); the latter, however, is entirely black except for the belly and in flight holds the head and neck below the level of the back.

Ecology ◈: Lowland to submontane districts with wetlands and water in the vicinity of the nesting grounds; it often forages for food in fields and meadows. In the non-breeding season it inhabits steppes and savannas. ∞: It may be seen when flying from one place to another. The nest is generally unconcealed and visible from a distance; as a rule one of the adults is beside it. NB: Individual birds or pairs may linger by the nest without nesting. In the non-breeding season it may be encountered by chance when foraging for food.

Bionomy ↔: It is migratory and is found at the nesting grounds in Mar.—Aug. Non-breeding birds and birds in the non-breeding season generally occur in groups or large flocks. ᴗ: The nest is a large (about 1 m across), permanent structure of twigs, situated on buildings, chimneys, electricity poles or on trees. The three to five white eggs (72.8×52.9 mm) are laid in Apr.—May. It has one brood a year, nesting solitarily as well as in small colonies, and incubates for 34 days. The young are tended by both parents and remain in the nest for 60 days. ◑: Frogs and other small vertebrates, large insects, caught by waiting motionless in shallows, by water, in fields.

Conservation A vulnerable species, generally on the decline. Locally numerous, but its numbers are decreasing and its range is diminishing; however, it is recolonising some places within its range. Partial aid consists in providing foundations for the nests, but no other means of conservation are known at present.

1

Spoonbill
Platalea leucorodia

Identification Size — appearance — behaviour
∗: Smaller than the stork (85 cm, wingspan
1.4 m), it has long legs, a long neck, and a flattened bill dilated at the tip into a spoon shape.
Adults are white throughout the year, with
black legs and bill; in breeding plumage they
have an area of yellow at the base of the neck
and a yellowish crest (1); ♂ = ♀. Juv. birds are
white with black-tipped wings (2), and have
a pinkish-brown bill and legs. ✦: It stands in
shallows, and sleeps with neck and head laid on
the back. It wades along in shallow water,
swinging its partly immersed bill from side to
side. It flies in a straight line with rapid wingbeats and neck and legs extended (2). ☉: Its
deep hoarse notes and occasional bill-clapping
may be heard only at the nesting grounds. ☜:
The Great White Heron (*Egretta alba*) occurs
in similar localities; its bill, however, is different in shape.
Ecology ◈: Extensive swamp vegetation and
shallow waters in lowland districts. ∞: The
nesting grounds may be located by the birds' regular occurrence and flights over the area; the
birds stay near the nests, which may be found
by scanning through the reeds. In summer,
non-breeding birds may also be seen away from
colonies. During the non-breeding season, look
out for Spoonbills also on smaller bodies of
water.
Bionomy ↔: It is migratory and is found at the
nesting grounds in Mar.—Aug. During the
non-breeding season it occurs singly or in small
groups. ᴥ: The nest, made of twigs and reed
stalks, is located in reeds, rarely in bushes or

trees. The three to six white eggs, speckled
rusty-brown (67.2×45.5 mm), are laid in
Apr.—June. The birds nest in colonies, rarely
solitarily, have one brood a year and incubate
for 25 days. The young are tended by both parents and remain in the nest 42 days. When fully
grown, they roam in all directions. ◖: Small invertebrates sieved through the bill from the
water and mud.
Conservation A vulnerable, declining species. It
is essential to protect its wetland environment
and ensure that it is undisturbed at the nesting
grounds.

2

1

**Greater or
Roseate Flamingo**
Phoenicopterus ruber

Identification Size — appearance — behaviour
✳: A large bird (132 cm, wingspan 1.5 m) with
a small head, characteristic, massive, down-
curved bill, and extremely long neck and legs.
Adults (1 — at right, taller bird) are white with
a pinkish tinge of varying intensity, and have
red legs; ♂ = ♀. Juv. birds have a greyish-
brown head, neck and back; they do not attain
the full adult coloration until the 3rd-4th year.
✦: It stands in shallow water, foraging for food
with the head or just the bill immersed in the
water and continually swinging the bill from
side to side. Its flight is slow, with regular wingbeats (2). ☉: At the nesting grounds it utters
a cackling *vrruk* and a long-drawn-out *kraau*; in
flight a loud trumpeting call. ♋: It is unmistakable. Specimens that have escaped from captivity are occasionally seen in Europe: the Carib-
bean Flamingo (*P. ruber ruber* — 1 at left),
which is brighter pink and has an orange, white
and black bill, and the Chilean Flamingo (*P.
chilensis*), which has grey legs with pink joints.
Ecology ◈: Shallow salt water, both on the sea
coast and at inland lakes; when roaming, it may
also be seen by freshwater lakes. ∞: The few
nesting colonies in Europe are well known and
are characterised by a large concentration of
birds. In the non-breeding season it may be encountered only by chance.
Bionomy ↔: It is resident as well as migratory,
and is found at the nesting grounds in
Mar.-Oct. ♈: The nest is a flattened cone of
mud and bits of vegetation located in shallow
water. The one to three yellow-green, thick-
shelled eggs (90.0×54.5 mm) are laid in May. It

nests in colonies, has one brood a year, and incubates for 32 days. The young remain in the
nest a mere four days, afterwards wandering in
the vicinity; they fledge only after several
months. ◐: Small animals and plants gathered
by dabbling in the shallow water and mud.
Conservation A vulnerable species and rare in
the non-breeding season. It is essential to provide total protective legislation and ensure that
it is not disturbed at the nesting grounds.

2

1

Whooper Swan
Cygnus cygnus

Identification Appearance — size — behaviour — voice

✳: The same size as the Mute Swan (150 cm, wingspan 2.3 m). It has a long neck, and the bill has no basal knob. Adults (1) are white, with a black and yellow bill; the yellow forms a wedge narrowing from the base of the bill to the nostrils (2). ♂ = ♀. Juv. birds are greyish-brown, gradually (2nd-3rd year) turning white. ✦: Mostly it swims on the water with neck held erect, perpendicular to the water's surface. It flies with neck extended and wings moving slowly and regularly; the wingbeats produce a loud whistling note. ☉: A sonorous, trombone-like *an-ghe* is quite often heard, and at the nesting grounds also makes other sounds. ☞: North-western Europe is the wintering ground of the very similar but smaller Bewick's Swan (*C. columbianus* — 3). Distributed throughout Europe is the Mute Swan (p. 51), which has an orange bill with a black knob, a curved neck, and is far less vocal.

Ecology ◈: Shallow large bodies of water bordered with reedbeds, from lowland to high elevations. In the non-breeding season it occurs also on rivers, by the sea coast, etc. ∞: It can be seen on open water. The nest is not very concealed, and families with young chicks do not hide either.

Bionomy ↔: It is migratory and is found at the nesting grounds in Apr.—Aug. It occurs in pairs and family groups, and non-breeding birds also in flocks. ꙍ: The nest is a large heap of vegetation located in reeds. The two to seven yellowish-white eggs (112.5×72.6 mm) are laid in Apr.—June. It has one brood a year and incubates for 70 days. The young leave the nest on hatching, are cared for by both parents, and fledge at the age of two months. ◑: Almost exclusively plants, which it plucks on the water or beneath the surface.

Conservation Following a long-term decline, its numbers are slightly on the increase. Protective legislation is sufficient, and active measures are not considered necessary.

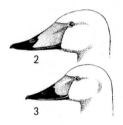

2

3

Mute Swan
Cygnus olor

Identification Appearance — coloration — behaviour

✳: A large bird (150 cm, wingspan 2.3 m) with a long neck, small head and stout bill. Adults are white; ♂ (1) is larger than ♀, and in the breeding season the knob at the base of his bill is more prominent. Juv. birds are greyish-brown, gradually becoming white over three years. ✦: Mostly it swims on water, ♂ often with partly raised wings, with the neck curved in an S shape (3). It climbs out on the shore with a swaying gait. It forages for food by submerging the head and upending. This swan flies relatively low, with outstretched neck (2) and regular wingbeats, the wings producing a deep, rhythmic throbbing sound. ☉: Occasionally it makes deep snorting, grunting and hissing sounds; the young keep up a continual piping. ♋: The Whooper Swan (4), found in the same localities, has a yellow and black bill, holds the neck erect, and has a resounding call. There is a close resemblance between it and the smaller Bewick's Swan (*C. columbianus* — 5), which winters in northwestern Europe.

Ecology ◈: Still or slow-flowing waters with a large surface expanse, rich in aquatic vegetation and with extensive reedbeds. On migration and in winter, it occurs chiefly on the sea coast, rivers and lakes. ∞: It can be seen without difficulty on open water. The nest is not particularly concealed, whether among reeds, on an islet or on the shore. ♂ usually keeps watch close by on the water. Families with chicks swim about on the open water at the nesting site. NB: Small chicks sometimes conceal themselves amongst the feathers on their parents' backs.

Bionomy ↔: It is resident or partly migratory, and is found at the nesting grounds in Mar.—Oct. During the past decades its numbers have increased markedly in Europe and it has expanded its range. It generally occurs in pairs or family groups, with non-breeding birds also in large flocks. ♥: The nest is a large mass of vegetation located on a bank or islet or in reeds; the surrounding reed stalks are nipped

out. It is bordered with down feathers. The two to twelve greenish-grey eggs (112.5×73.5 mm) are laid in Mar.—April. It has one brood a year; mostly ♀ incubates for 35 days. The chicks are grey (white in the form known as 'Polish' Swan). When they have dried, they leave the nest, are tended by both parents, and fledge after 4 ¹/₂ months. ◕: Soft aquatic plants; also various remnants floating on the water and on the shore.

Conservation It is often kept on small lakes for ornament. The great increase in its numbers poses problems in places with large concentrations; it is thus not recommended to promote their increase by feeding them excessively. In Britain, however, numbers have recently decreased greatly, largely through poisoning from anglers' discarded lead weights.

6

Identification Voice — appearance — behaviour — coloration

✳: A medium-sized goose (75 cm, wingspan 1.6 m) with the typical goose appearance: stout bill, long neck, plump body, short tail and legs, and broad, pointed wings. Adults (1) are dark greyish-brown; the bill is black and yellow, sometimes with some white at the base. ♂ = ♀. Juv. birds are duller. Subspecies differ mainly in the shape and coloration of the bill. Three are distinguishable in the wild: *A. f. fabalis* of northern Europe is larger, has a longer bill with a broad yellow band in the middle (2), and wings not extending beyond the tail when folded; *A. f. rossicus* of northeastern Europe is smaller, squatter, the wings extend beyond the tail when folded, and the bill is short and deep, slanting, with a narrow yellow band in the middle (3); *A. f. serrirostris,* which inhabits the Asian tundra and has a conspicuously elongate, slender bill (4). ✦: It swims well, and sleeps on the water or on the shore. It feeds in fields and grassy areas. It often flies in lines and V formations (6); when landing the formations break up and the birds descend with sharp loops and turns. In the non-breeding season they make regular morning and evening flights to and from the spot where they congregate to feed. ☉: Often heard, particularly in flight, is its loud honking *kayak-kayak.* ♋: The White-fronted Goose (p. 54), which is, however, smaller, has a white patch on the forehead, and has a different call. In western Europe in Oct.—Mar. one may encounter the Pink-footed Goose (*A. brachyrhynchus* — 5), which in Britain is much the commoner species.

Ecology ◈: It nests in the vicinity of water in the taiga and tundra; in the non-breeding season it may be seen in open areas (pastures, fields) near water. ∞: At the nesting grounds watch for the flights of birds overhead; the nest may be pinpointed by the behaviour of the birds and by searching the area. In the non-breeding season the birds may be found on water in the vicinity of their feeding grounds; they are best counted when they take off in the evening or on their return in the morning.

Bionomy ↔: It is migratory and is found at the nesting grounds in Mar.—Sept. The places where they congregate and the number of birds that gather there differ markedly during the course of the year, as well as over the years. In the non-breeding season the birds occur in family groups, as well as in flocks, often numbering thousands of geese. ♨: The nest is a shallow depression in the ground lined with down. The four to six dingy white eggs (84.0×55.9 mm) are laid in May—June. The birds nest solitarily, have one brood a year, and ♀ incubates for 28 days. The young leave the nest on hatching, are tended by both parents, and fledge after 50 days. ◖: Green vegetable matter obtained by grazing.

Conservation This is an important game bird, but hunting needs to be regulated. Where large numbers congregate, it may cause damage by grazing up young crops.

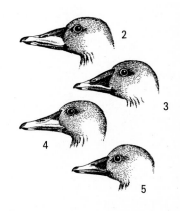

2

3

4

5

1

White-fronted Goose
Anser albifrons

Identification Voice — appearance — coloration — behaviour

✳: This is a smaller species of goose (71 cm). It is greyish-brown, the tail white with a black band just before the tip; adults (1) have a conspicuous white patch on the forehead and dark markings on the belly; ♂ = ♀. Juv. birds lack the white patch and the belly is without markings or with only a few. In Europe there are two subspecies: *A. a. flavirostris,* with a yellow bill, breeds in Greenland and winters in Ireland, west Scotland and west Wales; the Eurasian *A. a. albifrons,* with a pink bill, winters in the rest of Britain and Europe. ✦: It generally swims on water, where it also rests; it feeds on open tracts of land. It flies with regular wingbeats, often in lines and V formations. ☉: A far-carrying high-pitched *lyo-lyok,* often uttered in flight. ♋: The Bean Goose (p. 53) and Greylag Goose (p. 55) are larger, lack the white forehead patch, and their voice is different. Found in eastern Europe, but in very small numbers, is the Lesser White-fronted Goose (*A. erythropus* — 2).

Ecology ◈: It nests in swampy tundra above the forest limit; in the non-breeding season, it occurs on the sea coast and in open country with fields, pastures and meadows close to water. ∞: At the nesting grounds it can be found by its flights over the site and its behaviour; the nest can be discovered by walking about in the area. In the non-breeding season it generally occurs together with other geese, on the Continent mainly the Bean Goose, at traditional sites where the birds congregate.

Bionomy ↔: It is migratory and is found at the nesting grounds in Apr.—Sept. In the non-breeding season it generally forms flocks, whose numbers vary. ᴗ: The nest is a shallow depression in the ground lined with down. The four to six dingy white eggs (79.0×53.3 mm) are laid in May—June. It has one brood a year and nests solitarily; ♀ incubates for 28 days. The young leave the nest on hatching, are cared for by both parents, and fledge after 50 days. ◖: Green parts of plants and seeds obtained by grazing.

Conservation This is an important game bird. It is essential to make rational use of individual populations, including regulation of hunting.

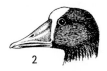

2

1

Greylag Goose
Anser anser

Identification Voice — appearance — coloration — behaviour
✳: This is a large goose (80 cm, wingspan 1.6 m) with a stout bill. It is pale greyish-brown, the upperwing appearing very pale in flight, the tail white with a broad black band just before the tip, and the bill is orange-yellow to pink. Adults have pale underparts vermiculated dark brown (1); ♂ = ♀ = juv. birds. ✦: It swims on water, bathes and upends, and rests on the shore (even some distance from water) or in shallow water. It flies with slow, regular wingbeats, in larger numbers in lines and V formations. It feeds in fields and pastures. ☉: It often utters loud calls similar to those of the farmyard goose — *gagaga*... etc. ☜: Most similar are the Bean Goose (p. 53), which is, however, smaller, generally darker, and has a black bill with yellow band, and the Pink-footed Goose (*A. brachyrhynchus*), which has a small bill with pink markings. Both species have different multisyllabic calls.
Ecology ◈: Shallow overgrown waters, sea coasts; in the non-breeding season, open country by water. ∞: At the nesting grounds, the birds may be detected from the time of their arrival in spring by their flights over the site and by their voice; the nest may be discovered by exploring suitable spots (♀ will fly up only when approached closely). In the non-breeding season it is conspicuous by its flights in the vicinity of the site where the birds congregate.
Bionomy ↔: It is migratory and is found at the nesting grounds in Feb.—Aug. After the young have fledged, it forms large flocks. ᴗ: The nest,

a mound of vegetation lined with down, is located on the ground, among vegetation, or in a tree. The two to ten whitish eggs (85.8×58.4 mm) are laid in Mar.—May. It has one brood a year; ♀ incubates for 28 days. The young are cared for by both parents outside the nest and fledge after 55 days. ◐: Green parts of plants and plant seeds obtained by grazing.
Conservation This is an important game bird. Where birds congregate in large numbers, farmers complain that they graze young crops and cereals. It is necessary to protect the nesting grounds and ensure that hunting is regulated wisely.

1

Canada Goose
Branta canadensis

Identification Appearance — coloration — voice — behaviour

✳: Markedly larger than the Greylag Goose (105 cm), and with a long neck and stout body. The neck and head are black, with a white half-moon across the throat (1). ♂ = ♀. Juv. birds are duller, browner. ✦: It swims in water, up-ends, feeds in open places, and regularly roams to graze in the vicinity of the nesting grounds and sites where the birds congregate. It flies with regular, slow wingbeats, in larger numbers in lines and V formations. ☉: It often gives a loud honking *aa-honk*, etc. ♋: It is unmistakable.

Ecology ◈: Bodies of water with vegetation and islets, mostly in open country with fields, pastures and meadows in the vicinity. In the non-breeding season it also occurs on the sea coast. ∞: The nesting grounds may be pinpointed by the constant occurrence of the birds and their flights over the area and to the immediate surroundings; often the nest is not particularly concealed. In the non-breeding season, the Canada Goose may be seen by chance or at sites where the birds congregate.

Bionomy ↔: It is dispersive and partly migratory; in the non-breeding season it generally forms flocks, only rarely occurring singly. ᴗ: The nest, a mound of plant material lined with down, is located in vegetation on the water or on the shore. The five to seven whitish eggs (86.0×56.2 mm) are laid in Mar.—May. It has one brood a year, nesting solitarily or several pairs together and incubating for 28 days. The young are tended by both parents outside the nest; they fledge after 45 days. ◐: The green parts and seeds of plants, obtained by grazing.

Conservation It was successfully introduced into Europe from North America. In northern Europe it is numerous and is continually expanding its range. European populations are not as yet hunted for sport; endangered populations or those beginning to establish themselves require protection both at and away from the nesting grounds.

1

Barnacle Goose
Branta leucopsis

Identification Appearance — coloration — behaviour — voice
✳: This is a small goose (63 cm) with a short, thick neck and a small bill. The crown, neck and breast are very dark, and the cheeks and forehead are white (1); in flight the white belly stands out in sharp contrast to the black-brown breast. ♂ = ♀. Juv. birds (June—Jan.) are more grey-brown, with grey markings also on the white cheeks. ✦: It swims well, and rests on dry land. It flies rapidly, with regular wing-beats, in flocks. It grazes on open tracts of land. ☉: It often utters a repeated short rhythmic *knak knak*... ☻: It is unmistakable.

Ecology ◆: During the nesting season, the arctic tundra and rocky upland plateaux near water; in the non-breeding season, sea coasts and very occasionally inland waters. ∞: The nesting grounds, as well as the grounds where the birds congregate in the non-breeding season, are locally circumscribed and well known. It is not difficult to determine the birds' presence.

Bionomy ↔: It is migratory and is found at the nesting grounds in Apr.—Sept. ᗑ: The nest is a small mound of grass lined with down on a cliff face or on the ground among stones. The four to five yellow-tinged whitish eggs (76.7×50.2 mm) are laid in May—June. It has one brood a year, nests in colonies, and incubates for 25 days. The young are cared for by both parents. They leave the nest as soon as they hatch, and fledge after 49 days. ◑: Green parts of plants and occasionally also plant seeds, obtained by grazing.

Conservation It is sporadic in occurrence; following a marked decline, its numbers are currently increasing. Until recently it was in the category of vulnerable species. Rational protection at the nesting and wintering grounds has proved sufficient, although it remains a necessity for the future.

1

Brent Goose
Branta bernicla

Identification Appearance — coloration — behaviour — voice

✳: The size of the Barnacle Goose (60 cm) and with the typical goose appearance. The bill is short, the head, neck and breast brownish-black, the upperwings dark with a black rear edge and wingtips, and the tail white with a dark terminal band (1). Within its western breeding range it occurs in two subspecies: *B. b. bernicla* of northern Europe has a black-brown belly, and *B. b. hrota* of Spitsbergen and Greenland has a grey-white belly. Adults of both subspecies have a white band on either side of the neck; ♂ = ♀. Juv. birds (July—Nov.) lack the white band on the neck and their wings have pale bars on the upper surface. ✚: It swims well, often resting on dry land. It flies rapidly, with regular wingbeats, in lines and V formations. ☉: A frequent ringing call, *rott rott rott.* ♋: It is unmistakable.

Ecology ◆: It nests on the tundra; in the non-breeding season it occurs on flat sea coasts. ∞: The nesting as well as the wintering grounds in Europe are limited to a number of sites, which are well known. As the birds do not conceal themselves, it is not difficult to determine their presence.

Bionomy ↔: It is migratory, forming flocks in the non-breeding season. It is found at the nesting grounds in Apr.—Sept. ᴗ: The nest is a hollow in a rocky place lined with down. The two to five yellow-tinged whitish eggs (70.7×46.7 mm) are laid in June. It has one brood a year, nests in colonies, and ♀ incubates

for 28 days. The young leave the nest as soon as they hatch, are tended by both parents, and fledge after 49 days. ◖: Green parts of plants, obtained by grazing as well as by plucking from the water.

Conservation Following a marked decline in its numbers, it was considered a vulnerable species until recently. Currently its numbers are on the increase. Total protection at the nesting and wintering grounds has proved sufficient, but must be continued in future years.

1

Ruddy Shelduck
Tadorna ferruginea

Identification Appearance — coloration — behaviour

✳: This small duck (65 cm) resembles a goose. It is reddish-brown with a paler neck and head, the tail is black, and the speculum is glossy green. ♀ is smaller than ♂ (1), lacks the black band around the neck, is browner, and the head is paler. Juv. birds have the same coloration as ♀ but duller, and the back is brown. ✦: It swims well, frequently leaving the water to rest on the shore or in open spaces in the vicinity, either in pairs or in small groups. It flies quite rapidly, with regular wingbeats. ☉: A loud nasal *shang* is uttered infrequently. ♋: It is unmistakable.

Ecology ◗: It occurs by shallow steppe lakes or larger rivers; in the non-breeding season also in open cultivated country. ∞: It can be seen on waters and shorelines; the nest may be located by the behaviour of adults and by searching through suitable sites. Families with young birds stay on the water.

Bionomy ↔: It is partly migratory and is found at the nesting grounds in Apr.—Sept. ᴗ: The nest is in a burrow in the ground or a tree cavity and is lined with down. The eight to twelve yellowish eggs (68.0×47.0 mm) are laid in May. It has one brood a year; ♀ incubates for 28 days. The young leave the nest as soon as they hatch, are tended by both parents, and fledge after 55 days. ◑: Seeds and green parts of plants, less often also small animals; it grazes and also gathers food on land, as well as on water.

Conservation It is declining in the wild; escapes from captivity are occurring in increasing numbers in western Europe. Total protection is necessary. The possibility of rearing and re-introducing the birds to the wild is being considered.

1

Common Shelduck
Tadorna tadorna

Identification Appearance — coloration

✳: Between a goose and a duck in size (62 cm), with a stout bill and pointed wings. The breeding plumage is predominantly white, black and dark green, with a rufous band across the breast; ♂ (1) has a red bill with basal knob, and is larger and more brightly coloured than ♀. In the non-breeding plumage ♀ and ♂ have a pinkish-red bill. Juv. birds have a grey-brown head and are entirely white below. ✦: It walks and rests on muddy ground, and swims well. It flies in a straight line with slow wing-beats. ☉: During the nesting period ♂ gives whistling calls and ♀ a repeated *eg-eg-eg*. ♋: It is unmistakable.

Ecology ◈: Flat muddy sea coasts. During the nesting period it seeks out sand dunes and rabbit burrows and in eastern Europe also steppe lakes. ∞: Adults may be observed in the appropriate habitats. Look for nests where the birds are permanently present; families with fully grown young can be seen on water.

Bionomy ↔: It is partly migratory; mass migrations of birds head for the North Sea from northwestern Europe to moult (June—Oct.). In the non-breeding season it forms flocks sometimes numbering thousands of birds. ॐ: The nest is in a cavity, most often in a burrow in the sand. The seven to twelve yellowish-white eggs (65.6×47.3 mm) are laid in May—June. It has one brood a year, nests solitarily, and incubates for 28 days. The young leave the nest as soon as they hatch, are tended by both parents, and fledge after 47 days. ◑: Almost exclusively marine molluscs and other smaller animals which

it gathers in the muddy bottom when the tide is out or when the water is at a lower level.

Conservation It is hunted only in some areas. It is essential to protect the nesting grounds and the grounds where the birds congregate on their moult migration.

1

Wigeon
Anas penelope

Identification Coloration — appearance — voice

＊: A smaller (48 cm) dabbling duck with a small head, high forehead and short bill. In flight (2), ♂ has a conspicuous white wing patch which has the shape of a V when viewed from the rear; the speculum in both sexes is green. In winter and spring ♂ (1) has a reddish-brown head with yellowish forehead and crown; ♀, ♂ in summer/autumn (eclipse plumage: June—Oct.) and juv. birds are rusty-brown with an inconspicuous white band on the flanks. ✦: It generally swims on water; it walks well on dry land, where it also feeds. It flies rapidly, in flocks. ☉: Quite frequently it utters a high-pitched descending whistling *wheeoo.* ☜: ♂ in winter and spring is unmistakable. The shape of the head and the wing pattern in eclipse plumage are characteristic.

Ecology ◈: Shallow bodies of water with marsh vegetation; in the non-breeding season, mainly flat sea coasts and larger bodies of water inland. ∞: Observe the birds on suitable waters, where they often draw attention to themselves by their calls. On the breeding grounds families remain hidden.

Bionomy ↔: It is mostly migratory. In the non-breeding season it forms flocks, which in winter on the sea coast number a great many birds. ☺: The nest is lined with down and located in marsh vegetation. The seven to ten creamy-yellow eggs (54.5×37.7 mm) are laid in May—July. It has one brood a year, nests solitarily, and incubates for 25 days. The young leave the nest on hatching, are cared for only by ♀, and fledge after 42 days. ◑: Green matter and plant seeds, obtained by grazing or by gathering it on dry land as well as on water.

Conservation Locally it is a numerous, intensively hunted species. Protective measures are not necessary at present.

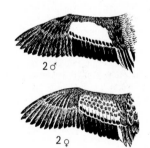

2 ♂

2 ♀

61

1

Gadwall
Anas strepera

Identification Appearance — coloration
✳: A medium-sized (50 cm), very plain dabbling duck with an inconspicuous white band towards the rear formed by the square white speculum, bordered with black and bronze, on the wings (2). ♂ in winter and spring (1) is a uniform grey with a black rear end; ♀ is mottled brown. ♂ in summer/autumn (eclipse plumage: June—Aug.) resembles ♀, as do the juv. birds, except that they are more brown and the underside of their body is darker. ✦: It generally swims on water, where it also forages for food. It rarely occurs on the shore, flies rapidly, and does not form cohesive flocks. ☉: Its call is not often heard: ♂ utters a deep-pitched whistle, ♀ calls *rek rek*. ♋: It differs from other duck species in its white speculum. A rather similar species in southern Europe is the rare Marbled Teal (*Marmaronetta angustirostris*).
Ecology ◈: Shallow bodies of water with marsh vegetation; in the non-breeding season also other waters. ∞: It can be seen on the water and among shore vegetation during the breeding as well as the non-breeding season. Look for the nest on islets and on the shore. Families stay well hidden from sight.
Bionomy ↔: It is partly migratory and is found at the nesting grounds in Feb.—Oct. It generally occurs in pairs, in the non-breeding season occasionally also in larger groups. ♥: The nest is generally sited on the shore or on an islet in thick vegetation and during incubation is lined with down. The seven to twelve yellowish eggs (53.6×38.5 mm) are laid in Apr.—July. It has one brood a year; ♀ incubates for 27 days.

The young leave the nest on hatching, are tended only by ♀, and fledge after 55 days. ●: Green parts and seeds of plants gathered on water.
Conservation Locally it is a game bird; special protective measures are not necessary. In some areas, e.g. Britain, its numbers are increasing.

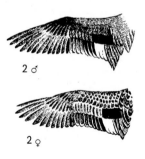

2 ♂

2 ♀

62

1

Common Teal
Anas crecca

Identification Size — behaviour — coloration — voice
∗: A small dabbling duck the size of a pigeon (36 cm) with a small head and short bill. It has a glossy green speculum bordered with white in front (2). ♂ in winter and spring (1) has a chestnut-brown head with a glossy green band across the eyes, and yellow rear end. ♀ is mottled brown. ♂ in summer/autumn (eclipse plumage: June—Oct.) and juv. birds resemble ♀.
✦: Mostly it swims on water, but often walks about on muddy shores and in shallow water. It flies very rapidly with jerky movements from side to side, often in large flocks. ☉: It utters a soft *krlik* (♂), especially when taking off; ♀ gives a *knek*. ❄: ♂ in winter and spring is unmistakable. In female and eclipse plumages it greatly resembles the Garganey (p. 66); the latter, however, has a pale upper forewing, the speculum is different, and there is also a pale spot at the base of the bill.
Ecology ◈: Marshes with short-stemmed vegetation from lowland to mountain elevations, meadows, watersides, etc. In the non-breeding season it is often found on the muddy shores of estuaries and lakes. ∞: Adults can be observed easily on water and on muddy shores. The nesting site can be located by the permanent presence of the birds, the nest by searching through the low vegetation in shallows and on the shoreline. Families remain hidden from sight.
Bionomy ↔: It is partly migratory. During the non-breeding season it mostly stays in flocks. It is found at the nesting grounds in Mar.—Oct. ✿: The nest is concealed in dense vegetation on the ground; during incubation it is lined with down. The eight to eleven yellowish eggs (45.5×32.8 mm) are laid in Apr.—June. It has one brood a year; ♀ incubates for 23 days. The young leave the nest on hatching, are tended only by ♀, and fledge after 30 days. ◖: Seeds and green parts of plants and small aquatic invertebrates, gathered near the water's surface and in mud.
Conservation Locally this is an important game bird. Its numbers are declining along with the disappearance of wetland environments, which should be preserved.

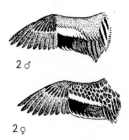

2 ♂

2 ♀

1

Mallard
Anas platyrhynchos

Identification Appearance — coloration — behaviour — voice

✳: A large (58 cm) dabbling duck with a large bill and violet, white-edged speculum (2). In winter and spring (Oct.—June) ♂ (1) has a glossy green head, chestnut breast, white neck-ring and yellow-green bill; ♀ is mottled brown, and has a dark grey-green bill with orange edges. In summer/autumn (eclipse plumage: June—Sept.) ♂ resembles ♀, but his bill remains yellow-green. Juv. birds resemble ♀.

✦: It mostly swims high on water, and upends; it nests and grazes on dry land. Its flight is rapid, with regular wingbeats. In city parks it often becomes tame. ☉: Its call may be heard frequently: ♀ generally utters a loud *qua qua*, like farmyard ducks; ♂ utters a high-pitched whistling *feeb*. ♋: ♂ in winter and spring is unmistakable; in other plumages the adults and juv. birds may be mistaken for other ducks. When distinguishing the birds it is always necessary to compare the size, shape, speculum, bill and voice.

Ecology ◆: Inland waters of all types and their vicinity, including small bodies of water in cities. ∞: It may be seen throughout the year on various waters. Look for the nest where adult birds are present.

Bionomy ↔: It is partly migratory and is found at the nesting grounds in Feb.—Aug. ∾: The nest is located in marsh vegetation, by the waterside as well as far from water, also in cavities in trees, etc. The duck lines it with down while incubating. The four to thirteen yellowish or greenish eggs (58.0×41.7 mm) are laid in Feb.—July. It has one brood a year; ♀ incubates for 26 days. The young leave the nest on hatching, are guided about by ♀ in shallow waters overgrown with vegetation, and fledge after 55 days. ◖: Mainly the green parts and seeds of plants gathered in water or obtained by grazing; also small aquatic animals.

Conservation This is an important game bird. It is abundant, and special protective measures are not necessary.

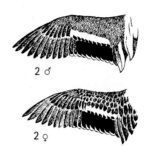

2 ♂

2 ♀

64

1

Common Pintail
Anas acuta

Identification Appearance — coloration
✳: A dabbling duck the size of the Mallard (58 cm), with a long neck held upright, long bill, rather long pointed tail, and an inconspicuous green speculum (2). ♂ in winter and spring (Oct.—June) (1) has a brown head interrupted by a gleaming white line extending up the sides of the neck from the breast and narrowing into a point at the top. ♀ in winter and spring, both sexes in summer and autumn (July—Sept.), and juv. birds are all mottled brown. ✦: It mostly stays on the water, upending often, and seldom comes on to land. It flies rapidly, with regular wingbeats. ☉: Its short whistle is heard only very occasionally. ♋: ♂ in winter and spring is unmistakable; in other plumages the long neck, bill, pointed tail, and dull speculum are characteristic.
Ecology ◈: Shallow bodies of water and marshland, also floodlands and estuaries. ∞: It may be seen on water or when flying from one site to another. Look for the nest by the waterside where Pintails occur regularly. ♀ and the young remain concealed in the vegetation.
Bionomy ↔: It is mostly migratory and is found at the nesting grounds in Mar.—Oct. In the non-breeding season it generally occurs in small flocks or pairs. ♡: The nest is a depression in the ground, generally on dry land and sometimes far from the water. ♀ lines it with down while incubating. The eight to ten yellowish eggs (55.4×38.3 mm) are laid in Mar.—June. It has one brood a year, nests solitarily, and incubates for 23 days. The young leave the nest on hatching, are guided about

only by ♀, and fledge after 42 days. ◖: Green parts and seeds of plants and small aquatic animals.
Conservation Locally this is an important game bird. Special protective measures are not necessary.

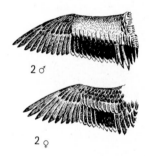

2 ♂

2 ♀

1

Garganey
Anas querquedula

Identification Appearance — coloration — voice

∗: A short-necked dabbling duck the size of a pigeon (38 cm). ♂ in winter and spring (Oct.—June) is grey and brown with a conspicuous white band on the brown head (1). ♂ in summer/autumn (eclipse plumage: June—Feb.), ♀ and juv. birds are light brown with dark markings. Discernible in all plumages is the paler forewing, especially in ♂ (2), where it is very pale grey-blue. The speculum is a dull green, bordered with white at front and at rear. ✦: It mostly swims on water, in pairs or small groups as a rule. It flies rapidly, in a straight line. ☉: In spring ♂ often utters a conspicuous crackling *rrrep*, ♀ a faint *knak*. ☜: ♂ in late winter and spring dress is unmistakable; in other plumages the adults and juv. birds resemble the Common Teal (p. 63), which, however, has darker wings, a different speculum and different manner of flight.

Ecology ◈: Wet meadows, marshland, shoreline vegetation by shallow bodies of water. ∞: It may be seen on water or when flying from one site to another. Finding the nest is difficult: you must walk around suitable sites and watch for the tightly sitting ♀. Families lead a very concealed life in the vegetation.

Bionomy ↔: It is migratory and is found at the nesting grounds in Mar.—Sept. ᴗ: The nest is located on the ground in thick, low vegetation, occasionally some distance from water, and is very well concealed. ♀ lines it with down during incubation. The six to twelve creamy-yellow eggs (45.7×32.9 mm) are laid in Apr.—June. It

has one brood a year, nests solitarily, and ♀ incubates for 23 days. The young are tended only by ♀, leave the nest on hatching, and fledge after 30 days. ◑: Small aquatic invertebrates, seeds and green parts of plants, gathered on the water's surface.

Conservation It is of little importance as a game bird. Its numbers are on the decline, and it is essential to protect its wetland environment.

2 ♂

2 ♀

1

Shoveler
Anas clypeata

Identification Appearance — coloration — behaviour
✱: A dabbling duck with a conspicuously long, spoon-shaped bill; slightly smaller than the Mallard (50 cm). ♂ in winter and spring (Oct.—June) (1) has a dark green head, reddish-brown flanks bordered with white, pale blue-grey upper forewings, and a green speculum (2). ♀ and juv. birds are mottled brown, with greyer upperwings; ♂ in summer/autumn (eclipse plumage: June—Aug.) is similar, but with wings blue-grey above. ✦: It mostly swims with the front end low and with bill resting on the water, often swimming in circles; it also upends. It flies rapidly, and on dry land keeps to the waterside. ⊙: It makes a loud quacking sound but is heard only rarely. ♋: It is unmistakable.
Ecology ◈: Shallow edges of bodies of water, wet meadows, flooded areas, etc. at lower elevations. ∞: It may be seen on water or by shore vegetation. Look for the nest by making a careful search of suitable sites by the waterside. Families remain hidden from view.
Bionomy ↔: It is mostly migratory. In the non-breeding season it occurs in small groups as well as flocks. It is found at the nesting grounds in Mar.—Nov. ღ: The nest is sited in thick low vegetation on the ground, usually on the shoreline, though sometimes even quite far from water, and is lined during the incubating period with down. The six to thirteen yellowish eggs (52.9×37.2 mm) are laid in Apr.—July. The birds have one brood a year, usually nest solitarily, and ♀ incubates for 23 days. The young leave the nest on hatching, are tended only by ♀, and fledge after 40 days. ◑: Plant seeds and small aquatic invertebrates, gathered on the water's surface.
Conservation This is not a very important game bird. It is declining in numbers, and it is essential to protect its wetland environment.

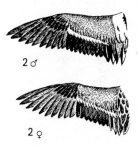

2 ♂

2 ♀

1

Red-crested Pochard
Netta rufina

Identification Appearance — coloration
✳: A diving duck about the same size as the Mallard (55 cm). ♂ in breeding plumage (Nov.—July) has a small reddish-yellow crest, but otherwise is strikingly black, white and brown (1). ♀, ♂ in eclipse plumage (May—Oct.) and juv. birds are brown, with white cheeks contrasting conspicuously with the dark cap (2). ♂ has a coral-red bill in both plumages, ♀ a grey bill with a red transverse band. A broad white band on the brown wings is visible in flight. ✦: It mostly swims high on water, upends, but rarely dives. Generally striking in flocks is the predominance of males. The flight is rapid and in a straight line. ☉: Very occasionally it utters a hoarse *karrr.* ♋: ♂ in breeding plumage is unmistakable. ♀, eclipse ♂ and juv. birds resemble ♀ Common Scoter (*Melanitta nigra* — 3), which, however, is darker and lacks the white band on the wings.
Ecology ◐: Bodies of water, not very deep, thickly overgrown with vegetation. ∞: It tends not to hide away and thus may be seen easily on water, where it also leads its family. Look for the nest in vegetation on the shoreline and on islets. The female sometimes guides the young of other species of ducks.
Bionomy ↔: It is partly migratory, and in the non-breeding season occurs in small flocks as well as singly. It is found at the nesting grounds in Feb.—Aug. ◡: The nest is near the water or in shoreline vegetation in the water; during incubation it is edged with a huge ring of down. Often several females lay their eggs in the same nest or the eggs may be laid in the nests of

other duck species. The four to twenty yellowish eggs (56.7×41.7 mm) are laid in Apr.—July. It has one brood a year, nests solitarily, and incubates for 27 days. The young leave the nest on hatching, are guided by ♀ on the water, and fledge after 56 days. ◖: Aquatic plants, which it gathers from the surface or nips off underwater.
Conservation It is essential to protect the nesting grounds. Numbers of Red-crested Pochards are currently showing a slight upward trend.

2

3 ♀

1

Common Pochard
Aythya ferina

Identification Appearance — coloration — behaviour

✳: A medium-sized (48 cm) diving duck with a large head, high forehead, and a broad pale band the whole length of the wing. ♂ in breeding plumage (1) has a reddish-brown head and a black breast. ♀, ♂ in eclipse plumage (June—Sept.) and juv. birds are brown with a grey back, and (except juv.) have a pale yellowish streak behind the eye. The downy nestlings (2) are mottled yellow-brown with yellow cheeks. ✦: Mostly it swims low on water and dives frequently; it commonly sleeps on the water, on the shore or on objects by the water's edge (stumps, tree trunks, etc.). ☉: Occasionally, particularly in flight, it utters a loud muffled *kurr kurr*. ☜: ♂ in breeding dress is unmistakable. In other plumages the birds are somewhat similar to the Tufted Duck (p. 70) and scoters, all of which are darker and have different head markings. Central and eastern Europe are sparsely inhabited by the similar Ferruginous Duck (*A. nyroca*).

Ecology ◈: Shallow inland waters with shoreline vegetation. ∞: It is easily observed on water. Look for the nest by searching through the shoreline marsh vegetation.

Bionomy ↔: It is migratory and dispersive and is found at the nesting grounds in Feb.—Oct. In the non-breeding season it generally occurs in larger groups. In June—July the males fly to their moulting grounds; the young, when they have fledged, also disperse in all directions. ☽: The nest is near open water in a clump of reeds, sedge, etc., lined during incubation with down. The five to twelve oval greenish eggs (59.0×42.8 mm) are laid in Apr.—July. It has one brood a year, nests solitarily, and ♀ incubates for 25 days. ◑: Aquatic plants and smaller invertebrates, hunted underwater.

Conservation This is an important game bird. Special protection is not necessary.

2

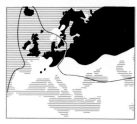

1

Tufted Duck
Aythya fuligula

Identification Appearance — coloration — behaviour

✳: A smaller (45 cm) diving duck with feathers extended into a drooping crest, and with a short neck and a relatively long, broad bill. The white band on the dark brown wings is conspicuous in flight. ♂ in breeding plumage (1) is black with white flanks and a longer crest; in eclipse plumage (June—Sept.) the crest is short, the head, upperparts and tail are blackish-brown, and the flanks are grey with dark barring. ♀ resembles eclipse ♂, but generally has a narrow white band rimming the base of the bill and darker flanks. Juv. birds resemble ♀, but have buff at the base of the bill. Ducklings in down feathers are uniformly blackish-brown (2). ✦: Mostly it swims on water, diving frequently; it flies in a straight line and very rapidly. ☉: It utters a hoarse *karrr*, mostly in flight. ☻: Mainly the Scaup (*A. marila*) in the more northern parts of Europe.

Ecology ◀: Still or slow-flowing inland waters with rich vegetation and islets; in the non-breeding season all kinds of waters. ∞: It may be easily seen on water throughout the year. The nest is readily found by searching through the shoreline vegetation. Families stay on open water.

Bionomy ↔: It is resident and migratory, and is found at the nesting grounds in Mar.—Oct. In the non-breeding season it usually occurs in flocks or smaller groups. ᴗ: The nest is located in shoreline vegetation, mainly sedge, and on islets, and is lined during incubation with down. The five to twelve greenish-grey eggs

(58.5×40.7 mm) are laid in Apr.—July. It has one brood a year, and ♀ incubates for 24 days. The young leave the nest on hatching, are guided about by ♀, and fledge after 49 days. ◑: Mostly molluscs obtained by diving underwater.

Conservation This is an important game bird. Although it is very common, rational hunting regulations are required in some areas.

2

Common Eider
Somateria mollissima

Identification Size — appearance — coloration — behaviour

✳: A large (60 cm) diving duck with a large head and massive bill extending onto the forehead in a straight line. ♂ in breeding plumage (1) is white, with a broad black band over the eye, black rear end, flanks and belly, black rear and outer wings, and a greenish area on the hindneck; in eclipse plumage (July—Nov.) it is mostly dark sooty-brown, with white forewings and variable whitish areas on the body. ♀ is brown with darker barring (2) and has a narrow white band on the wings. Juv. birds resemble ♀ but are duller and darker and lack any markings on the wings; in the 2nd—3rd year the coloration of ♂ gradually changes, with increasing expanses of white. ✦: Mostly it swims of water with head resting on its back, and dives frequently; it flies close above the water, often in line formations. During courtship ♂ ♂ make characteristic movements, including drawing the head backward. ☉: During the courtship period ♂ utters a hoarse *coo rooa*, and ♀ *korrr.* 🔊: In the arctic regions of Europe the King Eider (*S. spectabilis* — 3).

Ecology ◆: Flat sea coasts with little vegetation and islets; in the non-breeding season it also occurs on the open sea. ∞: It can be observed on water by the coast; the nest is not particularly well concealed and is readily located by walking about suitable sites. Families stay on open water.

Bionomy ↔: It is only partly migratory. 〰: The nest is placed on the ground and during incubation is richly lined with down. The four to ten grey-green eggs (77.8×51.1 mm) are laid in Apr.—July. It has one brood a year, often nests in colonies, and ♀ incubates for 28 days. The young leave the nest on hatching, are guided about only by ♀, and fledge after 56 days. ◑: Smaller animals, caught in shallow seas near the surface, also by diving.

Conservation This species is in some areas (e.g. Iceland) an economically important source of down feathers (eiderdown). It is essential to protect the nesting grounds.

2

3

71

1

Long-tailed Duck
Clangula hyemalis

Identification Coloration — appearance — voice — behaviour

✳: A medium-sized diving duck (50 cm) with an elongated, upward-slanting tail, particularly long in adult ♂. The plumage pattern varies greatly during the year, but white is always present in varying degrees on the head and flanks; the wings are brownish-black. ♂ in May—June (breeding) plumage (2) has the sides of the head whitish, otherwise the head, neck and breast are brownish-black; in non-breeding plumage (1) the head and neck are white, with pale grey around the eye and a dark area below it. ♀ in breeding plumage (3) has the top of the head, hindneck, chin and lower part of the neck dark and a large dark patch beneath the eye; in non-breeding plumage the crown is brown and there is a smaller brown patch beneath the eye. Juv. birds resemble ♀ in breeding plumage, but have a white patch in front of the eye and the chin and front part of the neck a pale colour. ✦: It swims on water, diving frequently and for long intervals. It flies in a straight line, rapidly, with shallow wing-beats and a rocking motion from side to side. ☉: ♂ quite frequently utters a loud, yodelling *a-owoolee* in display. ♋: It is unmistakable.

Ecology ◈: Tundra lakes; in the non-breeding season the sea, sometimes quite far from shore, and very occasionally also inland waters. ∞: It may be seen on waters by the shore and can be recognised also by its voice. Look for the nest around the shore.

Bionomy ↔: It is partly migratory and in the non-breeding season generally occurs gregar-

iously. It is found at the nesting grounds in May—Aug. ♡: The nest is located on the ground near water and is lined during incubation with down. The six to seven yellow-green eggs (53.7×38.4 mm) are laid in May—July. It has one brood a year, nests solitarily, at some places in larger numbers, and ♀ incubates for 24 days. The young leave the nest on hatching, are guided about only by ♀, and fledge after 35 days. ●: Aquatic invertebrates caught underwater.

Conservation Locally this is an important game bird. No special protection is necessary. In northern Europe it is very numerous.

2

3

72

1

Velvet Scoter
Melanitta fusca

Identification Appearance — coloration — behaviour

✳: This diving duck, almost the size of the Mallard (55 cm), has a large head and heavy, swollen bill, a short neck and short tail. ♂ is black, with a small white patch below the eye and a white speculum, the latter occasionally visible when on the water; ♀ (1, 2) is dark brown with a white speculum, and has a pale round patch in front of as well as behind the eye. Juv. birds resemble ♀ but are paler. ✦: It swims and dives well, often a whole flock submerging simultaneously. It flies close above the water, rapidly and following a straight course, on lengthier flights in lines. ☉: It is heard rarely: ♂ utters a whistling *huor-or*, ♀ rasping sounds. ♋: Commonly found in the same parts is the Common or Black Scoter (*M. nigra*); on rare occasions Europe is visited by the Surf Scoter (*M. perspicillata*) from North America.

Ecology ◑: Sea coasts, lakes and rivers in the taiga and tundra. In the non-breeding season it inhabits sea coasts, including stony and rocky shores. ∞: Observe scoters on open coastal waters. The nest can be located by the behaviour of the birds at the beginning of the breeding period and by exploring suitable sites. Families stay on the water.

Bionomy ↔: It is migratory; in the non-breeding season it generally occurs in small groups. It is found at the nesting grounds in Apr.—Aug. ♋: The nest is on the ground, sometimes also in holes in trees and far from the water; it is lined with down during incubation. The six to ten brownish-yellow eggs

(72.0×48.4 mm) are laid in May—June. It has one brood a year, nests solitarily, and ♀ incubates for 28 days. The young, which leave the nest on hatching, are guided about by ♀ for 35 days. ◑: Mostly aquatic molluscs obtained by diving.

Conservation No special protection is necessary.

2 ♀

1

Common Goldeneye
Bucephala clangula

Identification Appearance — coloration — voice — behaviour
✱: A smaller diving duck (46 cm) with a large triangular head with high forehead, and a slender, shortish neck. ♂ in breeding plumage (1) is black and white; in eclipse plumage (July—Oct.) his head is dark brown, the upperparts dark greyish-brown, and the underparts a paler brown with dark transverse markings. ♀ resembles the eclipse ♂, but often has a white collar around the neck; the white area on the wing is crossed by two black transverse bands, and the bill has a yellow band at the tip. Juv. birds resemble ♀ but lack the white collar. ✦: It swims buoyantly, and dives very often and for long intervals. It flies rapidly, in a straight line, with wings making a far-carrying whistling sound. From mid winter onwards ♂ performs pronounced courtship displays, throwing his head up and laying it on the back with bill jutting straight upward. Voice: ♂ whistles when tossing the head, otherwise he utters a hoarse *quee-reek*; ♀ a rattling *kurr*. ♋: Iceland is the home of the similar Barrow's Goldeneye (*B. islandica*); very rarely encountered in Europe is the Bufflehead (*B. albeola*) of North America.
Ecology ◈: Lakes, rivers and other kinds of water in wooded country. In the non-breeding season it also occurs on open waters and on coasts, often far from shore. ∞: It can be observed on various traditional waters throughout most of the year. The nest may be located by the behaviour of the birds and by examining holes in trees (those that are inhabited usually have down feathers clinging to the entrance). Families stay on open water.
Bionomy ↔: Generally it is migratory and is found at the nesting grounds in Apr.—Sept. ⊗: It lives in pairs on the nesting grounds. The nest is located in a tree hole or man-made nestbox, sometimes some distance from water; it is lined with down during incubation. The four to fourteen blue-green eggs (59.2×42.6 mm) are laid in Apr.—June. It has one brood a year, and ♀ incubates for 30 days. The young jump out of the nest and are immediately led to water, where they are guided about by ♀ for 50 days. ◐: Aquatic invertebrates obtained underwater.
Conservation Locally this is an important game bird. Nesting can be promoted by putting out nestboxes.

1

Smew
Mergus albellus

Identification Appearance — coloration

✻: A small duck (41 cm) with a short neck, rather large head with a slight crest, and a small slender bill. ♂ in breeding plumage (Oct.—May) is conspicuously white and black (1); ♀ (2) is greyish-brown with a reddish-brown cap contrasting with the white cheeks. ♂ in eclipse plumage (June—Oct.) resembles ♀ in her breeding plumage, but his back is darker and the white patch on the upperwing-coverts is larger. Juv. birds resemble ♀, but their upperwing-coverts are white with greyish-brown tips and the cap is paler. ✦: Mostly it swims on water, diving frequently. It flies rapidly, following a straight course, with neck stretched out in front, in flocks also in line formations. On dry land it walks upright. ☉: It is rarely heard: ♂ utters whistling sounds, ♀ a hoarse *kurr*. ☺: ♂ in breeding dress is unmistakable; it can be distinguished from ♂ Goldeneye (p. 74) from a distance by the white head. Birds that have not yet attained the full adult plumage may slightly resemble the Red-crested Pochard (p. 68) and the Common Scoter (*Melanitta nigra*).

Ecology ◈: Breeds on lakes and rivers in forests; in the non-breeding season various larger bodies of water, as well as estuaries. ∞: It may be found on water. When looking for the nest, examine tree holes by the waterside and watch for ♀ guiding the young.

Bionomy ↔: It is migratory and is found at the nesting grounds in Apr.—Sept. In the non-breeding season it occurs in small groups. ౿: The nest is in a tree hole, lined during incu-

bation with down. The six to nine creamy eggs (52.7×37.5 mm) are laid in May—June. It has one brood a year, nests solitarily, and ♀ incubates for 30 days. The young are immediately taken by ♀ to water; they apparently fledge at the age of 1 ½ months. ◐: Small aquatic animals, including fish, obtained underwater.

Conservation Locally this is a common species. Nesting should be promoted by putting out nestboxes.

2 ♀

1

Goosander
Mergus merganser

Identification Appearance — size — coloration
✶: A large diving duck (62 cm) with a long
body, slender neck, large head with crest on the
nape, and a long, slender bill. In breeding plumage (1) ♂ is black and white, with grey rump
and tail and a red bill, the inner wings being
white and the outer wings blackish; in eclipse
plumage (June–Nov.) the head and upper part
of the neck are brown, and the throat white. ♀
(2, 3) resembles eclipse ♂ but has a larger crest,
the body is almost entirely pale grey, and only
the rear half of the inner wings is white. Juv.
birds resemble ♀, but the crest is smaller, and
the coloration of the head and body less intense. ✦: Mostly it swims on water, diving frequently and for long intervals. It flies in
a straight line, very rapidly, and with extended
neck and head (4). ☉: When displaying,
♂ utters croaking sounds, ♀ a hoarse *kurr*.
♋: The Red-breasted Merganser (*M. serrator* –
5, 6, 7), commonly found throughout its entire
range.

Ecology ◈: Breeds on lakes and rivers in
wooded districts. In the non-breeding season it
often occurs on larger, open inland waters, and
sometimes on the coast in some areas. ∞: It
may be observed on water throughout the year.
When looking for the nest, investigate suitable
cavities in the vicinity of water. Families generally stay on the water, though sometimes they
hide in reeds.

Bionomy ↔: It is mostly migratory and is found
at the nesting grounds in Apr.–Aug. In the
non-breeding season it generally occurs in
groups, sometimes numbering hundreds of in-

dividuals. ∽: The nest is located in a tree hole,
in cavities under tree roots and in nestboxes; it
is lined with down during incubation. The
seven to thirteen creamy eggs (67.5×46.5 mm)
are laid in Apr.–July. It has one brood a year,
usually nests solitarily, and ♀ incubates for 35
days. The young are immediately taken to water
and guided there by ♀ for 35 days. ◖: Smaller
fish caught underwater.

Conservation It is locally numerous. Nestboxes
may be put out at the nesting grounds; no special protection is necessary.

76

1

Water Rail
Rallus aquaticus

Identification Voice — behaviour — appearance

✳: Slightly smaller than a partridge (28 cm) and with a long, almost straight, conspicuously red bill, long neck and legs, short wings and tail. The adult (1) is brown above, grey below with flanks barred black and white, and has red eyes; ♀ has a paler throat. Juv. birds are duller, with a pale face and mottled brown breast. ✦: It keeps well hidden in reedbeds, where it moves about at the lowest level near the water. When walking, it jerks its tail; it runs well, and occasionally swims. ☉: At the nesting grounds (Apr.—July) its conspicuous call may be heard often, even at night: loud squealing and growling sounds, usually ending with a descending scale of increasingly faster short notes. During courtship a soft *kik-kik* . . . ☻: Its voice is unmistakable. All other rails have a shorter bill.

Ecology ◈: Marsh vegetation, mainly reeds and sedges. In the non-breeding season it also occurs by small bodies of water, streams, springs, etc. ∞: At the nesting site it is easily recognised by its voice. The nest is hard to find: you must look carefully through the thick bottom layers of reeds, especially tufts of sedge. The sitting bird when flushed flies off very inconspicuously and quickly. In the non-breeding season it may be seen at the edge of or in paths cut through reedbeds.

Bionomy ↔: It is migratory, nests and mostly lives solitarily, and is found at the nesting grounds in Mar.—Oct. ᗡ: The nest is made of broader leaves and concealed in a clump of vegetation close above water. The six to twelve creamy eggs (34.3×25.5 mm), sparsely speckled reddish-brown, are laid in Apr.—Sept. It has two (three) broods a year and incubates for 20 days. The young are cared for by both parents, leave the nest after a short time but keep returning to it, and fledge after 50 days. ◕: Small animals caught among the vegetation near water's surface.

Conservation This is a declining species. It is essential to preserve its wetland environment.

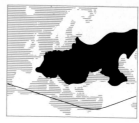

1

Little Crake
Porzana parva

Identification Voice — behaviour — appearance

✳: The size of a starling (19 cm) and with a short body, legs and tail, and a small head with a short bill. The adult is dark brown above with black and white streaks, the legs are green, and the bill yellow-green with red corners. ♂ has slate-grey underparts, ♀ is yellow-brown below (1); both have pale barring on rear flanks. Juv. birds resemble ♀ but have dark barring on the underside. ✦: It keeps concealed in marsh vegetation, where it moves about in the thick layer near the water. It generally walks or runs, very occasionally swims, and rarely flies. ☉: During the nesting period, the call of ♂ is a descending scale of increasingly rapid notes, *kvek-kvek*..., *ko-ko*,... and so on. The courtship call is a *kvek*. ☎: The voice is distinctive; when listened to for a while it is unmistakable. Baillon's Crake (*P. pusilla*) is very similar in appearance, but has heavier flank barring and no red on the bill.

Ecology ◆: Marsh vegetation, mainly reeds, sedges, etc. ∞: At the nesting grounds it may be recognised by its voice; the birds often call in the vicinity of the nest. If you remain motionless, you may observe it in gaps in the vegetation. The nest may be discovered by a careful search of the marsh vegetation. In the non-breeding season only the chance encounter may be expected.

Bionomy ↔: It is migratory and is found at the nesting grounds in Mar.—Oct. It nests and lives solitarily. ✿: The nest is located in a dense tangle of vegetation near the water's surface, concealed from view from above. The four to eight yellow-brown eggs (31.6×22.0 mm), densely speckled reddish-brown, are laid in Apr.—Aug. It has one or two broods a year, and incubates for 17 days. The young leave the nest on hatching, are tended by both parents and fledge after 45 days. ◑: Small animals, less frequently also parts and seeds of plants, gathered at the water's surface and in vegetation.

Conservation It is found only locally and is declining in numbers. It is essential to preserve its wetland environment.

1

**Moorhen or
Common Gallinule**
Gallinula chloropus

Identification Voice — appearance — behaviour

✳: The size of a partridge (33 cm) and with a small head, the base of the bill extending into a frontal shield, a short tail and long legs. Adults (1) are greyish-black and dark brown, with a white band on the flanks and white undertail; the bill is bright red, the legs green; ♂ = ♀. Juv. birds are pale on the underside and lack the red frontal shield. ✦: It often keeps well concealed in marsh vegetation, swimming out on the water close to the vegetation, where it immediately hides when alarmed. It swims buoyantly in the water, with the rear end pointing upward, jerking its head (2); it continually flicks its tail, thus flashing the white underside. It climbs up plants expertly, but flies for only short distances. ☉: It often utters its penetrating explosive *kirrr.* ☞: It is unmistakable.

Ecology ◈: Shallow, thickly overgrown waters, also small ponds by human habitations. In the non-breeding season it is also found on rivers with sparse shoreline vegetation and warm outflows. ∞: At the nesting grounds, listen for its call or watch by the water's surface by the edge of the vegetation for a time. The families generally keep in or at the edge of thick clumps of vegetation.

Bionomy ↔: It is partly migratory and is found at the nesting grounds in Mar.—Oct. ☙: The nest is a sturdy structure of flat leaves located in thick vegetation, generally (though not always) close to the water's surface; it is usually concealed from above by the surrounding vegetation. The five to eleven ochre eggs (41.9×

29.7 mm), speckled dark reddish-brown, are laid in Mar.—Sept. It has one to three broods a year, nests solitarily, and incubates for 21 days. The young remain two or three days in the nest, then hide in the vegetation, where they are tended by both parents. They fledge after 35 days. ◑: Leaves and fragments of plants, and small invertebrates, gathered on the water's surface or in marsh vegetation.

Conservation Locally it is of minor importance as a game bird. No special protection is necessary.

2

1

Eurasian Coot
Fulica atra

Identification Appearance — coloration — voice — behaviour

∗: This is a large member of the rail family (37 cm). When swimming, it rides high in the water with lowered rear end. Adults (1) are dark greyish-black with a white bill and frontal shield; ♂ = ♀. Juv. birds lack the frontal shield and the front of the neck is white. ✦: Mostly it swims on water with neck drawn back, and dives well; when flushed or taking off, it runs along the water's surface flapping its wings and leaving a distinct trail in its wake (2). It flies infrequently but rapidly and in a straight line, with legs hanging downward. It often comes up on shore. In spring its territorial behaviour is very striking, including fierce combats amongst rival males. ☉: It often utters a loud *kowk* and a penetrating, occasionally repeated *pix*. ☣: The similar Crested Coot (*F. cristata*) is found in southern Spain.

Ecology ◈: Shallow waters with vegetation; in the non-breeding season it also occurs on rivers, open waters on the sea coast and even in cities. ∞: It is readily seen on water during both breeding and non-breeding periods. The nest may sometimes be located by scanning from the shore; otherwise by searching through the vegetation by the edge, close to the water's surface. Parents guide and feed the young on the water near vegetation.

Bionomy ↔: It is partly migratory. In the non-breeding season it occurs in groups or large close-knit flocks. ∽: The nest is located in vegetation close to the water's surface, sometimes even almost freely on the water. It is made of leaves, often with a ramp to the water. The four to twelve yellowish-brown eggs (52.2× 35.9 mm), sparsely speckled black, are laid in Mar.—July. It has one to three broods a year, nests solitarily, and incubates for 23 days. The young soon leave the nest, are fed by the parents on the water, hide among the vegetation, and fledge after 56 days. ◐: Parts of plants, less often aquatic invertebrates, gathered on the water, underwater, as well as on dry land.

Conservation This is a less important game bird. No special protection is necessary, as it is very numerous.

2

1

Common Oystercatcher
Haematopus ostralegus

Identification Size — coloration — behaviour — voice

∗: A large wader (43 cm), larger than the Lapwing. It has short legs, a thick neck, a round head with long, straight bill, and a short tail. In breeding plumage (1) the upperparts are black, the underside white, and the bill and legs red; the broad white band on the wings, the white rump and the black terminal band on the tail are visible in flight (2). In the non-breeding plumage there is a white band across the throat; ♂ = ♀. Juv. birds are mottled buffish above, and have grey legs and a dull yellowish bill. ✦: It walks or runs about on the shore, probing with its bill in the mud and sand. Flocks fly in lines or V formations. ☉: It often utters a loud penetrating *kebeek*, and its alarm call is a repeated *pik-pik*; when courting, also a high-pitched, descending trill. ☜: It is unmistakable.

Ecology ◈: Sandy and muddy shores of seas, in some places also of larger rivers and lakes. ∞: It may be seen on open beaches or in places with short grass cover near water, mainly seashores. The nest may be located by the behaviour of the birds and by checking out the site, and the young by the behaviour of the adults.

Bionomy ↔: It is mostly migratory and is found at the nesting grounds in Mar.—Sept. In the non-breeding season it generally occurs in flocks. ᴥ: The nest is a shallow depression in sand, between stones, or in grass. The two to four ochre, dark-speckled eggs (56.5×39.8 mm) are laid in Apr.—July. It has one brood a year, nests solitarily, and incubates for 26 days. The

young are cared for by both parents, leave the nest on hatching, and fledge after 32 days. ◐: Small aquatic animals inhabiting shallows and flat shores, gathered while walking or probing.

Conservation It is very numerous in places. No special conservation measures are necessary, although its wintering grounds require protection.

2

1

Black-winged Stilt
Himantopus himantopus

Identification Appearance — coloration
✳: It vaguely recalls a small minute stork (38 cm). It has a long, slender neck, long bill, and extraordinarily long, bright red legs. ♂ has the back and wings black and the remainder of the plumage white, though the crown and nape vary from white to black (in non-breeding plumage often grey or brown). ♀ has a dark brown back and similarly variable head markings, but the head is often entirely white (1). Juv. birds usually have a dark brown nape and hindneck, the feathers on the back are edged with buff, and the legs are pinkish-grey. ✚: It wades in shallow water. Its flight is in a straight line with regular wingbeats and legs extending far beyond the tail. ☉: Its calls include a loud *kip kip* and a shrill *kyee*. ☃: It is unmistakable.
Ecology ◈: Shallow waters and lagoons with low vegetation, by the sea coast as well as inland. ∞: It may be seen easily in appropriate habitats. The nest may be located by looking for sitting birds. Newly-fledged birds may be discovered by the behaviour of the parents, but locating a young bird that is pressed close to the ground is difficult.
Bionomy ↔: It is migratory and is found at the nesting grounds in Mar.—Oct. Occasionally there are invasion migrations northward in spring, and individual pairs may then nest north of the usual boundaries of their range. ♡: Pairs nest solitarily as well as in loosely-knit groups. The nest is sited on a clump of vegetation or on the ground near water, or directly on the water. The three to five yellow-brown, dark-patterned eggs (44.0×31.0 mm) are laid in May—

June. It has one brood a year, and incubates for 26 days. The young leave the nest on hatching, are tended by both parents in the vicinity of the nest, and fledge after 32 days. ◑:Mostly small aquatic invertebrates, caught in shallow water or on the bottom.
Conservation Its numbers are declining; larger numbers occur in only a few places. It is essential to preserve its wetland environment and individual nesting grounds.

82

1

Eurasian Avocet
Recurvirostra avosetta

Identification Appearance — coloration — behaviour
✳: A large wader (43 cm) with long legs, long slender neck and long upturned bill. Adults are contrasting black and white (1); ♂ = ♀. In juv. birds the black areas are brownish. ✚: It wades in shallow water, capturing food with rapid sweeping movements of the bill. It flies in a straight line, with legs extending far beyond the tail. ☉: It often utters a soft melodious *klooeeit*; its alarm call is a *gig gig.* ⬡: It is unmistakable.
Ecology ◈: Flat shores of estuaries and sea bays and shallow salt as well as freshwater lakes. ∞: It is easily observed on shores. The nest may be located by watching sitting birds; locating young birds which are pressed closely to the ground is difficult.
Bionomy ↔: It is partly migratory and is found at the nesting grounds in Mar.—Sept. It generally occurs throughout the year in larger groups, less often also solitarily. ♡: The nest is a shallow, sparsely lined scrape in the ground near water. The three to four pale yellow-brown, dark-patterned eggs (50.6×35.0 mm) are laid in Apr.—July. It has one brood a year and incubates for 25 days. The young leave the nest on hatching, are tended by both parents, and fledge after 35 days. ◑: Small invertebrates, gathered on muddy bottoms of shallow waters.

Conservation It is numerous in places. Protection measures include preserving suitable habitats and ensuring that the birds are not disturbed at the nesting grounds.

Little Ringed Plover
Charadrius dubius

Identification Voice — appearance

✳: Its body is the size of a sparrow (15 cm). It has a large round head with yellow eye-rings and short bill, and a short tail and legs. There is no white bar on the wings (2). Adults (1) are brown above, white below, and have conspicuous black and white markings on the head and breast; ♂ = ♀. In juv. birds the markings on the head and breast are brown, and the white line behind the eye is absent. ✦: Mostly it runs about rapidly on flat shores, pausing after a short distance to pick up food, then running again; when alarmed, it bobs its head. It flies rapidly, close above the ground; during the courtship display it performs a wavering bat-like flight. At the nest it feigns injury when disturbed. ☉: It often utters a loud *dyu*, and in display flight a repeated *preea*. ♋: The Kentish Plover (*C. alexandrinus*) (3, 4), mainly on sea coasts, and the Ringed Plover (p. 85), which, however, is larger and has slightly different head markings, an orange-yellow bill and legs, and a distinct white bar on the wings.

Ecology ◆: Flat muddy, sandy or shingle shores of shallow inland waters. In the non-breeding season it also occurs on sea coasts. ∞: It occurs almost exclusively on flat shores; one often hears its voice and sees birds flying from one spot to another. Look for the nest as well as the nestlings according to the behaviour of the adult birds; because of the cryptic coloration of the eggs as well as the young birds, however, finding them is difficult.

Bionomy ↔: It is migratory and is found at the nesting grounds in Mar.—Sept. ♼: The nest is a sparsely lined hollow in the ground, generally not very far from water. The three to four pale sand-coloured eggs (29.8×22.2 mm) with tiny black-brown spots are laid in Apr.—July. It has one or two broods a year, nests solitarily, and incubates for 25 days. The young soon leave the nest, are tended by both parents, and fledge after 21 days. ◐: Small invertebrates, gathered on shores.

Conservation No special protection is necessary.

Ringed Plover
Charadrius hiaticula

Identification Appearance — behaviour — coloration

✳: About the size of a Skylark (18 cm), and with a large round head with short bill, short legs, and a short tail. The white wingbar (2) stands out in sharp contrast to the dark rear edge of the wing, the tail is dark, the bill is orange-yellow with a dark tip, and the legs orange-yellow. Adults (1) have conspicuous black and white markings on the head and breast; ♂ = ♀. The markings on the head of juv. birds are brown, and there are large brown patches on each side of the breast (usually not joining in the middle). ✦: It patters rapidly along muddy and sandy shores, frequently pausing, and crouching and bobbing when nervous. It flies leisurely, close above the ground. At the nest and with chicks, it feigns injury when disturbed. ☉: It often utters a melodious *too-ee*. ♋: It much resembles the Little Ringed Plover (p. 84), which, however, is smaller with less pronounced markings on the head, lacks the white wingbar, and has pale pinkish or greyish-brown legs and a dark bill.

Ecology ◀: Sea coasts, northern tundra, and locally inland waters or heathland; in the non-breeding season flat shores. ∞: It is best observed during the courtship and breeding period at the nesting grounds. The nest and young birds may be located by the behaviour of the adults and by watching a sitting bird. In the non-breeding season the birds can be observed running about on flat shores and flying from one site to another.

Bionomy ↔: It is both resident and migratory in Europe and is found at the nesting grounds in Mar.—Oct. In the non-breeding season it generally occurs in groups or flocks. ♋: The nest is a sparsely lined hollow in the ground. The three to four sandy yellow, dark-patterned eggs (35.2×25.6 mm) are laid in Mar.—July. It has one to three broods a year, nests solitarily, and incubates for 24 days. The young soon leave the nest, are tended by both parents, and fledge after 25 days. ◑: Small shoreline invertebrates.

Conservation The only measure of protection is to ensure undisturbed nesting grounds. At present it is relatively numerous.

2

1

Dotterel
Charadrius morinellus

Identification Appearance — behaviour — voice

*: A medium-large plover about the size of a Blackbird (21 cm). It has a short neck, large round head, short yellow legs and short tail, and long pointed wings without a white wing-bar. In breeding plumage (1) the head is dark grey and white, the throat is whitish, and the upper breast is grey with a white stripe separating it from the chestnut lower breast and black belly; ♂ usually duller than ♀. In non-breeding (2) and juv. plumages the birds are a nondescript greyish-brown, with whitish supercilia converging on the nape and a whitish band across the breast. ✦: Mostly it patters about on the ground, often stopping for a brief moment; it flies very rapidly and close above the ground. ☉: It often utters a repeated *pwit* and a whistling *uit-ee-vee*. ☜: In breeding dress it is unmistakable. In non-breeding plumage it resembles plovers of the genus *Pluvialis*, but the latter are larger, lack the pale band across the breast and the supercilia do not extend onto the nape.

Ecology ◈: Tundra or subalpine elevations in mountains, occasionally also at lower elevations. In the non-breeding season it occurs in fields, pastureland and steppes. ∞: At the nesting grounds it may be recognised by its voice; the nest and young birds may be discovered by watching the adults. In the non-breeding season check suitable (often traditional) localities; it may also be encountered by chance.

Bionomy ↔: It is migratory. In the non-breeding season it occurs also in small groups.

⚭: The nest is a shallow, sparsely lined hollow in the ground, usually beside a stone. The two to four olive-brown, mottled eggs (41.3×28.5 mm) are laid in May—June. It nests solitarily and has one brood a year, but polyandrous ♀♀ may have as many as three clutches; ♂ incubates for 24 days. The young soon leave the nest, are cared for mostly by ♂, and fledge after 30 days. ◗: Small invertebrates gathered on the ground.

Conservation It is not numerous. An expedient measure is protection of individual nests, as well as nesting habitat.

2

1

Grey Plover
Pluvialis squatarola

Identification Appearance — voice — behaviour — coloration
✳: Almost the size of the Lapwing (28 cm). It has a round head, robust body, rather long legs, and broad pointed wings. In breeding plumage (1), the underparts from the bill and cheeks to the belly are black, and the upperside of the body mottled silvery-white and dark grey; ♀ less contrasting than ♂. In non-breeding plumage, the upperparts are brownish-grey with pale feather fringes and the underparts are very pale whitish; ♂ = ♀. The juv. plumage resembles the non-breeding plumage but is more yellow-brown above and buffer below. In all plumages the rump is white, the tail is barred, and the wings have a pale bar above and are pale below with a black 'armpit' (2). ✦: It runs about on muddy and bare soil in pattering fashion, stopping every few steps, and flies rapidly in a straight line, though more leisurely than smaller plovers. ☉: It frequently utters a loud flute-like *dveeueekh*. ∾: The Golden Plover (*P. apricaria* — 3), which occurs in the same regions.
Ecology ◈: Tundra, mainly drier areas. In the non-breeding season mostly flat muddy shores on the sea coast, very occasionally also inland. ∞: It may be located by its voice and can be observed directly in typical habitats. The nest may be discovered by the behaviour of the birds and by searching the site. Non-breeding birds also occur well south of the nesting grounds in summer.
Bionomy ↔: It is migratory and is found at the nesting grounds in May—Aug. In the non-breeding season it occurs in small groups. ☙: The nest is on the ground. The four brownish, dark-patterned eggs (52.0×36.3 mm) are laid in June—July. It has one brood a year, nests solitarily, and incubates for 26 days. The young are cared for by both parents outside the nest for 40 days.
Conservation No special protection is necessary.

2

3

1

Lapwing
Vanellus vanellus

Identification Appearance — coloration — voice — behaviour

✳: A large wader (30 cm) with a short neck and legs, a long stiff crest and broad róunded wings. Adults (1) are contrastingly dark and white, and in flight (2) the dark upperside of the wings, white base of the tail and white underside of the inner wing are well visible. ♀ has pale spots in the dark-coloured crown, chin and throat, and in winter both sexes have the chin and throat white. Juv. birds have a shorter crest and their dark colouring is more brownish and intermingled with white. ✦: It runs about on the ground, stopping every now and then, holding itself erect and bowing, and often flying from one spot to another. It is skilful in flight, its wingbeats rather leisurely; during the courtship display in spring it performs acrobatic dives, turns and somersaults. ☉: It often utters a loud wailing *keeu-wit;* on migration also a *keeit.* ☜: It is unmistakable.

Ecology ◈: Meadows, pastures, fields, mainly near water, muddy shores. ∞: At the nesting grounds it can be recognised by its unmistakable voice and flight; the nest may be located by the behaviour of the birds (the eggs as well as young birds are provided with excellent cryptic coloration). In the non-breeding season it occurs on farmland and flat muddy shores.

Bionomy ↔: It is partly migratory. In the non-breeding season it occurs in flocks, sometimes very large ones. ◡: The nest is a sparsely lined hollow in the ground; often several pairs nest close to each other. The three to four olive yellowish-brown eggs with dense dark markings

(46.6×33.3 mm) are laid in Feb.—June. It has one brood a year and incubates for 24 days. The young soon leave the nest, are tended by both parents, and fledge after 33 days. ◑: Small invertebrates, gathered on the ground.

Conservation Its eggs used to be collected for food. At present it is numerous, but it is essential to protect its habitats.

2

1

Sanderling
Calidris alba

Identification Appearance — coloration — behaviour

✳: This sandpiper, about the size of a Skylark (20 cm), has short legs and a straight bill the same length as the head. In flight (2), the conspicuous white bar on the wings, and the grey tail with white on either side at the base and dark down the centre are obvious. In breeding plumage the birds are rusty-brown (♀ greyer) above, with a white belly. The non-breeding plumage is very pale: the underparts are entirely white, and the upperparts are pale whitish-grey, with the bend and tip of the wings dark; ♂ = ♀. The juv. plumage (1) is streaked blackish on the crown, the upperparts have bold black and rusty-yellow markings, and the breast has dark-speckled buff patches at the sides. ✦: It runs lightly and rapidly at the water's edge, fleeing from incoming waves, and flies rapidly. ⊙: When disturbed, it utters a *pit pit* in a burst; close to, a soft *trrr* may be heard. ♋: In size and appearance it resembles other sandpipers of the genus *Calidris*, e.g. the larger Knot (*C. canutus* — 3), the Purple Sandpiper (*C. maritima* — 4) and the smaller Little Stint (p. 90), but its coloration, its wingbar and its behaviour are characteristic.

Ecology ◆: Arctic tundra and sandy shores; in the non-breeding season flat shorelines, especially sandy sea coasts. ∞: At the nesting grounds the nest may be located by the behaviour of the adults and by searching the site. In the non-breeding season it may be seen on flat coastal shores in traditional areas.

Bionomy ↔: It is migratory and is found at the nesting grounds in May—Aug. In the non-breeding season it generally occurs in groups. ♡: The nest is a sparsely lined hollow in the ground. The three to four olive-green darkly patterned eggs (35.6×24.6 mm) are laid in June—July. It has one brood a year, nests solitarily, and incubates for 24 days. The young soon leave the nest, are cared for by both parents, and fledge after 30 days. ◑: Small invertebrates, gathered at the edge of water.

Conservation No special protection is necessary.

2

3

4

89

1

Little Stint
Calidris minuta

Identification Appearance — size — coloration — voice

∗: About the size of a Wheatear (14 cm) and with short legs and a straight, slender bill shorter than the head. In flight (4), the narrow pale bar on the wings and the greyish-white tail with dark feathers down the centre can be seen. The legs are black. In breeding plumage the upperparts are rusty and blackish and the breast dark-speckled rufous, while the non-breeding plumage (2) is grey-brown above with greyish breast; in both plumages the belly is white; ♂ = ♀. Juv. birds (July—Nov.) have rusty-brown on the sides of the breast, and are rusty and black above with white markings on the shoulders forming a characteristic V (1). ✦: It moves about agilely on muddy shores by the edge of water; it flies often and rapidly. ☉: It frequently utters a thin, high-pitched *tit-tit*. ☺: In Europe chiefly Temminck's Stint (*C. temminckii* — 3, 5).

Ecology ◈: Marshy tundra; in the non-breeding season flat muddy shores, including inland on migration. ∞: At the nesting grounds it can be located by its behaviour; the nest may be discovered by searching the site. In the non-breeding season it occurs on flat shores and at muddy inland sites, usually with other waders.

Bionomy ↔: It is migratory and is found at the nesting grounds in June—Aug. In the non-breeding season it generally occurs in small groups. ♡: The nest is a sparsely lined hollow in a drier spot. The four olive-brown dark-mottled eggs (29.0×20.7 mm) are laid in June—July. It nests solitarily, and incubates for 20 days. The young

leave the nest on hatching and are tended by both parents. ◖: Small invertebrates, gathered at the edge of water.

Conservation This is a little-known species even though it is quite numerous. It is essential to provide protection at the nesting grounds as well as during the non-breeding season.

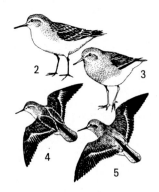

1

Dunlin
Calidris alpina

Identification Size — appearance — coloration ✳: This medium-sized sandpiper (18 cm) has the bill curved slightly downward at the tip and longer than the head, and short legs. In flight (2), the pale wingbar, white sides to the rump and the dark-centred tail are visible. The breeding plumage (1) is rusty and blackish above with a black belly. In the non-breeding plumage the upperparts are brownish-grey, and the underparts whitish with a grey breast; ♂ = ♀. Juv. birds are blackish, brown and chestnut above, and have blackish spots on the flanks. ✦: It walks about on flat shores and often wades in shallows. It flies rapidly, and flocks execute abrupt turns. It often occurs in the company of other species (Little Stint, Curlew Sandpiper, and others). ☉: It often utters a harsh wheezing *keerr;* during courtship a purring trill. ♋: Mainly the Curlew Sandpiper (*C. ferruginea* — 3), quite common throughout Europe. In eastern Europe the rare Broadbilled Sandpiper (*Limicola falcinellus* — 4).
Ecology ◆: Marshlands and moors; in the non-breeding season muddy shores and muddy areas inland. ∞: At the nesting grounds, watch the conspicuous behaviour of the adults in the vicinity of the nest and young and search the site. In the non-breeding season it can be observed well on mudflats.
Bionomy ↔: It is migratory and is found at the nesting grounds in Apr.—Aug. In the non-breeding season it forms flocks, often very large ones. ᴗ: The nest is a sparsely lined hollow in grass. The four (five) olive yellowish-brown eggs with darker markings (34.6×24.3 mm) are laid in May—July. It has one brood a year, nests solitarily, and incubates for 17 days. The young leave the nest on hatching, are tended by both parents, and fledge after 26 days. ☻: Small invertebrates, gathered on dry ground and mud.
Conservation In the southern parts of its breeding range it is an endangered and disappearing species; elsewhere it is numerous. It is essential to protect its nesting grounds.

2

3

4

1

Ruff
Philomachus pugnax

Identification Appearance — coloration
✳: A larger wader (♂ 28 cm, ♀ 22 cm) with long legs and neck, and a relatively short bill the same length as the head. Visible in flight (2) is the conspicuous white oval patch on each side of the rump, forming a white V when viewed from the tail end. In breeding plumage ♂ has a large and striking ruff and ear tufts of varying coloration, each bird being different, very striking (white, chestnut, black, purple, in varying combinations). ♀ (1) is pale brown; ♂ in non-breeding plumage resembles ♀, but is bigger. Juv. birds are similar to ♀, but are scaly above with blackish feathers edged with buff and are warm buff below. ✦: It walks slowly in shallow water or on flat muddy shores. It flies rapidly, flocks often gliding. In spring the males wage fierce fights. ☉: It is rarely heard, even at the nesting grounds; when alarmed, it may utter a muffled *gaga*. ☜: ♂ in breeding dress is unmistakable; in non-breeding plumage ♀ and juv. birds differ from common species of *Calidris* by their long orange, yellow, green or grey legs, and from birds of the genus *Tringa* by their rump pattern.
Ecology ◈: Wetlands, damp meadows, moors; in the non-breeding period also muddy coastal and inland areas. ∞: At the nesting grounds it may be recognised by its behaviour during courtship and in the vicinity of the nest and young. In the non-breeding season it can be found in appropriate habitats (often traditional sites).
Bionomy ↔: It is migratory and is found at the nesting grounds in Apr.—Oct.; during the nest-

ing period non-breeders may be found throughout much of Europe. In the non-breeding season it forms flocks, sometimes numbering thousands. ♒: It generally nests in small groups. The nest is a sparsely lined hollow in grass. The three to four olive-greenish eggs with dense dark markings (43.5×30.6 mm) are laid in May—June. It has one brood a year, and ♀ incubates for 21 days. The young soon leave the nest, are tended by both parents, and fledge after 26 days. ◗: Small invertebrates, gathered in mud and in grass.
Conservation It is numerous in places. At the southern edge of its range it is necessary to protect its nesting grounds.

2

92

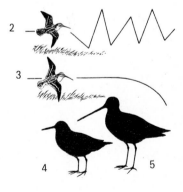

Common Snipe
Gallinago gallinago

Identification Behaviour — appearance — voice
✳: This smaller snipe, about the size of a Blackbird (26 cm), has short legs, a short neck and a very long bill. Adults (1, 5) are mottled brown, their wings have a very narrow white rear inner edge, and the sides of the tail are narrowly edged with white. ♂ = ♀ = juv. ✦: It stands by the edge of water probing with its bill into the mud. It rises abruptly when disturbed, and flies very rapidly and on a zigzag course (2). During courtship it flies about its territory, alternately swooping up and down. ☉: When alarmed it utters a scratchy *ech-ech*. During the courtship display, the vibration of the outer tail feathers as it dives causes a sound like the bleating of a goat; it also sings a repeated *tikeh tikeh*... ♋: The Great Snipe (*G. media*), less common in Europe and differing in size, markings, and mainly style of flight (3), and the smaller Jack Snipe (*Lymnocryptes minimus* — 4), with a much shorter bill.
Ecology ◈: Marshes, moors, wet meadows, muddy shores. ∞: At the nesting grounds it may be recognised by the striking sounds it makes during courtship. Locating the nest is difficult; it is necessary to explore suitable sites and flush the sitting bird. In the non-breeding season it may be seen probing in muddy areas or may be flushed when walking through marshy places.
Bionomy ↔: It is partly migratory and is found at the nesting grounds in Mar.—Oct. ✎: The nest is a sparsely lined hollow in grass. The four olive-green, dark-patterned eggs (39.2×28.3 mm) are laid in Mar.—July. It has one, perhaps two broods a year, nests solitarily, and ♀ incubates for 19 days. The young leave the nest on hatching, are tended by both parents, and fledge after 20 days. ◑: Small invertebrates, gathered from the ground or from mud.
Conservation This is a less important game bird; it is disappearing in cultivated countryside. It is necessary to protect the nesting grounds and possibly also to regulate hunting at the wintering grounds.

1

Woodcock
Scolopax rusticola

Identification Habitat — appearance — behaviour — voice

✳: Its body is the size of a Lapwing (34 cm). It has a small head with a long straight bill, eyes placed high on the head, short neck, robust body, short tail and short legs. Its plumage is dark brown, heavily barred and mottled (1). ♂ = ♀; juv. birds have a spotted forehead. ✦: It stays concealed, alone, in damp locations almost exclusively in woods. It is conspicuous only during the courtship period; its flight resembles a bat's, with movements from side to side. ☉: It utters its typical call almost continually only when flying around its territory: a relatively thin, high-pitched whistling followed by a deep gobbling sound — *psee psee, kvorr kvorr.* ♋: It is unmistakable.

Ecology ◈: Forests and woodland from lowland elevations to the upper forest limit, primarily in damp locations. In the non-breeding season it is found also in more open country. ∞: It can be located both by sight and by its voice as it flies around its territory. These flights take place above woodland clearings and along the edge of forests only for a brief period at dusk when the stars begin to show, in spring or after the arrival from wintering grounds or when nesting a second time (June—July). The paths of these flights are well known, but the birds do not necessarily nest there; the lengthier presence of the birds is a sign of their nesting. Finding the nest is very difficult; it may be discovered by searching the area very thoroughly (the bird flies up at the last moment).

Bionomy ↔: It is mostly resident but partly migratory, and is found at the nesting grounds in Mar.—Sept. ☽: The nest of dry leaves is located on the ground by a tree trunk, tree stump, or under bracken. The four yellowish, brown-mottled eggs (44.0×33.6 mm) are laid in Mar.—July. It has one or two broods a year, nests solitarily, and ♀ incubates for 21 days. The young leave the nest on hatching, and when danger threatens ♀ carries them elsewhere; they fledge after 40 days. ◖: Worms, earthworms and other animal life in the ground, caught by probing in the soil with its beak.

Conservation This is an important game bird but declining in numbers. We do not know precisely the reasons for its decline or how to protect it, but habitat preservation and regulation of hunting are important.

Black-tailed Godwit
Limosa limosa

Identification Size — appearance — behaviour — voice

✳: This large wader (42 cm) has a small head with a very long, almost straight bill, long neck and legs and a short tail. The broad white wing-bar and the white tail with a black terminal band are conspicuous in flight (2). In breeding plumage (1) the head, neck and breast are red-dish-brown and the upperparts dark brown and rust-coloured; ♀ is duller than ♂. In non-breeding plumage the upperparts, neck and head are greyish-brown and the underparts whitish; ♂ = ♀. The juv. plumage is similar to breeding plumage but very much paler. ✦: It walks slowly, and flies rapidly and in a straight line with legs extending beyond tail. During the courtship period, and when danger threatens the nest, it flies about the territory with loud cries. ☉: Its resounding *kvu-eeay* in display resembles the call of the Lapwing; when alarmed it utters *ketekeek,* during courtship a plaintive fluty *dyedyodyedyo.* ♋: Throughout Europe mainly the Bar-tailed Godwit (*L. lapponica* — 3).

Ecology ◈: Wet meadows, pastures, edges of water with low vegetation, and the like. In the non-breeding season muddy shores. ∞: The nesting site may be located by the calls of court-ing birds. The nest is readily found by search-ing the site thoroughly; the newly-fledged young press tightly to the ground when alarmed and difficult to find. Adults are most likely to be seen when walking or in flight.

Bionomy ↔: It is migratory and is found at the nesting grounds in Mar.—Sept. In the non-breeding season it generally occurs in groups. ♥: The nest is a sparsely lined depression on the ground. The four green eggs mottled blackish-brown (55.1×37.8 mm) are laid in Apr.—June. It has one brood a year, and incu-bates for 23 days. The young leave the nest on hatching, are tended by both parents, and fledge after 30 days. ◑: Small invertebrates, gathered from the ground and in mud in shal-low water.

Conservation This is a declining species. It is es-sential to protect its wetland environment.

1

Curlew
Numenius arquata

Identification Voice — size — appearance
✱: A large wader (55 cm) with a small head, very long downcurved bill, and a rather long neck and legs. Adults (1) are pale brown with dark streaks, and in flight show a conspicuous white rump; ♂ = ♀. Juv. birds are slightly paler and have a shorter bill. ✦: It walks leisurely about on the ground; its flight is not particularly rapid. During courtship it flies about the nesting territory in circles. ☉: Its voice is often heard, and includes a loud fluty *koorlui,* a *kwu-kwu-kwu* and, especially during courtship, a liquid and bubbling trill. ♋: Throughout Europe mainly the less common and smaller Whimbrel (*N. phaeopus* — 2); in eastern Europe the very rare Slender-billed Curlew (*N. tenuirostris*).
Ecology ◆: Damp meadows, pastures, moorland, sometimes also fields; in the non-breeding season flat muddy shores and coastal fields. ∞: The nesting site may be located by the birds' calls during courtship; however, sometimes a territory is defended by birds that do not nest. The nest may be located by the behaviour of the birds and by exploring the site; newly-fledged young are hard to find, despite the loud and aggressive behaviour of the adults. In the non-breeding season, the Curlew may be located by its voice or may be observed walking and foraging for food on flat muddy shores.
Bionomy ↔: It is generally migratory and is found at the nesting grounds in Mar.—Aug. In the non-breeding season it usually occurs in groups and flocks. ᰦ: The nest is a hollow in the ground, generally located in thick grass and near water. The three to four greenish-brown,

dark-mottled eggs (67.8×47.5 mm) are laid in Mar.—June. It has one brood a year, nests solitarily, in suitable sites sometimes with a few pairs together, and incubates for 28 days. The young soon leave the nest, are guided about by both parents, and fledge after 40 days. ◖: Small invertebrates, found in soil and mud.
Conservation Its numbers are declining in cultivated countryside. It is necessary to protect its nesting grounds and major wintering grounds.

2

96

1

Spotted Redshank
Tringa erythropus

Identification Appearance — voice — coloration

✱: This bird, about the size of the Mistle Thrush (30 cm), has long legs, long bill, and long slender neck. The legs are dark red, and the bill is slender and blackish with a red base to the lower mandible. The fairly uniform colour of the upperwing and the white of the rump extending onto the back between the wings are well visible in flight (2). Adults in breeding plumage are almost black, with white spotting above (1); ♀ may be distinguished by her less intense colouring and faint pale feather fringes. The non-breeding plumage is greyish-brown above and white below; ♂ = ♀. The juv. plumage resembles the non-breeding plumage but is conspicuously darker with more markings, particularly on the underside. ✚: It walks about on the ground or in water; its flight is very rapid. Striking features of the courtship are the flights and calls. ☉: Its call is often heard; when alarmed it utters a loud *chuvik*. ♋: In non-breeding and juvenile plumages mainly the Redshank (p. 98), which, however, is more mottled, has a conspicuous white band on the wings, and has a different voice.

Ecology ◈: Swampy forest-tundra; in the non-breeding season flat muddy estuaries as well as fresh waters. ∞: The nesting site may be located by the calls and behaviour of adults, the nest discovered by observation and exploration of the site. In the non-breeding season the Spotted Redshank may be identified by its voice and by observation at suitable (often traditional) sites.

Bionomy ↔: It is migratory and is found at the nesting grounds in May—Sept. In the non-breeding season it mostly occurs singly or in small groups. ♋: The nest is a depression in grass on the ground. The three to four grey-green, darkly mottled eggs (47.1×32.3 mm) are laid in May—June. It has one brood a year, and generally nests solitarily. The young soon leave the nest and are tended by both parents. It is not known how long the birds incubate and care for the young. ◑: Small invertebrates gathered on the ground and on muddy shores and underwater.

Conservation This is a common species and no special protective measures are necessary.

2

1

Redshank
Tringa totanus

Identification Voice — appearance — coloration — behaviour

∗: A medium-sized wader (28 cm) with a long bill and legs, a long slender neck, and a short tail. The bill base and legs are bright orange-red. The white bar on the rear edge of the wings, the white rump and the greyish-brown tail are conspicuous in flight (2). Adults (1) are brown, darkly patterned above, and white with brown streaking below; ♂ = ♀. Juv. birds are more heavily patterned and duller, with yellower legs. ✦: It walks about on the ground, wades in water, and flies rapidly. During the courtship period it flies around the nesting territory in circles. ☉: It is often heard, its calls including a loud fluty *chu*, a three-syllable *chu-hu-u* and in alarm a repeated *chewk*; its song includes a repeated *tooli*. ♋: The Spotted Redshank (p. 97) in non-breeding and juvenile plumages, which, however, has darker red legs, lacks the white bar on the wings, and has a different voice.

Ecology ◈: Wet meadows, pastures, edges of water with low vegetation; in the non-breeding season mainly flat muddy shores. ∞: The nesting site may be located by the calls and behaviour of the adults and by patient observation; young birds pressed close to the ground in grass are very inconspicuous. In the non-breeding season adult birds are easily observed at suitable sites and identified by their voice.

Bionomy ↔: It is resident or migratory and is found at the nesting grounds in Mar.—Aug. In the non-breeding season it occurs in flocks or in small groups. ♥: The nest is a depression in

grass on the ground. The four yellow-brown, darkly patterned eggs (44.1×31.0 mm) are laid in Mar.—June. It has one brood a year, usually nests solitarily, and incubates for 24 days. The young soon leave the nest, are cared for by both parents, and fledge after 30 days. ◗: Small invertebrates, gathered from the ground or muddy bottoms.

Conservation This is a declining species. It is essential to protect the nesting and wintering grounds.

2

1

Greenshank
Tringa nebularia

Identification Voice — size — coloration
✶: The size of a Mistle Thrush (31 cm) and with a very long, slightly upturned bill, long neck and long legs. In flight (2) the wings are a uniform dark colour above, the white rump extends in a wedge to the middle of the back, and the tail is white barred with grey. The breeding plumage (1) is pale brown with dark markings above, the breast spotted blackish; the non-breeding plumage is slightly paler above and whitish below. ♂ = ♀. Juv. birds are browner, with more markings. ✦: It walks about on dry land and on shores, often wading up to its breast in water and even swimming; when pursuing small fish, it quickens its movements. Its flight is rapid. ☉: Its call is a frequent loud, fluty *chu-chu-chu*, sometimes monosyllabic; when disturbed, a penetrating *kiyk-iyk*. ☾: In eastern Europe the relatively rare Marsh Sandpiper (*T. stagnatilis*), which is smaller, paler in colour, and gives weaker calls which include a trilled *bibibi*...
Ecology ◈: Tundra and forest-tundra; in the non-breeding season flat shores of seas and fresh waters. ∞: The nesting site may be identified by the calls and behaviour of the birds. The nest and young may be located by the behaviour of the adults, by observing them or by exploring the site; young birds pressed close to the ground are very inconspicuous. In the non-breeding season the birds may be identified on the shore either by sight or by voice.
Bionomy ↔: It is migratory and is found at the nesting grounds in Apr.—Aug; non-breeders commonly occur in more southerly regions during this period. In the non-breeding season it occurs singly or in scattered groups. ♆: The nest is a depression in grass on the ground. The four yellow-brown, darkly patterned eggs (50.8×34.5 mm) are laid in Apr.—June. It has one brood a year and incubates for 24 days. The young soon leave the nest, are tended by both parents, and fledge after 30 days. ◑: Smaller animals obtained from the ground, mud and water.
Conservation No special protective measures are necessary.

2

1

Wood Sandpiper
Tringa glareola

Identification Appearance — behaviour — voice — coloration

✳: The size of a thrush (20 cm) and with bill longer than the head and quite long yellow legs. In flight (2), the wings are dark above, pale on the undersurface, the rump is white, and the tail is finely barred with grey. In breeding dress the birds are dark brown and finely patterned above, pale with browner markings on the breast, and the belly is white. The non-breeding plumage is similar but less patterned; ♂ = ♀. Juv. birds (1) are more brown, their feathers edged a yellowish colour. ✦: It walks about on flat shores or in shallow water and flies rapidly. During courtship it flies repeatedly around the nesting territory; near the young it is aggressive. ☉: It frequently utters a resounding soft multisyllabic *didi-dididi*; in display a repeated loud *didldidl*. ♋: Throughout Europe mainly the Green Sandpiper (*T. ochropus* — 3).

Ecology ◈: Moorland, wet meadows, flooded areas. In the non-breeding season marshes and flat shores, mostly by fresh waters. ∞: The nesting site may be located by the birds' behaviour and calls during the courtship period, the nest may be discovered by exploring the site; the young are difficult to locate outside the nest. In the non-breeding season the birds may be identified by their voice and by observation in suitable localities.

Bionomy ↔: It is migratory and is found at the nesting grounds in Apr.—Aug. Non-breeders occur also in more southerly districts during this period. In the non-breeding season it oc-

curs mainly in groups and larger flocks. ∾: The nest is a depression in grass on the ground. The four pale ochre, darkly patterned eggs (38.4×26.4 mm) are laid in Apr.—June. It has one brood a year, nests solitarily, and incubates for 23 days. The young leave the nest on hatching, are tended by both parents, after 10 days usually by only one parent. ◖: Small invertebrates obtained from the ground and from mud.

Conservation It is numerous. No special protection is necessary.

2

3

1

Common Sandpiper
Actitis hypoleucos

Identification Appearance — behaviour — voice — coloration

✳: A small bird the size of a Starling (20 cm) and with very short legs, bill the same length as the head, a conspicuous white wingbar and white sides to the tail (2). In breeding plumage (1) the birds are dark greyish-brown above, with white underparts and greyish-brown breast and throat; the non-breeding plumage is more brown and less patterned. ♂ = ♀. In the juv. plumage the yellow-brown feather edges produce a bolder pattern on the upperparts. ✦: It walks about on the shore with body bent forward, continually pumping its tail up and down and often jerking its head. It flies swiftly close above the water, with rapid shallow wingbeats interrupted by short stiff-winged glides in which the wings are bowed downward. During courtship it flies around the boundaries of the nesting territory. ☉: It frequently utters a clear penetrating *heedidi*, especially during the courting period. ♋: It differs from small members of the genus *Tringa* by its shorter legs, and from members of the genus *Calidris* by its longer bill, behaviour and voice.

Ecology ◈: Shores of fresh waters, mainly sandy and gravelly alluvial deposits, also the muddy bottoms of bodies of water. In the non-breeding season also marshes and the sea coast. ∞: It may be located by its voice and by observation. The nest as well as young are difficult to find, despite the conspicuous behaviour of the adults both during courtship and with the young. In the non-breeding season it may be located by its voice, particularly in the evening, by flushing the bird or by observation.

Bionomy ↔: It is migratory and is found at the nesting grounds in Apr.—Aug. On migration it occurs singly or in small flocks. ♒: The nest is a sparsely lined depression on the ground, usually in a clump of grass. The three to four yellow-brown eggs with greyish-brown markings (36.1×25.8 mm) are laid in Apr.—July. It has one brood a year, nests solitarily, and incubates for 22 days. The young soon leave the nest, are tended by both parents, and fledge after 27 days. ◑: Small invertebrates obtained at the water's edge.

Conservation It is numerous. Its riverside nesting grounds are endangered by the regulating of watercourses.

2

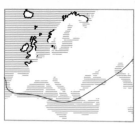

1

Turnstone
Arenaria interpres

Identification Appearance — coloration — behaviour

∗: A smaller wader the size of a thrush (23 cm), it has a short neck and legs, and a conical, slightly upturned bill shorter than the head. The two white wingbars, the white rump and the black and white tail are obvious in flight. The breeding plumage (2) is contrastingly variegated in black, grey, white and chestnut: ♂ has the top of the head almost white and the breast black, ♀ has the head more streaked and the black and chestnut areas duller. In non-breeding plumage (1, 3) the entire upperparts are blackish-brown, the breast darkly patterned, the chin white and the legs orange. The juv. plumage resembles the adult non-breeding plumage, but is browner with more pronounced markings and the legs are yellowish. ✦: It walks about on flat shores, turning over weeds and smaller stones with its bill. During courtship the males wage fierce combats and make low reeling flights above the nesting territory. ☉: Often heard, especially in the evening and at night during the migration period, is its harsh *khya, kea;* other calls include a harsh *khihkhihkhih* and a *tiyktiyktiyk rurrurrurrur.* ☺: It is unmistakable.

Ecology ◈: Flat sea coasts, mainly gravelly and stony shores, but also sandy and muddy shores (rarely inland). ∞: The nesting site may be located by the conspicuously loud courtship call, the nest by observing and by exploring the site, and the young by the behaviour of the adult birds. In the non-breeding season birds are easily observed on the shore.

Bionomy ↔: It is migratory and is found at the nesting grounds in Apr.—Sept. In winter it occurs in flocks. ♡: The nest is a depression in the ground between stones. The three to four brownish-green eggs with olive markings (40.7×29.2 mm) are laid in May—July. It has one brood a year, nests solitarily, and incubates for 23 days. The young soon leave the nest, are tended by both parents, and fledge after 20 days. ◐: Small shoreline invertebrates.

Conservation No special protection is necessary. It is quite numerous by the sea coast.

2

3

1

Red-necked Phalarope
Phalaropus lobatus

Identification Appearance — behaviour — coloration

✳: A smaller wader (16 cm) with a short neck, short legs, and a narrow bill the same length as the head. There is a conspicuous white wingbar, and the rump and tail are blackish-brown with white sides to the rump. In breeding plumage the upperparts are dark grey with feathers bordered rusty-brown, the underside is white except for the grey breast, the chin is white, and an orange-red band extends from the eye, down the neck sides to the lower foreneck; ♂ is duller, browner. The non-breeding plumage is pale grey above with darker wings, white below, and there is a dark patch behind the eye; ♂ = ♀. The juv. plumage (1) is much darker than the non-breeding adult plumage, blackish-brown above with prominent rusty-yellow stripes on the back. ✦: Mostly it swims, riding buoyantly high up in the water (2); when foraging for food, it spins around on the surface. It flies lightly and rapidly. ☉: It utters a sharp, penetrating *kit* and *kirrek*. ☜: In non-breeding plumage it resembles the Grey Phalarope (*P. fulicarius*) of the Arctic, a scarce migrant in west Europe, which has a bigger head and thicker bill.

Ecology ◈: Small lakes and marshes in the tundra; in the non-breeding season the open sea, rarely other kinds of water. ∞: The nesting grounds may be located by the courtship and behaviour of adults, the nest by exploring suitable sites and by observation. In the non-breeding season it may be encountered by chance observation.

Bionomy ↔: It is migratory and winters on the open sea, rarely occurring inland. It is found at the nesting grounds in May—Aug. In the non-breeding season it occurs singly or in small groups. ☙: The nest is a depression in grass tussocks. The four olive-brown eggs with dense dark markings (29.5×20.7 mm) are laid in May—June. It has one brood a year, generally nests in small colonies, and ♂ incubates for 20 days. The young soon leave the nest, are tended only by ♂, and fledge after 20 days. ◐: Small invertebrates picked from the surface of the water.

Conservation It is not very numerous. However, no special protection is necessary, apart from protection of its nesting habitats and ensuring freedom from disturbance there.

2

1

Great Skua
Stercorarius skua

Identification Appearance — size — coloration
✳: The size of a Pheasant (56 cm) and with
a strong bill, robust body, and a short, slightly
wedge-shaped tail (2). Adults (1) are dark
brown with paler markings and a conspicuous
white flash on the wings at the base of the primaries; ♂ = ♀. Juv. birds are a darker and
more uniform colour, blacker above, and the
white flash on the wings is smaller. ✦: It flies
leisurely with slow wingbeats, occasionally gliding; when pursuing birds carrying prey, it flies
more rapidly and zigzags, plummeting to catch
food they drop or disgorge. It swims buoyantly.
At the nesting grounds it is very aggressive.
☉: It is heard occasionally; when attacking it
utters a guttural *tak tak,* also a harsh *skirr* and
low-pitched barking *ok ok.* ♋: In northern Europe three other skuas, all smaller and differing
in the shape of the tail: the Arctic Skua (*S. par-
asiticus* — 4), Pomarine Skua (*S. pomarinus* —
3), and Long-tailed Skua (*S. longicaudus* — 5).
Ecology ◈: It breeds on northern moorlands
and tundra; in the non-breeding season it stays
out at sea, less often by the coast, and very occasionally on inland waters. ∞: The nesting
grounds may be located by the concentration of
birds and their flights over the site; the birds'
behaviour is very striking and aggressive; the
nest is unconcealed. During the non-breeding
season the birds may be encountered by chance
or at particular coastal migration watchpoints.
Bionomy ↔: It is migratory and winters in the
Atlantic. It is found at the nesting grounds in
Mar.—Sept. In the non-breeding season it occurs singly or in loose groups. ♒: The nest is

a scrape in the ground. The one to two olive
greenish-brown eggs with brown markings
(73.0×49.4 mm) are laid in May—July. It has
one brood a year, nests in small colonies, and
incubates for 29 days. The young remain in the
vicinity of the nest, are tended by both parents,
and fledge after 44 days. ◖: Various vertebrates
stolen from gulls, terns, etc., as well as carrion
and offal.

Conservation A rare species. It is essential to
provide protective legislation and to ensure that
the nesting grounds are undisturbed.

1

Little Gull
Larus minutus

Identification Size — coloration
✳: The smallest gull (28 cm), about the size of the Collared Dove. It has a round head, weak bill, and rounded wings. In breeding plumage (2) the head is coal-black, this colour extending well down the nape, the upperwings are grey, and the underwings blackish with a white rear edge; in non-breeding plumage the head is pale grey with a black patch behind the eyes and greyish-black crown. ♂ = ♀. In juv. birds (1, 3) the head is the same as in the non-breeding plumage, the underwings are white and the upperwings are grey with a black band forming an angled M when viewed from the rear. ✦: It flies well, generally close above the water, occasionally higher, and executing abrupt turns. It swims buoyantly, riding high in the water. It is often seen in the company of other gulls. ☉: It utters an abrupt *kek,* sometimes repeated in succession. ☜: In the breeding plumage it is unmistakable. Juv. birds resemble the Black-legged Kittiwake (p. 110).
Ecology ◈: Waters overgrown with marsh vegetation, generally seashores, less often inland waters. ∞: The nesting grounds may be located by observing adults in suitable habitats (though they may be non-breeding individuals), the nest by noting where the birds alight and by checking out the spot. In the non-breeding season these gulls may be observed on water.
Bionomy ↔: It is migratory and is found at the nesting grounds in Apr.—Sept. ◡: The nest is located on water or in vegetation, often in colonies of Black-headed Gulls or Common Terns. The three olive-brown, darkly patterned

eggs (41.5×30.1 mm) are laid in May—June. It has one brood a year, nests in colonies, and incubates for 22 days. The young keep close to the nest, are tended by both parents, and fledge after 24 days. ◕: Mostly small invertebrates obtained on the water's surface or in flight over reedbeds.
Conservation It is relatively numerous. It is necessary to protect the nesting grounds.

2

3

1

Black-headed Gull
Larus ridibundus

Identification Size — appearance — coloration — voice

✳: A small gull (35 cm) about the size of a pigeon. It has a rather small head with a slender bill; the bill and legs are red and the rear outer wings are black. In breeding plumage (1, 3) the chocolate-brown colour of the head does not extend to the nape; in non-breeding plumage the head is white with pale grey crown and a dark brown spot behind the eye. ♂ = ♀. The juv. plumage (2) resembles the non-breeding plumage but there are brown and blackish feathers on the wings and a black terminal band on the tail. ✦: It flies well, occasionally gliding in circles; when travelling greater distances flocks fly in V-formation. It swims buoyantly and walks and runs about adroitly on the ground. At the nesting grounds it is extremely aggressive and noisy. ☉: It frequently utters a loud chuckling *creep,* a cry of alarm *kverr, kriririp,* and other calls. ⚏: The Mediterranean Gull (*L. melanocephalus*), relatively common in southeastern Europe, in which the hood is black and extends onto the nape and the wings lack black.

Ecology ◈: Marshes, bodies of water with islets. In the non-breeding season it occurs also on other inland waters and on the sea coast, sometimes flying far from water and often being found in cities. ∞: In the above-mentioned places it can be seen and heard without any difficulty.

Bionomy ↔: It is generally dispersive and migratory and is found at the nesting grounds in Mar.—July, afterwards dispersing in various directions. In the non-breeding season it occurs in flocks, less often singly. ⌀: The nest is located on water, in vegetation, as well as on the ground. The three eggs, generally dark green with dense dark markings (51.9×36.7 mm), are laid in Apr.—July. It has one brood a year, nests in colonies, and incubates for 23 days. The young stay near the nest, are tended by both parents, and fledge after 27 days. ◐: Mostly small animal life, to a lesser extent also seeds and fruits (e. g. cherries) and refuse. It obtains its food on the ground, in trees, in or on water, as well as in the air.

Conservation In some places it is reaching plague numbers. No special protection is necessary.

2

3

1

Common or Mew Gull
Larus canus

Identification Size — appearance — coloration
✳: Visibly larger than the Black-headed Gull
(40 cm). It has a round head, a bill that is not
particularly strong, and a rounded tail. The
adult plumage (1, 3) is white and grey, the
wingtips are black with white markings, the bill
yellowish, the legs yellow-green; ♂ = ♀. Juv.
birds (2) have the top of the head pale brown,
the back buffish, the upperwings brown, grey-
brown and blackish-brown, and the tail white
with a broad dark brown terminal band. ✦: It
flies more slowly than the Black-headed Gull,
with more leisurely wingbeats. It swims and
walks well, and often stands on the shore. ☉: It
utters a rather high-pitched penetrating *keke,
kie* and similar calls, but is less vocal than most
other gulls. ♋: Throughout Europe the similar
Herring Gull (p. 109), which, however, is larger
and has a stout bill. In flocks of Black-headed
Gulls the Common Gull is distinguished by its
larger size, round head with high forehead and
stouter bill, juv. birds by their brown coloration.
Ecology ◈: During the breeding season mostly
sea coasts, vicinity of lakes, low moors, and
hills near the shore. In the non-breeding season
it stays near shores, often occurring also inland,
mainly around large rivers, large ponds and
valley lakes. ∞: It is easily observed beside
water, including birds flying about at the nesting grounds and sitting on the nests.
Bionomy ↔: It is mostly migratory and is found
at the nesting grounds in Apr.—Oct. In the
non-breeding season it forms loose groups.
♺: The nest is located on the ground, in

semi-cavities, in old nests in trees, very occasionally on rocks. The three olive-brown,
darkly patterned eggs (56.2×40.8 mm) are laid
in May—June. It has one brood a year, nests in colonies, and incubates for 23 days. The young
stay near the nest, are cared for by both parents, and fledge after 35 days. ◑: Small invertebrates, obtained from the ground and from
water.
Conservation It is locally numerous, and its
numbers are on the increase. Protection is not
necessary.

2   3

1

Lesser Black-backed Gull
Larus fuscus

Identification Appearance — size — coloration
∗: A large gull (53 cm) with a stout bill and
long wings. Adults have the head, underside
and tail white, and the upperside of the body
and wings slate-grey (*L. f. graellsii*) to black
(*L. f. fuscus* — 1); the bill is yellow with a red
spot, the legs yellow. ♂ = ♀. Juv. birds have the
head and underparts pale brown, the back and
upperwings patterned dark brown. In the second year the back is darker; in the third year
so, too, are the upperwings, but some dark
markings may still show on the underparts and
tail. ✦: It flies leisurely, with slow wingbeats,
often rests on the shore, and runs a short way
before taking to the air; it follows ships. It
swims well. ☉: It often utters loud mewing,
barking and chuckling sounds. ☜: Throughout
Europe the Herring Gull (p. 109) — juv. birds
of which are practically indistinguishable; in
more northerly parts of Europe the Great
Black-backed Gull (*L. marinus*; 2 — adult, 3 —
juv.).
Ecology ◈: It is found mainly on flat sandy sea
coasts. In the non-breeding season it occurs on
the open sea, also at reservoirs, rubbish tips.
∞: It may be observed mainly on the sea coast,
or inland on larger bodies of water; the nesting
grounds may be located by the direction in
which the birds fly and by their behaviour.
Bionomy ↔: It is mostly migratory, and occurs
in loose groups. It is found at the nesting
grounds in Apr.—Oct. ♡: The nest is located
on the ground in grass, sand, between stones.
The three olive-brown darkly patterned eggs
(67.0×46.7 mm) are laid in Apr.—July. It has

one brood a year, nests in colonies, and incubates for 27 days. The young stay near the nest,
are tended by both parents, and fledge after 35
days. ◑: Various marine animals, offal and refuse, obtained from the water and on the shore.
Conservation It preys on other birds on the
shore. No special protection is necessary.

2

3

1

Herring Gull
Larus argentatus

Identification Size — appearance — coloration — behaviour

✳: About the size of the Lesser Black-backed Gull (56 cm) and likewise has a stout bill, rounded tail and white head, but adults (1) have the upperwings and back variably pale to darker grey (2). The bill is yellow with a red spot. The legs of south European subspecies (*L. a. cachinnans, L. a. michahellis*) and some north European populations (the *'omissus'* group) are yellow; in others they are flesh-coloured. ♂ = ♀. Juv. birds in their first year are very like the young of the Lesser Black-backed Gull; in their second year their back begins to turn grey. ✦: It flies leisurely, with slow wingbeats, and follows ships. It often rests on the shore, where it feeds on marine animals and scraps; it runs briefly before taking to the air, and swims well. ☉: It often utters loud chuckling, mewing and barking sounds. ♋: Mainly the Lesser Black-backed Gull (p. 108), juv. birds of which are practically indistinguishable.

Ecology ◀▶: Sea coasts, inland large bodies of water and rubbish tips. ∞: It is easily observed on the sea coast and at other suitable sites; the nesting grounds may be identified by the concentration of birds, their flights in the vicinity and their behaviour, and by checking on the nests.

Bionomy ↔: It is a resident as well as partly migratory species, occurring in greater numbers as a rule in the non-breeding season. It is found at the nesting grounds in Apr.—July. ౿: The nest is located on the ground or cliffs, but sometimes also on buildings. The three olive yellow-brown eggs with dark markings (70.5×49.1 mm) are laid in Apr.—June. It has one brood a year, nests mostly in colonies, and incubates for 26 days. The young stay near the nest, are tended by both parents, and fledge after 37 days. ◑: Various marine animals, the eggs of birds and their young, and refuse, obtained on the ground and on water.

Conservation It has overmultiplied in some areas. It preys on other birds. Protective measures are not required; its numbers are locally regulated.

2

1

Black-legged Kittiwake
Rissa tridactyla

Identification Size — appearance — coloration
＊: Slightly larger than the Black-headed Gull
(41 cm), and with a round head with slender
bill and short legs. Adults (3) are white, with
a grey back and upperwings and black wingtips;
♂ = ♀. Juv. birds (1, 2) have a white head with
a black band on the hindneck, a black zigzag
band on the upperwing (shaped like a wide-
angled M when viewed from the rear), and
a black band on the tail. ✦: Its flight is light
and effortless, like that of terns; it often flies
close above the water. It swims buoyantly. ☉: It
is hardly ever heard away from the nesting
grounds; at the nesting grounds it utters the
characteristic *kittiveek.* ♋: The Common Gull
(p. 107) resembles adult Kittiwake but it has
white markings at the ends of the black wingtips and a more rounded tail. The Little Gull
(p. 105) resembles juv. birds but it is smaller,
has the top of the head black and lacks the
black band on the nape.
Ecology ◈: Seas; it nests on coastal cliffs as
well as on buildings at the seaside. ∞: It may be
found chiefly on the sea coast; the nesting
grounds may be located by the concentration of
birds, the direction of their flights and their behaviour, and the nest by observation.
Bionomy ↔: It is migratory and dispersive. In
the non-breeding season it forms flocks that
remain on the open Atlantic for most of the
time. It is found at the nesting grounds in
Apr.—Aug. ◡: The nest is located on rock
ledges. The two pale greenish-brown dark-patterned eggs (50.6×41.2 mm) are laid in May—
June. It has one brood a year, nests in colonies,

and incubates for 27 days. The young stay at the
nest, are tended by both parents, and fledge
after 43 days. ◖: Various marine animals
obtained from the water's surface.
Conservation No special protection is necessary
away from the nesting grounds.

2

3

Common Tern
Sterna hirundo

Identification Appearance — behaviour — size — coloration — voice

✳: A medium-sized tern (35 cm) with a slender body, long pointed wings, short legs and a long, deeply forked tail. The breeding plumage (1) is white with grey upperparts and a black cap, red bill tipped with black, and red legs; in the non-breeding plumage the forehead is white, and the legs and bill are dark coloured. ♂ = ♀. The juv. plumage is like the non-breeding plumage, but the upperparts and wings have brown and blackish markings and the base of the bill and legs are pinkish-orange. ✦: It lives gregariously, and often rests on the shore or on objects in the water (e.g. on buoys). It flies (2) very effortlessly, with a slight upward swing every wingbeat and abrupt changes of direction, frequently hovering before plummeting into the water. In flight it is often seen carrying a fish in its bill. ☉: It frequently utters a penetrating *kirr kirr, krrierr*; when attacking an intruder a piercing *kikikiki.* ♋: Very similar are the Arctic Tern (*S. paradisaea* — 3) of northern Europe, and the Roseate Tern (*S. dougallii*), sparsely distributed on the coasts of the British Isles.

Ecology ◈: Marshland, shallow waters with islets, rivers and sea coasts. ∞: It may be identified by its voice and by observing birds in flight. At the nesting grounds they sit, stand guard and fly from one place to another in some numbers; to locate the nest, however, it is necessary to check out the site.

Bionomy ↔: It is migratory and is found at the nesting grounds in Apr.—Oct. ॐ: The nest is a scrape among vegetation on the shore, etc.

The two to four olive brownish-yellow eggs with dark markings (41.5×30.5 mm) are laid in Apr.—Aug. It has one brood a year, nests in colonies, and incubates for 24 days. The young stay at the nest, are tended by both parents, and fledge after 28 days. ◐: Aquatic animal life, including small fish, captured underwater.

Conservation A declining species. It is vital to protect the nesting grounds, and to provide flat artificial islets.

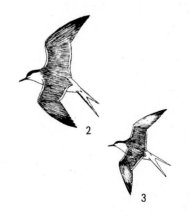

1

Little Tern
Sterna albifrons

Identification Appearance — size — coloration
✳: The smallest tern, about the size of a Starling (23 cm), and with a short, slightly forked tail (2), yellow bill tipped with black, yellow legs, and grey back and upperwings. In breeding plumage (1) it has a black cap and white forehead; in the non-breeding plumage the crown also is white. ♂ = ♀. Juv. birds have brown markings on the forewings and back.
✦: It flies faster than larger terns, with more rapid wingbeats, and frequently hovers in one spot above the water. It plunges into the water with a splash in pursuit of prey (3). ☉: It frequently utters a loud penetrating *krit krit.* ♋: It is unmistakable.
Ecology ◆: Sandy and gravelly seashores, islets, locally inland on rivers; in the non-breeding season also other waters. ∞: At the above habitats birds may be observed mainly in flight; they may be identified also by their voice. The nesting site may be located by observing the flights of the birds, their concentration and their behaviour; to discover the nest it is necessary to check out the site.
Bionomy ↔: It is migratory and is found at the nesting grounds in Apr.—Oct. In the non-breeding season it occurs in loose groups as well as singly. ☽: The nest is a depression in bare ground. The two to three greyish-ochre, darkly patterned eggs (32.3×23.8 mm) are laid in May—July. It has one brood a year, nests in colonies, and incubates for 21 days. The young remain in the vicinity of the nest, are tended by both parents, and fledge after 20 days. ◑: Exclusively aquatic animal life, mainly crustaceans and small fish and to a smaller extent molluscs and insects.
Conservation Locally it is a regular breeder but not very numerous. It is declining in numbers, the reasons for this being not known. It is vital to protect the nesting grounds.

2

3

1

Black Tern
Chlidonias niger

Identification Appearance — behaviour — coloration
✳: A smaller tern the size of a Blackbird (24 cm) and with a short, slightly forked tail. In breeding plumage (1, 2) the head and body are black, the tail and wings dark grey. In the non-breeding plumage (4) the body is white, and on the head only the crown and a patch on either side of the hindneck are black. The intermediate plumage has variegated markings (3). The bill and legs are always dark. ♂ = ♀. In the juv. plumage (5) the upperparts are patterned dark brown and the markings on the head are the same as in the non-breeding plumage. ✦: It generally flies close above the water, frequently changes direction, and occasionally turns and drops to the surface to capture prey. As a rule it occurs in loose groups, resting on objects in the water; at the nesting grounds it is aggressive. ☉: It frequently utters a plaintive *klieh,* an abrupt *kitt;* when attacking an intruder at the nesting grounds, *kitkitkitkyeh.* ♋: In eastern Europe mainly the White-winged Black Tern (*C. leucopterus* — 6); in southern and southeastern Europe locally the Whiskered Tern (*C. hybridus* —7). Juv. birds may perhaps be mistaken for the Little Gull (p. 105).
Ecology ◈: Inland marshes, old arms of rivers, bodies of water, etc.; in the non-breeding period also sea coasts. ∞: The birds are most easily observed in flight, as a rule close above water. The nesting grounds may be identified by the concentration and behaviour of the birds, the nests sometimes being visible from afar; note the frequent occurrence of non-nesting birds.

Bionomy ↔: It is migratory and is found at the nesting grounds in Apr.—Oct. ♋: The nest, generally made of coarse bits of plants, is located on a mass of floating vegetation. The two to three yellow-brown, darkly patterned eggs (34.8×25.2 mm) are laid in May—July. It has one brood a year, nests in colonies, and incubates for 16 days. The young are tended by both parents and fledge after 28 days. ◑: Mainly insects caught in the water and above the water's surface.
Conservation This is a declining species and it is essential to protect the nesting grounds; it is possible to provide man-made floating foundations for the construction of the nests.

113

1

Common Guillemot
Uria aalge

Identification Appearance — coloration — behaviour

∗: It resembles a small penguin (40 cm). It has a long, slender neck, short wings, tail and legs, and wedge-shaped head extending into a long slender bill (4). The breeding plumage (1) is black above and white below; the head is entirely black, and in some birds there is a narrow white ring around the eye with a line extending backwards from it. The non-breeding plumage is similar, but the throat and cheeks are white and there is a narrow black stripe behind the eye. ♂ = ♀. The juv. plumage is scaly dark brown above. ✦: It occurs in flocks. It nests on the rocky ledges of cliffs in colonies together with other bird species. It swims and dives extremely well; it flies (2) rapidly in a straight line, often in line formations. ☉: It utters a loud, variously modulated *errr,* mostly at the nesting grounds. ♋: Brünnich's Guillemot (*U. lomvia* — 3), commonly found in northern Europe, which differs in having a stouter bill with a white stripe at the base, and the Little Auk (*Alle alle*), which differs in size (5).

Ecology ◈: It is a seabird. ∞: The nesting grounds are on rocky coastal cliffs, mainly on islands, and are conspicuous from afar. In the non-breeding season it may be encountered only by chance.

Bionomy ↔: It is partly migratory, wintering in the Atlantic. It is found at the nesting grounds in Jan.—Aug. ∞: It has one brood a year and does not build a nest. The single egg is laid on a bare rocky ledge; it is pear-shaped, greenish, darkly mottled (81.5×49.7 mm), and is laid in May—June and incubated for 32 days. The young birds remain in the nest 20 days, then leap into the sea and are tended by the parents until they fledge. ◕: Almost exclusively fish caught underwater.

Conservation It is very numerous. In some places it is hunted and its eggs are gathered, and it is also a frequent victim of oil spillages. Apart from regulating exploitation and control of pollution, no other protective measures are necessary for the time being.

2

3

4

5

Razorbill
Alca torda

Identification Size — appearance — coloration
✳: In size (40 cm) and appearance it resembles
the Common Guillemot, but has a large flat
head and stout compressed bill. The breeding
plumage (1) is black above with a narrow white
rear edge to the wing, and white below. The
non-breeding plumage is similar, but the chin
and cheeks are also white. ♂ = ♀. The juv. plumage resembles the non-breeding plumage but
lacks the white markings on the bill. ✦: It
stands upright on cliffs. It flies rapidly (3), at
sea usually close above the surface in formations. It swims very well (2), and dives often.
☉: It makes growling and rumbling sounds at
the nesting grounds. ♋: Occurring in the same
localities are the equally large and similarly coloured Common Guillemot (p. 114), Brünnich's
Guillemot (*Uria lomvia*) and pigeons.
Ecology ◈: It is a seabird. ∞: It nests on cliffs
on the sea coast together with other alcids and
gulls. These bird cliffs can be readily spotted by
the concentration of birds. In the non-breeding
season it may be encountered only by chance.
Bionomy ↔: It is partly migratory, wintering in
groups as well as singly in the Atlantic, Baltic
Sea and the Mediterranean. It is found at the
nesting grounds in Jan.—Aug. ᗯ: It does not
build a nest; the single egg is laid on a rock
ledge, in a rock crevice, under an overhang, or
in a cleft. The egg, white with dark blurred
markings (75.3×47.8 mm), is laid in May—
June. It has one brood a year, nests in colonies,
and incubates for 36 days. The young remain in
the spot where they hatch for 20 days and then
jump off into the sea, where they are tended by
both parents until they fledge. ◑: Smaller fish,
less often also other aquatic animals, captured
underwater.
Conservation In some places the eggs are gathered at the nesting grounds and it is hunted for
its meat; it also falls victim to oil spillages.
Apart from control of exploitation and oil pollution, no other protective measures are necessary.

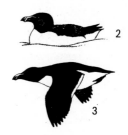

1

Identification Appearance — coloration — size — behaviour

✳: A medium-sized alcid (33 cm) with a long slender neck and a small head extending into a long, slender, straight bill. The breeding plumage (1, 3) is entirely black with a large white wing patch; in the non-breeding plumage (2) the black upperparts are mixed with white, the underside is white, but the wing pattern remains the same. ♂ = ♀. Juv. birds have black feathers in the white wing patch. ✦: It stays more on the coast than other alcids, generally on rocky shores. It swims well, dives, and flies in a straight line with extremely rapid wing-beats close above water. ☉: A high-pitched rattling *vee-vee*, uttered more frequently in early spring. ☜: It differs from alcids of the genus *Uria* occurring in the same localities mainly in the wing pattern in all plumages.

Ecology ◈: Sea coasts with rocky shores and cliffs; in the non-breeding period inshore seas. ∞: It can be observed at appropriate sites around the coast; locate the nest by the calls and behaviour of the birds and by exploring the locality where they are permanently present.

Bionomy ↔: It is mainly dispersive, wintering around the coasts of the northern Atlantic and Baltic. It is found at the nesting grounds mostly in Mar.—Sept. Throughout the year it occurs singly or in small groups. ☽: The nest is located on the ground between boulders, in cliff crevices or crannies. The two greenish dark-patterned eggs (58.1×39.5 mm) are laid in May—June. It has one brood a year and incubates for 30 days. The young are cared for by both par-

ents and remain at the nest for 40 days. ☜: Mostly small fish caught underwater.

Conservation It is numerous in certain places, where it is sometimes hunted for its meat and the eggs are gathered. No special protection is necessary.

2

3

Puffin
Fratercula arctica

Identification Appearance — coloration — behaviour

∗: A smaller alcid (30 cm) with striking, deep, compressed, brightly coloured bill, short neck, and short wings and tail. The breeding plumage (1) is black above, and white on the underside and on the cheeks; in the non-breeding plumage the cheeks are grey. ♂ = ♀. In juv. birds (2) the bill is much smaller and duller, and the cheeks are dark grey. ✦: It swims well, holding the neck erect, and dives well. It flies rapidly, often in line formations close above water. The fish carried to the nest in the bill hang crosswise (like whiskers). The birds often rest upright on cliffs. ☉: It is heard only at the nesting grounds, where it utters a guttural growling *orrr*. ♋: It is unmistakable.

Ecology ◈: It is a seabird, nesting on coasts with grassy slopes. In the non-breeding season it stays in flocks on the open sea; only very occasionally is it seen inland. ∞: It can be observed on sea coasts and also by chance on the open sea. The nesting grounds may be found by the constant presence of a greater number of birds, by the direction of their flight and by their behaviour; the nest may be located by exploring suitable sites.

Bionomy ↔: It is partly migratory and is found at the nesting grounds in Mar.—Aug. ♒: It nests in ground burrows — rabbit holes, the burrows of shearwaters and petrels, or under boulders. The single greyish-white egg with delicate dark markings (60.8×42.3 mm) is laid in Apr.—June. It has one brood a year, nests in colonies, and incubates for 39 days. The young remain in the nest 40 days and are cared for by both parents. ◐: Small fish caught underwater.

Conservation In and around the places where it nests it is very abundant. In some regions its meat, fat and eggs are used by man. It is necessary to provide for rational exploitation, and to control oil pollution.

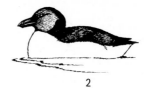

2

Raptors and owls

Raptors (Falconiformes) and owls (Strigiformes) were formerly considered to be closely related birds of prey, the one group diurnal and the other nocturnal. Their superficial similarities — sharp beak and talons — are, however, the result of adaptations to hunt, seize and devour prey. Otherwise their bodily features are different, and there is no relationship between the two groups. Owls are unmistakable birds. They have a thick layer of soft, fluffy feathers, a large round head and large eyes adapted to seeing even in dim light. They are typified by the Tawny Owl (1). In the wild they may be seen only by chance, but their presence is betrayed during the nesting period by their eerie cries, audible over long distances in the stillness of the night.

Raptors are a much more diverse group in terms of species, size and method of hunting. Systematically they are currently divided into four families: the American or New World vultures (Cathartidae); the cosmopolitan Old World vultures, hawks, eagles, kites and harriers (Accipitridae); the Osprey (Pandionidae); and the falcons (Falconidae). The Accipitridae family includes the following three types. Extremely large species with broad wings that move almost exclusively in long soaring and gliding flight high up in the sky and feed on carrion; these are typified by the Griffon Vulture (2). Species that are only slightly smaller in size, have broad wings with primaries spread apart like fingers, usually have a short tail, and which are typified by the Golden Eagle (3); besides gliding, they also fly normally to capture live prey. And thirdly, medium-sized species with rather broad rounded wings and rather long tail that alternate gliding and active flight and attack live prey; these are typified by the Goshawk (4). The Pandionidae family contains a single species, the Osprey, which hovers above water and then dives for fish. Raptors of the Falconidae family include smaller to very small species typified by the Eurasian Kestrel (5), with narrow pointed wings and tail of varying length, which attack prey in very swift flight. In all the above groups the male is smaller than the female. The dimensions given for each species are average values regardless of sex.

Raptors and owls are in the main declining to greatly endangered species. One reason for this is direct human persecution, another the accumulation in their bodies of pesticide residues from their food.

1

Honey Buzzard
Pernis apivorus

Identification Appearance — behaviour

✳: A medium-large raptor the size of the Common Buzzard (55 cm, wingspan 1.4 m), with a slender body and a small jutting head. The adult (1) is variably dark grey-brown, generally with a grey head, the wings are darkly barred on the underside and have a dark hind edge, and the tail has two dark bands and a dark terminal band (2); ♀ is slightly larger, usually darker and browner. Juv. birds are variably coloured from pale to dark. ✦: It flies slowly, occasionally gliding, and from time to time soars. Characteristic are the courtship flights (Apr.—June) of pairs, during which they occasionally clap their wings loudly above the body. When foraging for food, it walks about on the ground. ☉: Early in spring at the nesting grounds, it utters a high-pitched *kee-eh* or *pi-iy-ah.* ☜: The Common Buzzard (p. 129) is very similar, but has broader wings, a shorter tail, a less jutting head, and circles more often in flight.

Ecology ◁▶: Wooded regions, occasionally open countryside. ∞: The nesting grounds may be located by the birds' regular flights from one place to another, mainly during the courtship period; the nest may be discovered by carefully exploring suitable sites. In July—Aug. the newly-fledged young fly in circles around the nesting grounds together with the parents, constantly uttering loud cries. In the non-breeding season the Honey Buzzard may be encountered only by chance.

Bionomy ↔: It is migratory; on migration it may be seen also in larger loose groups. It is found at the nesting grounds in Apr.—Sept. ♡: The nest is located mostly in a tall broad-leaved tree where a branch joins the trunk, and its rim is continually decorated with fresh green twigs. The one to two yellowish eggs with dense dark markings (51.5×41.3 mm) are laid in May—July. It has one brood a year, nests solitarily, and incubates for 35 days. The young are tended by both parents, leave the nest after 40 days but return to it for another 14 days. ◑: Hymenopteran insects and their larvae, chiefly wasps, which the bird digs from the ground.

Conservation A declining species. Full protection is necessary.

2

1

Black Kite
Milvus migrans

Identification Appearance — behaviour
✳: The size of the Common Buzzard (58 cm, wingspan 1.7 m) but it has a very long, forked tail (2), less projecting head, and longer, narrower wings. The adult (1) is dark brown; ♂ < ♀. Juv. birds are paler, especially on the underside of the wings, with dark markings. ✦: It flies slowly and relatively close to the ground, frequently circling and occasionally hovering in one spot. ☉: At the nesting grounds it occasionally utters a rising *ayee*, followed by a descending *trrr,* also a repeated *kiki-ki* and mewing sounds. ♋: The Red Kite (*M. milvus* — 3), which, however, has an extremely long, deeply forked tail, the fork clearly evident even when the bird spreads its tail wide.

Ecology ◈: Parklands interspersed with woods, open spaces and water, in some places also near human habitations. ∞: It is conspicuous when it flies from one place to another in the vicinity of the nesting site; the nest may be discovered by searching the site, and is usually permanent. In the non-breeding season the Black Kite may be encountered by chance, especially near water or at rubbish tips.

Bionomy ↔: It is migratory. In the non-breeding season it occurs singly or in loose groups. At the nesting grounds, where it is found in Mar.—Oct., the birds stay in pairs, occasionally forming colonies. ∽: The nest, located high up in a tree where a branch joins the trunk, is relatively small (about 50 cm across), and littered inside with bits of cloth, leather, etc. The two to four greyish, brown-patterned eggs (54.0

×43.0 mm) are laid in Apr.—May. It has one brood a year, and incubates for 32 days. The young are cared for by both parents and remain in the nest 46 days. ◑: Frequently dead fish and other carrion, also smaller animals, mainly small mammals and insects, and refuse, gathered and hunted on the ground as well as on water.

Conservation Locally this is a declining species. It is necessary to provide it with year-round protection, including protection of the nesting grounds.

2

3

1

White-tailed or Sea Eagle
Haliaeetus albicilla

Identification Size — appearance — behaviour
✳: A large raptor (80 cm, wingspan 2.2 m). It
has a short body, broad, long wings with primaries spread like fingers, a short wedge-shaped
tail and a huge bill. The adult (2) is dark brown
with a white tail; ♂ = ♀. Juv. birds (1) have
a dark brown tail that gradually becomes white
in the second to fifth year. ✦: It perches on
trees, on the ground or on ice. Its flight is leisurely, with slow wingbeats; occasionally it
glides, and flies close above the ground in pursuit of prey. ☉: During the courtship period
and at the nesting grounds it utters a repeated
kliklikli and a softer barking *kakaka.* ⚲: It is
practically unmistakable. Only in extreme eastern Europe the rare Pallas's Sea Eagle (*H. leu-
coryphus*).
Ecology ◈: Countryside with plenty of water
— sea coasts, lowland country bordering rivers,
larger bodies of water. ∞: The nesting grounds
may be located by the regular occurrence and
courtship behaviour of adult birds (note that
there may also be non-breeding birds in the vicinity); the nest is a permanent structure that
can be discovered even in winter. In the non-
breeding season the White-tailed Eagle may be
encountered only by chance.
Bionomy ↔: It is resident and partly migratory,
sometimes roaming far from the nesting
grounds. In the non-breeding season it is often
found singly, but at the wintering grounds there
may also be a greater number of birds in
a small area. ◡: The huge nest is located in
a tree, at the top or by the trunk, or on a cliff
ledge; it is used for several years. The one to

two chalk-white eggs (74.7×57.9 mm) are laid
in Feb.—Mar. It has one brood a year, nests solitarily, occasionally several pairs close to one
another, and incubates for 40 days. The young
are tended by both parents, 90 days in the nest
and a further 30 days outside the nest. ◖:
Mainly dead animals as large as a hare; seized
in flight close above the ground or on water.
Conservation This is a greatly endangered species. Essential measures are full protection by
law, and active protection of the nests to ensure
undisturbed nesting; in some areas (e. g. west
Scotland), young birds raised in captivity have
been re-introduced into the wild.

2

1

Griffon Vulture
Gyps fulvus

Identification Size — appearance — behaviour
✳: One of the largest European raptors
(100 cm, wingspan 2.6 m). It has broad, stiff,
rounded wings, a long neck covered only with
down and with a ruff at the base, a small head,
and a stout bill. The adult (1) is brown, with
blackish-brown flight feathers and tail; the underwing-coverts are paler with dark markings,
and the ruff, neck and head are whitish;
♂ = ♀. In juv. birds the underside of the wings
is paler, contrasting with the dark flight feathers. ✦: It circles high up in the sky, expertly
soaring and gliding (2); on the ground the birds
converge on carcasses; it takes off into the air
cumbersomely after several hops. ☉: In groups
it utters hissing and deep croaking sounds.
♋: It is unmistakable. Other species of vultures
found in southern Europe are rare and/or differ in appearance: the European Black Vulture
(*Aegypius monachus* — 3), the Egyptian Vulture
(*Neophron percnopterus* — 4), and the Lammer-
geier (*Gypaetus barbatus* — 5).
Ecology ◈: Relatively uncultivated regions,
mainly mountains and foothills. When roaming
the countryside it occurs in various environments. ∞: The nesting grounds may be determined by the more regular occurrence of the
birds and by exploring suitable sites (their location in Europe is generally known to ornithologists). In the non-breeding season it may be
encountered by chance.
Bionomy ↔: It is mainly a resident species, but
roams widely in the vicinity of the nesting
grounds and regularly far from the nest.
♥: The nest is located on a rock ledge or cave

on precipices. The single chalk-white egg
(92.4×69.7 mm) is laid in Feb.—May. It has
one brood a year, nests solitarily as well as in
small colonies, and incubates for 52 days. The
young are cared for by both parents, 90 days in
the nest and a further 25 days outside the nest.
◐: Mainly carcasses of large animals searched
for in flight.
Conservation This is a rare, greatly endangered
species. Necessary measures are full protection
by law, protection of the nesting grounds, and
possibly also the providing of food.

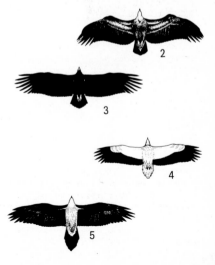

2

3

4

5

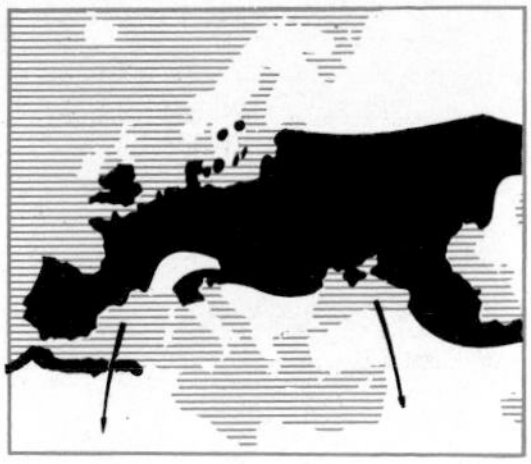

Montagu's Harrier
Circus pygargus

Identification Appearance — behaviour
✱: Smaller and more slender than the Common Buzzard (45 cm, wingspan 1.1 m). The adult ♂ (1) is pale grey with long slender wings, and has dark primaries throughout their length and a dark bar at the base of the secondaries (3). In juv. birds the underside of the body is a vivid rusty-brown without markings, in ♀ it is whiter with dark streaks. The pale collar around the neck in ♀ is only faintly discernible (6) or absent. ✦: It flies slowly close above the ground, wings held in a shallow V, with frequent abrupt changes of direction and descents to the ground. ⊙: At the nesting grounds it infrequently utters a *kekeke* and other sounds. ♋: The Hen Harrier (*C. cyaneus*) is very similar. ♂ is pale blue-grey above, with sharply defined white rump (uppertail-coverts); all the primaries are pale at the base so that the dark wingtip is demarcated by a line perpendicular to the body axis (2). In ♀ and juv. birds the underside of the body is brownish-white with dark streaks; in ♀, the pale collar around the neck is distinct but narrow and often darkly streaked (5). ♂ Pallid Harriers (*C. macrourus* — 4) have the front part of the body very pale but the rump is never white; the dark wingtip is narrowly conical. In juv. birds the underside of the body and underwing-coverts are rusty-brown and unstreaked. ♀ has a broad pale collar around the neck, and the sides of the neck streaked longitudinally (7).
Ecology ◗: Open countryside, mainly with damp meadows, mostly at lower elevations. ∞: The nesting grounds may be located by the more frequent occurrence of the birds, by their voice and by their dropping out of sight onto the nest; the nest may be discovered by searching the presumed site. In the non-breeding season chance observation is the only possibility.
Bionomy ↔: It is migratory. In the non-breeding season it occurs singly. ◡: The nest, made of dry stalks, is located on the ground in thick low cover. The three to five greyish-white eggs (41.7×32.5 mm) are laid in Apr.—July. It has one brood a year, nests solitarily, in suitable sites also with several pairs relatively close together, and incubates for 29 days. The young are cared for by both parents, 40 days in the nest and a further 12 days outside the nest. ◑: Mostly small mammals, hunted in low flight close above the ground.
Conservation This is a vulnerable species. Locally it is relatively numerous, but generally its numbers are decreasing. It is essential to provide full protection by law and ensure undisturbed nesting at the breeding grounds.

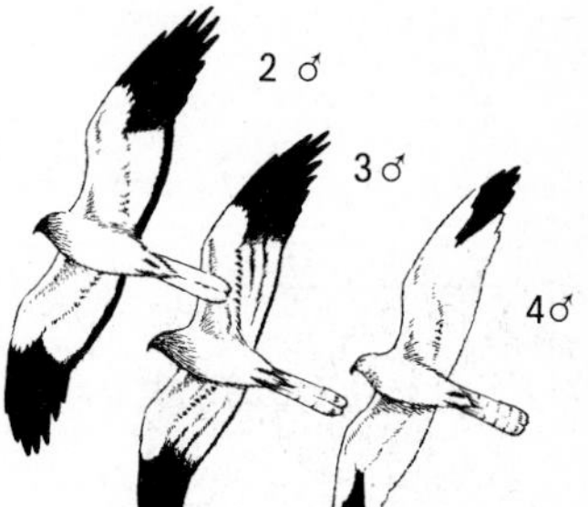

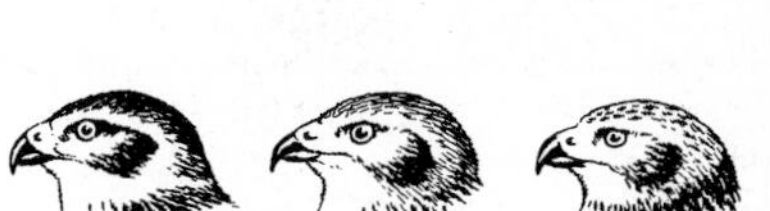

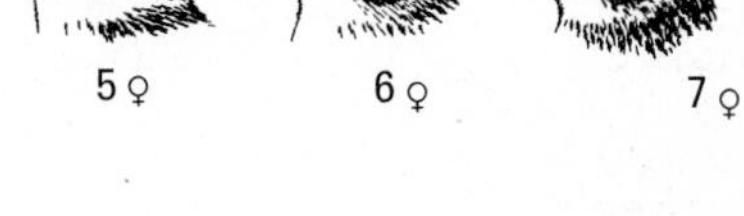

1

Marsh Harrier
Circus aeruginosus

Identification Habitat — appearance — behaviour

∗: Slightly smaller than the Common Buzzard (52 cm, wingspan 1.2 m) and with a slender body, long, relatively narrow wings with rounded and 'fingered' tips and a long tail. Adults are brown; ♂ (2) has a pale head, a large pale grey expanse on the wings, and a pale tail, while ♀ (1, 3) is entirely brown with a pale yellowish head and fore edge of wings. Juv. birds resemble ♀, but generally lack the pale fore edge of the wings and sometimes also the pale markings on the head. ✦: It flies close above the ground, relatively slowly with abrupt turns, occasionally circling, and dropping to the ground or into vegetation. ☉: At the nesting grounds it utters a shrill *whay-ee*. ☎: It is distinguished from other harriers by its coloration; it never has a white rump.

Ecology ◈: Reedbeds and their vicinity; in the non-breeding season also other open countryside, including fields. ∞: It may be seen at possible nesting grounds, where it drops down onto the nest; to pinpoint the nest it is necessary to search through the vegetation. In the non-breeding season it may be observed by chance.

Bionomy ↔: It is mainly migratory and is found at the nesting grounds in Mar.—Oct. In the non-breeding season it lives solitarily or in loose groups; sometimes a greater number of birds roost together. ᴥ: The nest, made of dry twigs, reeds and herbage from the neighbourhood, is located in larger reedbeds on flattened or broken reeds, occasionally also on the ground. The four to five whitish eggs

(49.1×37.7 mm) are laid in Apr.—June. It has one brood a year, mostly nests solitarily, and ♀ incubates 33 days. The young are cared for by both parents, 40 days in the nest and for a longer period outside the nest. ◑: Vertebrates as large as a gull, captured in low flight by pouncing on them on the ground.

Conservation Locally it is quite numerous and is increasing in numbers. In areas with intensive breeding of small game it may cause local damage. It is necessary to provide full protection, including protection of the nesting grounds.

3♀

2♂

126

1

Goshawk
Accipiter gentilis

Identification Appearance — size — behaviour — voice

∗: A medium-sized raptor (55 cm, wingspan l. 1 m) with short, broad, rounded wings and a long tail. The adult is grey with a dark upperside (3), pale underside with dark bars (2), and orange eyes. Juv. birds (1) are brown, the pale underparts being patterned with tear-drop streaks, including the straw-coloured breast and underwings. The south European race (*A. g. arrigonii*) is very dark, the north European race (*A. g. buteoides*) light-coloured. ✦: It watches for prey from a tree. In flight it alternates several wingbeats with brief glides; it also soars. As a rule it flies relatively low around the edge of the forest and among the treetops. ⊙: During the courtship period it utters a resounding *gigigi*. ♋: ♀ Sparrowhawk (p. 128) is almost the same size as ♂ Goshawk; when gliding, the rear edge of the Sparrowhawk's wing is straighter, less bulging.

Ecology ◈: Forests, from lowland elevations to the upper forest limit. ∞: At the nesting grounds it may be recognised by its voice in early spring (Jan.—Mar.) as it circles its territory; the nesting grounds are permanent, and it is possible to find remnants of prey in the territory. An occupied nest may be recognised by the feathers of the moulting female scattered around the nest and by the droppings beneath the nest. In the non-breeding season it may be seen by chance even in less wooded countryside, including the outskirts of cities.

Bionomy ↔: It is resident, roaming the countryside around the nesting territory; northern pop-

ulations also fly farther south for the winter. It is a solitary bird. 👁: The nest is located in a treetop next to the trunk. The three to four pale greenish-yellow eggs (57.2×45.1 mm) are laid in Mar.—May. It has one brood a year, nests solitarily, and ♀ incubates 37 days. The young are cared for by both parents, 38 days in the nest and 30 days outside the nest. ◑: Birds and mammals as large as a domestic hen, caught in flight amidst the treetops as well as on the ground.

Conservation In game preserves with intensive breeding of small game it may cause local damage, though on the other hand it regulates the numbers of crows. Its numbers depend markedly on the extent to which it is persecuted. Protection is possible mainly by regulating hunting.

2 ♀

3 ♂

1

Sparrowhawk
Accipiter nisus

Identification Appearance — size — behaviour — voice

∗: About the size of a pigeon (33 cm, wingspan 65 cm). The perched bird has long legs and a robust body. The wings are broad and rounded (2), the tail long, and the head small. The adult ♂ (1) is grey above, with underparts densely streaked reddish-brown. ♀ is greyish-brown above with a white stripe above the eye, and has whitish underparts with dark brown barring. Juv. birds resemble ♀, but the brown colouring is more rusty. ✦: It often perches on solitary trees or at the edge of woods. It flies at a relatively low height among the treetops, around the edge of forests, and quite frequently also over open expanses. ☉: Adults utter a penetrating *kikiki*; the young make plaintive whistling sounds. ♋: The Goshawk (p. 127), which, however, has the rear edge of the wing angled at the junction of the primaries and secondaries, forming an S shape. In southeastern Europe the rarer Levant Sparrowhawk (*A. brevipes*).

Ecology ◆: Wooded areas from lowland elevations to the upper forest limit. ∞: At the nesting grounds it may be recognised by its voice in early spring (Feb.—Apr.) and when raising the young (May—June). Occupied nests are full of down feathers and scattered around them are individual wing or tail feathers from the moulting female. Near the nest there are a number of spots where the birds pluck their prey and which contain remnants of the victims. In the non-breeding season it may be seen by chance, even outside forests and frequently also in cities. The loud agitated cries of small birds betray their presence.

Bionomy ↔: It is a resident, solitary bird, which roams in the vicinity of its territory; some birds journey for the winter as far as southern Europe. ♒: The nest is located by the trunk in the dense crown of a tree. The four to five greenish, brown-patterned eggs (40.5×32.5 mm) are laid in Apr.—June. It has one brood a year, nests solitarily, and ♀ incubates for 35 days. The young are tended by both parents, 27 days in the nest and a further 25 days outside the nest. ◑: Small birds as large as a Blackbird, caught skilfully in flight in thickets and treetops.

Conservation Locally it is numerous, but in some areas it is endangered by the increasing saturation of the environment with chemicals. One means of protection is by regulating hunting, which is illegal in many countries.

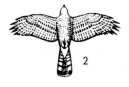

2

Common Buzzard
Buteo buteo

Identification Size — appearance — behaviour — voice

✳: The commonest central European medium-sized raptor (55 cm, wingspan 1.2 m). It has broad, rounded wings and a short, rounded (often spread), barred tail (2). Its coloration exhibits marked variation: generally it is dark brown with paler underwings; ♂ = ♀ = juv. ✦:It flies slowly, often soaring in circles without moving the wings; very occasionally it hovers in one spot. It perches on trees, high poles, elevated spots, as well as on the ground (1). ☉: It often utters a resonant *keeah-keeah*; newly-fledged young keep up a continual piping. ♋: In more northerly Europe the locally abundant Rough-legged Buzzard (p. 130), which, however, has the base of the tail whitish, and in southeastern Europe the rare Long-legged Buzzard (*B. rufinus* — 3). The Honey Buzzard (p. 120) is also very similar, but it is more slender, with a smaller head, and has a longer tail with characteristic markings.

Ecology ◈: Wooded and open country from lowland elevations to the upper forest limit. ∞: The nesting grounds may be located by the constant presence of buzzards conspicuously circling overhead, engaging in aerial acrobatics, and uttering loud cries. Look for the nest by exploring suitable sites; it is usually permanent. In the non-breeding season one can readily see both flying and perched birds in open country.

Bionomy ↔: It is partly migratory and is found at the nesting grounds in Feb.—Sept. ☽: The nest is usually located by the trunk in treetops, sometimes in a solitary tree, on cliffs as well as (rarely) on the ground. The three to four bluish, brown-patterned eggs (56.2×44.6 mm) are laid in Mar.—June. It has one brood a year, nests solitarily, and incubates for 35 days in the nest and 50 days outside the nest. ◐: Mostly small mammals caught on the ground.

Conservation This is an important predator of the common vole and the rabbit; it causes negligible damage, and only locally, to wild game. Protection consists of regulating hunting. It is very numerous.

1

Rough-legged Buzzard
Buteo lagopus

Identification Appearance — size — behaviour
∗: In size (58 cm, wingspan 1.4 m) as well as
general appearance it resembles the Common
Buzzard; ♂ < ♀. It has broad, rounded wings,
a short, broad tail, and legs feathered down to
the toes. The adult (1) is dark brown above with
the tail white at the base, the underparts brown
intermingled with white, and the underwings
mostly white with a characteristic conspicuous
dark patch at the bend (2). ♂ = ♀ =juv. ✦: It
flies leisurely with slow wingbeats, frequently
circling; over short distances from one place to
another, it flies close above the ground. It often
hovers in one spot. It perches on elevated spots
on the ground. ☉: Rarely, it utters a plaintive
keeah. ☎: The Common Buzzard (p. 129), in
which, however, the base of the tail is not white
and which is usually darker. In southeastern
Europe the Long-legged Buzzard (*Buteo rufinus*).
Ecology ◈: Open country: rocky tundra, fields,
etc. ∞: The nesting grounds may be determined
by the constant presence of the birds and their
flights from one place to another; the nest may
be found by searching through suitable sites. In
the non-breeding season it may be readily observed in flight, as well as perched in open
country.
Bionomy ↔: It is migratory, and nests and lives
solitarily (occasionally several birds congregate
in one spot). It is found at the nesting grounds
in Apr.—Sept. ♥: The nest is located on the
ground or on a cliff. The three to four bluish,
darkly patterned eggs (55.3×44.3 mm) are laid

in Apr.—June. It has one brood a year, and ♀
incubates for 30 days. The young are cared for
by both parents, 40 days in the nest and 30 days
outside the nest. ◖: Small mammals and birds
caught in flight close above the ground.
Conservation It is plentiful but its numbers exhibit marked fluctuations. It preys on smaller
vertebrates, at its wintering grounds mainly on
the common vole. When the snow cover is very
thick and the vole population is small, it may
cause local damage to small game in places
where it occurs in some numbers. Possible protection consists of regulating hunting.

2

1

Lesser Spotted Eagle
Aquila pomarina

Identification Appearance — size — behaviour
✳: A small eagle (63 cm, wingspan 1.5 m),
slightly larger than a buzzard. It has relatively
long, broad wings; in flight their edges are
straight and the primaries spread like fingers
(3). The adult is dark brown, with the upperside
of the wings contrastingly lighter; the white
patch at the base of the primaries and frequently the pale uppertail-coverts in the shape
of a U are visible in flight; ♂ < ♀. Juv. birds
(1) are browner with a whitish patch on the
nape and white-tipped upperwing-coverts,
secondaries and tail feathers; visible in flight is
the white patch at the base of the primaries and
the paler upper- and underwing-coverts. In
their 2nd—4th year they have intermediate plumage. ✦: It perches on trees and on elevated
spots on the ground, walks adroitly, and flies
slowly, often soaring in circles. ☉: At the nesting grounds it utters a barking *yef yef* and
whistling *kyu*. ♋: In eastern Europe the very
similar Spotted Eagle (*A. clanga* — 2). Also
larger eagles of the genus *Aquila,* mainly the
Steppe Eagle (*A. rapax*) and Imperial Eagle
(*A. heliaca*).
Ecology ◈: Forests, mainly in areas with
marshes. When hunting and in the non-breeding season it may be seen in open country.
∞: At the nesting grounds, it betrays its presence following its arrival (Apr.—May) by its
constant occurrence and by its nuptial flights
accompanied by piercing cries. The nest may be
discovered by a thorough search of the nesting
site and by checking on large nests.

Bionomy ↔: It is migratory, lives solitarily, and
is found at the nesting grounds in Apr.—Aug.
◡: The nest is located in treetops, by the trunk
or in the fork of a branch, and is decorated
with fresh green twigs. The two whitish, brown-
patterned eggs (62.9×50.7 mm) are laid in
Apr.—May. It has one brood a year, nests solitarily, and incubates for 40 days. The young are
cared for by both parents, 55 days in the nest
and 25 days outside the nest. ◖: Smaller animals, particularly small mammals, caught on
the ground.
Conservation It is not very numerous, even
though it is the commonest European eagle. It
is essential to provide it with full protection, including protection of its nesting grounds.

2

3

Golden Eagle
Aquila chrysaetos

Identification Appearance — size — behaviour
✳: A large eagle (82 cm, wingspan 2.1 m), one of the largest European raptors. It has broad, rounded wings with primaries spread like fingers (2), and a short, rounded tail. Adults (1) are dark brown, with the rear of the head a paler colour, buff to yellowish; ♂ < ♀. Juv. birds have a dark head, a long white band on the underwings formed by the white bases of the flight feathers and appearing on the upperside as a patch on the inner primaries, and a white base to the tail. In the 2nd—3rd year the white colour gradually disappears. ✦: Its flight is leisurely, with deep wingbeats, interspersed with long intervals of gliding; it often soars for long periods. It perches on the ground with body held horizontally and head up (1). ☉: Occasionally it utters a loud *hieh* and *kye kye kye.*
☎: In southern and eastern Europe the sparsely distributed Imperial Eagle (*A. heliaca* — 3) and the rare Steppe Eagle (*A. rapax* — 4). In those parts it is necessary to watch out also for smaller eagles — the Lesser Spotted Eagle (p. 131) and Spotted Eagle (*A. clanga*) — for, particularly in flight and at a distance, estimate of size is deceptive.

Ecology ◈: Wooded and rocky places from lowland to subalpine elevations in mountain districts, where it is currently most numerous. ∞: The nesting grounds may be located by the constant presence of the birds and their flights from one place to another. The nest is usually permanent; to find it requires a thorough search of possible nesting sites and checking on large nests. Bear in mind the possible occur-

rence of non-nesting birds. In the non-breeding season it may be observed by chance in open country.

Bionomy ↔: It is resident, dispersive and migratory, and is a solitary bird. It is found at the nesting grounds in Feb.—Sept. ☾: The nest is sited on a cliff or in a tree, mainly in conifers. The two to three yellowish eggs with diverse brown markings (75.5×58.0 mm) are laid in Mar.—May. It has one brood a year, nests solitarily, and incubates for 40 days. The young are cared for by both parents, 70 days in the nest and 90 days outside the nest. ◑: Vertebrates as large as a fox, hunted in flight close above the ground. A trained Golden Eagle will even attack a wolf.

Conservation This is a declining species. It is essential to provide full protection for existing individuals and ensure protection of the nesting grounds.

1

Osprey
Pandion haliaetus

Identification Appearance — size — behaviour — habitat
∗: This raptor (57 cm, wingspan 1.6 m) has a slender body, long, rounded wings and a short tail (2). The adult (1) is a contrast in blackish-brown and white, with a white head and a dark band through the eye; ♂ < ♀. In juv. birds the feathers on the upperside have pale edges. ✦: It often perches on trees by water. It flies slowly, flapping its wings several times and then gliding or soaring a longer while; it also hovers above the water in one spot, plunging after its prey feet first. ☉: At the nesting grounds it utters short whistling notes, e.g. *kai kai*; during the courtship flight a loud penetrating *tyib, tyib*. ♋: It is unmistakable.
Ecology ◈: Larger bodies of water with undisturbed wooded surroundings. ∞: At the nesting grounds it may be identified by its constant presence, its flights from one spot to another, and its strikingly noisy courtship flights. Individual birds and even pairs sometimes remain at the nesting grounds but do not breed. The nest may be discovered by exploring suitable sites and checking on large nests. In the non-breeding season the Osprey may be observed at all kinds of water.
Bionomy ↔: It is migratory and is found at the nesting grounds in Mar.—Aug. In the non-breeding season it occurs singly or in loose groups. ᗱ: The nest is permanent, usually in the top of a solitary tree, also on high poles. The two to three bluish eggs, heavily spotted dark brown (61.8×46.2 mm), are laid in Apr.—May. It has one brood a year, nests soli-

tarily, and incubates for 37 days. The young are cared for by both parents, 53 days in the nest and a further 30 days or so outside the nest.
◕: Exclusively fish, captured at or just below the water's surface by plunging from the air.
Conservation Its numbers are few, and it is a declining species. It is essential to provide it with full protection and to ensure undisturbed nesting at the breeding grounds.

2

1

Eurasian Kestrel
Falco tinnunculus

Identification Appearance — behaviour — voice

∗: A small raptor (33 cm, wingspan 75 cm), only slightly bigger than a Turtle Dove. It has slender, pointed wings and a long tail. The adult ♂ (1) has a grey head and tail and buffish, spotted underparts; ♀ is larger and is entirely reddish-brown above (3) with dense markings, the underside being heavily patterned (2). Juv. birds resemble ♀, but have paler markings. ✈: It flies at a relatively low height and not very rapidly, alternating fast wingbeats with occasional gliding; it soars, and frequently hovers in one spot. It perches upright on trees, high poles, etc. ☉: A loud *kikiki*, uttered frequently even in the pre-nesting period as well as when rearing the young. ♋: Common in southern Europe is the very similar Lesser Kestrel (*F. naumanni* — 4). It is also necessary to watch out for smaller common raptors — the Hobby (p. 137), Merlin (p. 136), and Sparrowhawk (p. 128).

Ecology ◆: Cultivated country and parkland; it is occurring with increasing frequency in cities. ∞: At the nesting grounds it may be identified by the regular occurrence of the birds and their flights in the vicinity, in spring by its voice, and also later by the newly fledged young. The nest may be discovered by exploring suitable sites (there are bird droppings beneath the nest). In the non-breeding season it is easily observed in open country: perched and, particularly, hovering birds are conspicuous.

Bionomy ↔: It is partly migratory and is found at the nesting grounds in Feb.—Aug. In the non-breeding season it leads a solitary life. ♒: It nests in the old nests of crows, etc., in tree cavities, on buildings, in earth banks and on cliffs. The three to seven yellow-brown, brown-patterned eggs (39.0×31.4 mm) are laid in Mar.—July. It has one brood a year, nests solitarily, and incubates for 28 days. The young are cared for by both parents, 30 days in the nest and a further 30 days outside the nest. ◑: Smaller animals, mainly small mammals and birds, caught mostly on the ground.

Conservation This is a beneficial species. It is necessary to provide full protection; nesting may be promoted by putting out larger man-made nestboxes.

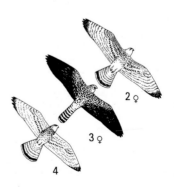

2 ♀

3 ♀

4

1

Red-footed Falcon
Falco vespertinus

Identification Appearance — behaviour — coloration
✳: Roughly the size of the Eurasian Kestrel (30 cm, wingspan 70 cm). It has a slender body, long pointed wings and a very long tail. The adult ♂ (2) is dark slate-grey with rufous-red 'trousers'; ♀ (1) is slightly larger and very different, being barred grey above, and a pale rusty-buff below (3) including the underwing-coverts. Juv. birds resemble ♀ but are browner above and streaked below. ✦: It perches on trees and wires, flies not very rapidly and close above the ground, and often hovers in one spot; frequently several birds flock together, adroitly catching insects in the air. ☉: At the nesting grounds it utters a repeated *kikiki.* ♋: ♀ in appearance and juv. birds also in their colouring resemble the Hobby (p. 137), which, however, never has a pale crown and forehead and has a shorter tail. In southern Europe ♂ resembles the dark phase of Eleonora's Falcon (*F. eleonorae*).

Ecology ◈: Steppes and forest-steppes, cultivated country with fields and groves of trees. ∞: Nesting grounds may be located by the regular occurrence often of larger numbers of birds.
The nest may be discovered by exploring suitable sites such as Rook colonies, groves in fields, etc. In the non-breeding season it may be observed in open areas.

Bionomy ↔: It is migratory and is found at the nesting grounds in May—Sept. In the non-breeding season it occurs singly, as well as in groups. ᴗ: It nests in the old nests of Rooks, raptors, etc., in trees, very occasionally in cavities or on the ground, frequently in colonies. The three to four rufous eggs with dark markings (36.8×29.2 mm) are laid in May—June. It has one brood a year and incubates for 22 days. The young are tended by both parents, 28 days in the nest and ten days outside the nest. ◑: Mostly insects, caught with the talons in flight high in the air or close above the ground.

Conservation This is apparently an endangered species. It is essential to provide it with full protection, including protection of the nesting grounds, and aid by constructing foundations for nests and placing them in suitable spots.

2 ♂

3 ♀

1

Merlin
Falco columbarius

Identification Appearance — size — behaviour
✻: Smaller than the Kestrel (28 cm, wingspan
60 cm) and with long, narrow, pointed wings
and a short tail (2, 3). The adult ♂ is blue-grey
above, and rufous below thinly streaked
darker; ♀ (1) is larger, dark brown above, and
whitish below with conspicuous dark brown
markings resembling tear-drops. Juv. birds resemble ♀ but are darker, with a whitish patch
on the hindneck. ✦: It flies rapidly and generally at a low height, alternating rapid wingbeats with brief intervals of gliding with wings
pressed close to the body, so that its flight is undulating; it expertly attacks fleeing prey. It
perches upright in spots with a good view (on
trees, etc.). ☉: At the nesting grounds it utters
a rapid, relatively high-pitched *kikiki* similar to
the call of the Eurasian Kestrel. ♋: The Hobby
(p. 137) is very similar in appearance, but is only
a summer visitor to Europe between Apr. and
Oct., and has darker upperparts, a darker moustachial streak, and reddish 'trousers'. Almost
the same size but less similar are the Eurasian
Kestrel (p. 134) and Sparrowhawk (p. 128).
Ecology ◈: Tundra, forest-tundra, moorland
and fells. ∞: At the nesting grounds it may be
recognised by the constant presence of the
birds, their flights from one place to another,
and their calls; the nest may be discovered by
exploring suitable sites. In the non-breeding
season it may be observed in open country.
Bionomy ↔: It is migratory and is found at the
nesting grounds in May—Sept. It occurs singly.
♒: The nest is located on the ground, on
cliffs, as well as in trees. The three to five

rufous-tinged eggs thickly patterned brown
(40.0×31.0 mm) are laid in May—June. It has
one brood a year, nests solitarily, and incubates
for 30 days. The young are cared for by both
parents, 26 days in the nest and a further 20
days outside the nest. ◖: Mostly smaller birds
captured after being flushed, in flight, less
often also on the ground.
Conservation A declining species, it is essential
to provide it with full protection.

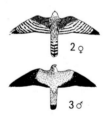

2 ♀

3 ♂

136

Hobby
Falco subbuteo

Identification Appearance — size — behaviour
✳: The size of a Kestrel (33 cm, wingspan
85 cm) and with long, narrow, pointed wings
and a short tail (2). The adult ♂ is blue-black
above, has a prominent moustachial streak on
the white cheeks, pale darkly streaked underside and rufous-red 'trousers'; ♀ (1) is larger
than ♂, but otherwise similar in appearance.
Juv. birds are blackish-brown above with feathers edged paler; the 'trousers' are buff. ✦: It
generally flies rapidly at a low height, interspersing wingbeats with gliding flight, skilfully
captures insects and birds on the wing, occasionally soars in circles, and very rarely it
hovers. It perches upright on trees (the wings
extend to the tip of the tail). ☉: At the nesting
grounds it utters a loud, high-pitched alternately rising and falling note *kikiki*. ☜: The
similar Merlin (p. 136), occurring also in winter,
but its coloration does not exhibit such con-
trasts and it does not have a well-defined moustachial streak. Also similar are ♀ and juveniles
of the Red-footed Falcon (p. 135), and in southern Europe Eleonora's Falcon (*F. eleonorae*).
Ecology ◈: Parkland and open country with
smaller woods, mainly in lowlands and foothills. ∞: The nesting grounds may be located,
as with other raptors, by the regular occurrence
of the birds, their flights from one place to another, and their calls; the nest by exploring suitable sites and examining larger nests. In the
non-breeding season it may be observed on the
wing flying from one spot to another.
Bionomy ↔: It is migratory and is found at the
nesting grounds in Apr.—Sept. ৺: It nests in
old crow nests in treetops. The two to four yellow-brown, brown-spotted eggs (41.8×32.6 mm)
are laid in May—June. It has one brood a year,
nests solitarily, and incubates for 29 days. The
young are tended by both parents, 31 days in
the nest and a further 35 days outside the nest.
◕: Insects and small birds captured in flight.
Conservation Its numbers are on the decline. It
is essential to provide it with full protection, including protection of the nesting grounds.

1

Peregrine Falcon
Falco peregrinus

Identification Appearance — size — behaviour
✴: A robust raptor the size of a crow (42 cm, wingspan 1 m) and with long, relatively broad, pointed wings and a short tail (3). The adult (1) is slate-grey above, with a striking moustachial streak on the white cheeks. The underparts are pale with dark barring: in the north European race *F. p. calidus* they are entirely white, in *F. p. peregrinus* of central Europe they are somewhat brownish, and *F. p. brookei* of southern Europe has the breast coloured pale rusty-brown. ♂ < ♀. Juv. birds are blackish-brown above with feathers edged paler, and pale brownish on the underside with heavy streaks.
✦: It flies high, with leisurely wingbeats interrupted by intervals of gliding flight, rapidly increasing its speed and plummeting in a dive when attacking prey. It also soars, and hangs on the wind. It perches in places with a good view.
☉: At the nesting grounds it utters a loud *kiki-ki.* ⬡: In northern Europe the Gyrfalcon (*F. rusticolus* — 4); in eastern Europe the Saker Falcon (*F. cherrug* — 5); in southern Europe the Lanner Falcon (*F. biarmicus* — 2); also smaller falcons.
Ecology ◆: Wooded tundra, steppes, upland areas and coastal cliffs, as well as cultivated country. ∞: At the nesting grounds it may be located by the constant presence of the birds, their flights from one place to another and their calls, the nest by exploring suitable sites. In the non-breeding season it may be observed when flying from one place to another in open country.
Bionomy ↔: It is resident, dispersive and migra-

tory and is found at the nesting grounds in Feb.—Aug. ⬡: It nests on cliffs, very occasionally in old crow nests in trees, sometimes also on the ground. The nesting sites are permanent. The three to four yellowish eggs, heavily patterned with brown (51.4×40.4 mm), are laid in Mar.—Apr. It has one brood a year, nests solitarily, and incubates for 30 days. The young are cared for by both parents, 40 days in the nest and a further 60 days outside the nest. ◑: Birds as large as a duck, captured in flight.
Conservation This is a severely endangered species. It is essential to provide full protection, including protection of the nesting grounds; breeding in captivity and release in the wild is also a helpful conservation measure.

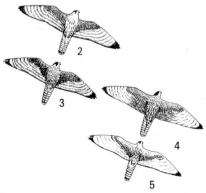

2

3

4

5

1

Barn Owl
Tyto alba

Identification Voice — habitat — behaviour — appearance

✳: A medium-sized owl (34 cm) with a large round head and a striking facial disc, broad, rounded wings and a short tail. Adults (1) are pale yellowish and whitish-grey with a white facial disc; the underparts of the west European race *T. a. alba* are white, in *T. a. guttata* of central and eastern Europe they are buffish and spotted. ♀ is generally more spotted than ♂. Juv. = adults. ✦: It flies silently in wavering flight with slow wingbeats, close above the ground. The Barn Owl is active in the evening and at night; in the daytime it perches by the nest or in a concealed spot. ☉: It utters a loud, hoarse shriek, *krééi.* ♋: Both its appearance and its voice are unmistakable; when bird-watching in the evening it is necessary to watch out for other owls of the same size.

Ecology ◈: Farmland and open country at lower elevations, also churchyards and built-up areas. ∞: It may be discovered by its voice at night, usually at the site of the nest; throughout the year examine barn attics, church towers, etc., where you may come across either the nest, perched birds, or its characteristic large regurgitated pellets, often in quantities, on the floor.

Bionomy ↔: It is resident or dispersive and occurs singly. ﮞ: The nest is located in rock crevices, nowadays with increasing frequency in church towers, haylofts, etc. The four to ten white eggs (39.7×30.7 mm) are laid in Feb.—Nov. It has one to three broods a year, nests solitarily, and incubates for 30 days. The young are tended by both parents, 50 days in the nest and a further 28 days outside the nest. ☀: Almost exclusively small mammals captured by pouncing on them on the ground.

Conservation It is not very numerous and has greatly declined in numbers. It is an important predator of field pests, especially voles. It is vital to provide it with full protection, including protection of the nesting grounds.

Eurasian Eagle Owl
Bubo bubo

Identification Voice — habitat — size — appearance

∗ : The largest European owl (70 cm, wingspan 1.7 m). It has a large round head with large ear tufts, broad, rounded wings, and a short tail.. The adult (1) is yellowish-brown with dark markings and orange eyes; ♂ = ♀. Juv. birds have short ear tufts and the breast is less streaked. ✦ : It is active mostly by night. It flies silently, with slow wingbeats interrupted by intervals of gliding flight. In the daytime it perches hidden from sight on a rock or tree. ☉ : Heard frequently and throughout the night during the courtship period is its barking note *hoo* (♂) and a short *hu* (♀). ☟ : It is unmistakable; in northern Europe it is necessary to watch out for other owls of the same size.

Ecology ◈ : Wooded country with rocks and open expanses. ∞ : The nesting grounds may be located by the birds' calls during the courtship period (Jan.—Apr.), but not all hooting owls are breeding. The nest, especially one with larger nestlings, may be discovered by exploring suitable sites; ledges in the vicinity of cliff nests are greatly soiled. In the non-breeding season the Eagle Owl may be seen by chance; sometimes its presence is revealed by the alarm calls of small birds.

Bionomy ↔ : It is resident; in the non-breeding season it roams in the vicinity of the nesting grounds. ᗡ : It nests on rock ledges, very occasionally on the ground or in old tree nests. The one to four white eggs (60.2×49.4 mm) are laid in Feb.—Apr. It has one brood a year, nests solitarily, and ♀ incubates for 35 days.

The young are cared for by both parents, 55 days in the nest and a further 100 days outside the nest. ◑ : Small to medium-sized vertebrates as large as a hare, captured in low flight at night.

Conservation This is a vulnerable species. It is not numerous; in Europe it has become extinct in some parts and in others it has been re-introduced. In districts with intensive breeding of small game, it causes damage around its nesting sites. It is essential to provide it with full protection by law, including protection of the nesting grounds.

Snowy Owl
Nyctea scandiaca

Identification Appearance — size — behaviour
✳: A robust owl (60 cm) the size of the Eagle
Owl, with a large round head, broad, rounded
wings, a short tail and yellow eyes. The adult ♂
is pure white except for a few black-brown
spots on the upperside. ♀ (1) has dark spots
and barring on most of the body. Juv. birds resemble ♀ but are even more heavily patterned.
♂ < ♀. ✦: It is active throughout the day. Its
flight is leisurely with slow wingbeats, very
adroit when attacking prey. The Snowy Owl
often perches on an elevated spot on the ground.
☉: At the nesting grounds ♂ utters a loud *krau
au*. ☟: It is unmistakable. In northern Europe
the smaller Hawk Owl (*Surnia ulula* — 2) and
equally large Great Grey Owl (*Strix nebulosa*)
occur, but both are much darker.
Ecology ◈: Tundra; in the non-breeding season
other open country. ∞: The nesting grounds
may be recognised by the constant occurrence
of the otherwise shy birds and their flights
from one spot to another. Look for the nest by
watching adult birds and then by exploring the
site. In the non-breeding season it may be seen
by chance in open areas.
Bionomy ↔: It is partly migratory and dispersive and is found at the nesting grounds in
Mar.—Sept. It occurs singly. ᴥ: It nests on
the ground. The three to nine white eggs
(57.0×45.0 mm) are laid in May—June. It has
one brood a year, nests solitarily, and ♀ incubates for 32 days. The young are tended by both
parents, 45 days in the nest and a further
25 days outside the nest. ◖: Small as well as
medium-sized vertebrates as large as a rabbit,

but mostly lemmings and voles, captured in low
flight.
Conservation This is a rare species. Consistent
legislative protection is evidently insufficient.

1

Pygmy Owl
Glaucidium passerinum

Identification Voice — habitat — appearance
✳: The smallest European owl (17 cm), the size of a Starling. It has a rather large, flat head, short rounded wings and a short tail. Adults (1) are dark brown above with minute pale markings; ♂ = ♀. Juv. birds are a darker, duller colour, their upperparts, wing-coverts and brown sides of the breast lacking markings. ✦: It is active mostly at night, but often also in the daytime. It flies swiftly, with rapid wingbeats interrupted by intervals of gliding flight with wings pressed close to the body. It perches concealed in cavities and in trees; when nervous, it wags its tail up and down. ☉: At the nesting grounds ♂ utters a soft monotonous whistling note *tyeei tyeei*; ♀ the same but higher-pitched. ♋: The voice resembles that of the Bullfinch (p. 243). Watch out for Tengmalm's Owl (p. 147) and the Little Owl (p. 143), which, however, are larger and have a different voice. In southern Europe the common Scops Owl (*Otus scops* — 2) which, however, occurs in a different habitat.
Ecology ◈: Large forests with old coniferous stands in damp places, often in the mountain forest belt. ∞: At the nesting grounds (in Feb.—Apr., occasionally also in Sept.—Nov.) it may be identified by its voice, most often at dusk and at dawn. It can be enticed to call by playing a tape or by imitating its call. The nest may be pinpointed by the voice of ♀; usually scattered beneath the nesting cavity are the feathers of small birds. In the non-breeding season it may be seen only by chance.
Bionomy ↔: It is resident; in the non-breeding season it roams near the nesting grounds. It oc-

curs singly. ☁: It nests in tree cavities made by woodpeckers. The three to seven white eggs (28.5×23.2 mm) are laid in Apr.—May. It has one brood a year, nests solitarily and ♀ incubates for 29 days. The young are cared for by both parents, 30 days in the nest and a further 25 days outside the nest. ◐: Small birds and mammals captured in treetops and on the ground.
Conservation This is a scarce species. The preservation of old forest stands in suitable localities is essential for its continued well-being.

2

142

1

Little Owl
Athene noctua

Identification Voice — appearance — behaviour

✳: A small owl (22 cm) the size of a Blackbird and with a large, relatively flat head, short rounded wings and a short tail. Adults (1) are greyish-brown with white mottlings; ♂ = ♀. Juv. birds are paler with less distinct markings and with a plainer crown. ✦: It is active by night, and frequently also during the day. It perches in trees, on buildings, as well as on the ground; when nervous, it bobs up and down. It flies swiftly, alternating several rapid wingbeats with brief intervals of gliding flight. ☉: At the nesting grounds it utters a loud plaintive *kooo, ooo*; when alarmed, *kit ket* and similar notes. ☜: Its voice is practically unmistakable. In some parts of Europe the Tengmalm's Owl (p. 147), which, however, is larger, has a round head with eyes and bill forming a right-angled triangle, occurs in different habitats and has a different voice.

Ecology ◈: Farmland, parkland with fields, meadows, tree avenues, buildings, stony areas, also built-up areas at lower elevations. ∞: At the nesting grounds in spring (Feb.—June) it may be located by its voice, the nest by examining cavities. Knocking on the tree trunk is all that is needed to flush the bird. In the non-breeding season it may be seen by chance observation.

Bionomy ↔: It is resident and occurs singly. ᪥: It nests in tree cavities, occasionally also in underground burrows. The four to six white eggs (34.8×29.3 mm) are laid in Mar.—May. It has one brood a year, nests solitarily, and ♀ in-cubates for 27 days. The young are tended by both parents, 35 days in the nest and a further 30 days outside the nest. ◑: Larger insects, worms, small birds and mammals, captured in low flight and on the ground.

Conservation Currently it is rapidly declining in numbers. It is essential to provide it with full protection and during the nesting period to put out nestboxes.

143

1

Tawny Owl
Strix aluco

Identification Voice — appearance — habitat
✳: A medium-sized owl (38 cm, wingspan 1 m)
with a characteristic large round head. Adults
(1) are grey- or rusty-brown with brownish-black
markings (2 — feather from the breast, 4 —
from the tail). ♂ = ♀ =juv. ✦: It is active at
night, remaining hidden during the day in
a tree cavity or on a branch next to the trunk.
Its flight is leisurely but it is very adroit, especially when attacking prey. ☉: At the nesting
grounds one can often hear its loud melan-
cholic hooting note *hoo hoo oo* (♂) and shrill
kioo-vit (♀); young birds outside the nest make
plaintive, hoarse whistling notes. ☙: The Ural
Owl (*S. uralensis*), which is slightly larger and
with fewer markings, clearly evident mainly on
the feathers from the breast (3) and tail (5); the
Great Grey Owl (*S. nebulosa*), with a striking
dark pattern on its large head (6).
Ecology ◈: Woods, parkland, as well as old
gardens in built-up areas. ∞: At the nesting
grounds it may be located by its calls
(Dec.—Apr.) with the onset of dusk, sometimes
also during the day, and in May—June by the
cries of the young birds; the nest by exploring
the site and examining suitable cavities. Merely
knocking on the trunk of the tree, however, is
not always sufficient to flush the bird. In the
non-breeding season it may be seen only by
chance; quite often it is possible to tell its
whereabouts by the alarm calls of small birds.
Usually scattered on the ground beneath the
places where the owls regularly perch are the
relatively large grey pellets regurgitated by the
birds.

Bionomy ↔: It is a resident bird, at most roaming in the vicinity of the nesting grounds in the
non-breeding season. Paired birds remain together the entire year. ᴎ: It nests in tree cavities or in chimneys of buildings in woodland.
The three to five white eggs (47.4×39.1 mm)
are laid in Feb.—May. It has one brood a year,
nests solitarily, and ♀ incubates for 29 days.
The young are cared for by both parents, 35
days in the nest and a further 90 days outside
the nest. ◖: Small mammals and birds, captured in low flight between trees or above the
ground.
Conservation It is a predator of small mammals.
It is necessary to provide full protection; active
aid is possible in the form of putting out larger
nestboxes.

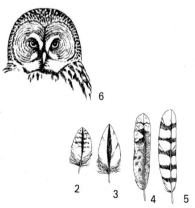

6

2   3   4   5

144

Long-eared Owl
Asio otus

Identification Voice — appearance — behaviour
✳: About the size of the Tawny Owl (36 cm) but with a slender body, round head, long ear tufts, rounded wings, a short tail, and orange eyes. Adults (1) are yellowish-brown with dark streaks; ♂ = ♀. Juv. birds have smaller ear tufts, greyer plumage and a darker facial disc. ✦: It is active at night. It flies relatively low, with slow wingbeats followed by a glide, and abrupt dives to the ground after prey. During the day it rests hidden in a treetop next to the trunk with body held upright. ☉: At the nesting grounds, ♂ utters a deep muffled *ooh*, repeated for a long time at regular three-second intervals; the young make squeaky piping sounds. ♋: Throughout Europe the similar Short-eared Owl (p. 146), which, however, is a paler colour, has smaller ear tufts (2) and roosts on the ground in fields, meadows and marshlands. A rare visitor to southern Spain is the African Marsh Owl (*A. capensis*).
Ecology ◈: Parkland with small woods, city parks, cemeteries, etc. from lowland elevations to the upper forest limit. ∞: At the nesting grounds it can be recognised by its calls (Mar.—June); during courtship ♂ also claps his wings. Nesting birds may be flushed by knocking on the tree trunk. At the wintering grounds they may be observed when they fly out at dusk; also look for regurgitated pellets beneath trees.
Bionomy ↔: It is partly migratory, and in winter it occurs in groups. ☙: It nests in the old nests of crows and raptors. The three to six

white eggs (40.0×32.4 mm) are laid in Feb.—June. It has one, sometimes possibly two, broods a year, nests solitarily, and ♀ incubates for 27 days. The young are tended by both parents, 30 days in the nest and a further 60 days outside the nest. ◗: Small mammals captured in flight close above the ground.
Conservation This is an important predator of small rodents. It is essential to provide it with full protection.

2

1

Short-eared Owl
Asio flammeus

Identification Appearance — behaviour — voice

✳: The size of the Long-eared Owl (38 cm), it has a slender body, smaller round head, and short ear tufts. Adults (1) are pale yellow-brown with dark brown streaks, the belly being almost white. ♂ = ♀ = juv. ✦: It is active at twilight and in the daytime. It rests on the ground in thick low herbaceous vegetation, and flies at a low height, buoyantly with slow wingbeats and abrupt changes of direction; during courtship it occasionally claps its wings. ☉: Its call is a high-pitched barking *kev kev*, particularly at the nesting site; during the courtship flight a hollow *boobooboo*; newly-fledged young birds a sneezing *kshiya*. ☜: The Long-eared Owl (p. 145), which, however, is darker, with longer ear tufts, has a different voice and occurs in a different habitat. In southern Spain it may be mistaken for the very similar African Marsh Owl (*A. capensis*).

Ecology ◆: Tundra, moorland, marshes, wet meadows, farm country with fields. ∞: The nesting grounds may be located by the constant occurrence of the birds and by the courtship display with its characteristic flights and calls. The nest may be discovered by walking through damp meadows and marshes and flushing sitting birds. In the non-breeding season it may be observed mainly by chance flushing.

Bionomy ↔: It is partly migratory and is found at the nesting grounds in Mar.—Oct. In the non-breeding season it generally occurs in groups. ☙: It nests on the ground in thick low vegetation, solitarily or in loose groups. The five to nine white eggs (40.0×31.3 mm) are laid in Mar.—June. It has one brood a year; when food is more than plentiful, it occasionally has a second brood in autumn (Oct.—Nov.). ♀ incubates for 26 days; the young are cared for only by ♀ for 26 days; after the 12th day they scatter in the vicinity, but continue to be cared for by ♀ a few weeks longer. ◕: Small mammals captured in low flight above the ground.

Conservation It is an important predator of small rodents, mainly voles. It is essential to provide full protection and to avoid disturbance at the nesting grounds.

1

Tengmalm's Owl
Aegolius funereus

Identification Voice — habitat — appearance
✳: The size of the Little Owl (25 cm), it has
a large, round, flat-topped head, and yellow
eyes forming a right-angled triangle with the
bill. The wings are broad and rounded, the tail
not very long, and the tarsi feathered. Adults
(1) are dark brown above with prominent white
markings, and whitish on the underside with
brown spotting; ♂ = ♀. Juv. birds are dark
brown above without any markings on the
crown and back. ✦: It is active by night. During the day it perches in tree cavities and thick
branches. Its flight consists of alternating wingbeats with intervals of gliding; it is very skilful
when attacking prey. ☉: At the nesting grounds
its call is a rapidly ascending *poo poo poo*, similar to the Hoopoe's; occasionally it may also be
heard in the non-breeding season. ♋: The relatively similar Little Owl (p. 143) has a less flattened head, different voice, and inhabits a different environment; the Pygmy Owl (p. 142),
though found in the same localities, is smaller
and has a different voice.
Ecology ◈: Larger forests, mainly coniferous,
with old stands of trees, generally at higher
elevations. ∞: At the nesting grounds in
Feb.—May it may be recognised by its calls, uttered throughout the night; it may be enticed to
call by playing a taped voice. It can be encouraged to nest by putting out nestboxes;
otherwise the nest may be found by examining
suitable cavities.
Bionomy ↔: It is resident, occasionally roaming
far from the nesting grounds in the non-breeding season, and leads a solitary life. ཀ: It nests

in tree holes made by the Black Woodpecker.
The four to seven white eggs (32.5×26.5 mm)
are laid in Mar.—May. It has one, occasionally
perhaps two, broods a year, nests solitarily, and
♀ incubates for 29 days. The young are cared
for only by ♀, 32 days in the nest and a further
35 days outside the nest. ◑: Small birds and
mammals captured while flying among the
trees and close above the ground.
Conservation This is a scarce species. It is essential to provide it with full protection; active aid
may be provided by putting out nestboxes.

147

Songbirds

Songbirds are the largest group of birds, with the greatest number of species. A characteristic they have in common is the possession of a vocal organ called the syrinx: this enables them to produce a wide range of notes, which in some species are extremely varied. The song is very characteristic for most species, often very melodious to the human ear, and thus generally serves as a valuable aid in identifying the species. Another characteristic songbirds have in common is their usually small size: the largest European songbird is the Raven, and the Goldcrest is the smallest (in fact the smallest of all European birds). All songbirds furthermore have short legs and a rather short bill, but otherwise they are very different in appearance and particularly in coloration.

Songbirds include among their number a great many very similar species, e. g. warblers, and also pairs that are practically if not completely indistinguishable (known as sibling species) such as the Marsh Warbler and Reed Warbler, or the Treecreeper and Short-toed Treecreeper. Most similar species, however, may be distinguished by their voice, above all by their song.

The House Sparrow (2) with its short legs and tail and short conical bill typifies the seed-eaters. The Pied or White Wagtail (5) has short slender legs, a long tail and, being an insectivorous bird, a slender bill. The Nuthatch (4) with its straight, strong bill and short legs and tail is adapted for climbing up and down tree trunks and branches. The Blackbird (3) is representative of medium-sized songbirds that have no special adaptations and can feed on a wide variety of foods. The Carrion Crow (1) is a similar omnivorous type, but large in size.

1

Crested Lark
Galerida cristata

Identification Appearance — voice — behaviour

✳: Larger than a sparrow (16 cm) and with a robust body, pointed erectile crest on the head, broad wings and a rather short, slightly forked tail. Adults (1) are greyish-brown with heavily streaked upperparts and breast; ♂ = ♀. Juv. birds have paler markings on the upperparts and a shorter crest. ✦: It runs about rapidly with small steps; its flight is leisurely with slow wingbeats; in spring it flies in broad circles above the nesting site. ☉: It frequently utters a soft call, *dyuyi deedidooh.* Its song resembles the Skylark's, but is simpler, shorter, with soft plaintive notes; it also imitates the voices of other birds. It sings in flight as well as on the ground. ♋: In southern Spain the Thekla Lark (*G. theklae*), a sibling species which is almost identical to the Crested Lark.

Ecology ◈: Open country with short grass cover in lowlands and foothills, roadsides, often also built-up areas. ∞: Listen for its voice; it may be observed without difficulty in a great variety of places. The nesting grounds may be located by the constant presence and behaviour of the birds. The nest is best discovered while it is being built or when the adult birds are feeding their offspring; they fly with the food in their bill to within 2—3 m of the nest and then walk the remainder of the way.

Bionomy ↔: It is resident practically throughout its range. In the non-breeding season it occurs in small groups or in pairs. ♡: The nest is located on the ground, generally by a clump of grass. The three to five yellowish, darkly patterned eggs (22.5×16.7 mm) are laid in Mar.—July. It has one to two broods a year, nests solitarily, and ♀ incubates for 13 days. The young are tended by both parents, nine days in the nest and a further ten days outside the nest. ◐: Plant seeds and small invertebrates, gathered from the ground.

Conservation It is quite numerous but is declining in places. Methods of protection are not known as yet.

1

Woodlark
Lullula arborea

Identification Voice — behaviour — appearance

✳: As large as a sparrow (15 cm). There is a slight indication of a crest on the head, and the wings are broad and triangular. Adults (1) are brown above with dark markings, pale below with a streaked breast, the pale supercilia join on the nape, and the short tail is not edged with white; ♂ = ♀. Juv. birds are more spotted and have the feathers on the upperside edged with buff. ✦: It runs about on the ground and perches in trees. It flies with leisurely wing-beats, often describing wide arcs, and flies around the boundaries of its territory in 'bat-like' flight while singing. ☉: It often sings; its song is a fluty *lululudaduldadul . . .*, very long, loud and melodious and particularly attractive at night. Its call in flight is a liquid *deedlui*. ♋: Its song is unmistakable (NB: the Nightingale also sings at night); the similar Skylark (p. 152) is larger, has a longer tail edged with white, its song is different and it inhabits a different environment.

Ecology: ◆: Open woods and their edges, woodland clearings, heaths, mainly on sandy soils from lowland elevations to the upper forest limit. In the non-breeding season also meadows and fields. ∞: At the nesting grounds it may be recognised by its song and the behaviour of the birds. The nest is hard to find: walk around suitable sites, and watch for adult birds feeding the young. In the non-breeding season you may locate it by its voice or flush the birds by chance.

Bionomy ↔: It is partly migratory. In the non-

breeding season it also occurs in small flocks, sometimes together with Skylarks. It is found at the nesting grounds in Mar.—Oct. ω: The nest is located on the ground by a clump of grass, under a shrub, etc. The four to five whitish-pink, darkly patterned eggs (21.2×15.7 mm) are laid in Mar.—July. It has one to two, occasionally three, broods a year, nests solitarily, and ♀ incubates for 14 days. The young are cared for by both parents, 12 days in the nest and several more days outside the nest. ◖: Seeds and small bits of plants and small invertebrates, all gathered on the ground.

Conservation This is an important songbird, often kept in captivity in former days. It is greatly declining in numbers but no sensible methods of protection are known as yet, apart from protection of its habitat.

1

Skylark
Alauda arvensis

Identification Voice — behaviour — appearance

∗: Larger than a sparrow (18 cm). There is a barely discernible crest on the nape, the wings are broad and pointed, the tail short. Adults (1) are dark-streaked above, pale below with streaked breast, and the tail is edged with white; ♂ = ♀. Juv. birds are scaly above. ✦: It runs about on the ground. It flies leisurely, flutters earthward and upward again while singing, circles or hovers, then flutters downward or drops in plummeting flight. In spring pairs often chase one another close above the ground. ☉: Its song consists of the well-known melodious trilling and warbling in flight; its call is a dry *trruit,* etc. ♨: Its voice is unmistakable. It resembles the Woodlark (p. 151), which, however, is smaller, has a shorter tail without white edges, and has a different voice. Similarly coloured pipits (*Anthus* spp.) are slender, with a longer tail, and have different voices and manner of flight.

Ecology ◈: Open country with fields, meadows, etc., from lowland to subalpine elevations. ∞: At the nesting grounds it is readily recognised by its song (Jan.—July) and by the behaviour of the birds. The nest is difficult to find: you must walk about and flush a sitting bird or observe birds feeding their young. In the non-breeding season observe the birds on the ground or in flight, flush them, or listen to their calls.

Bionomy ↔: It is resident and migratory and is found at the nesting grounds in Feb.—Oct. In the non-breeding season it generally occurs in small flocks. ᴗ: The nest is located on the ground, generally in grass. The three to five brownish, darkly patterned eggs (22.8×16.9 mm) are laid in Mar.—Aug. It has one to two, possibly even three, broods a year, nests solitarily, and ♀ incubates for 11 days. The young are tended by both parents, 11 days in the nest and a further eight days outside the nest. ◑: Seeds and small invertebrates gathered from the surface of the ground.

Conservation No protective measures are necessary; it is numerous.

152

1

Sand Martin
Riparia riparia

Identification Appearance — behaviour — voice
∗: Smaller than a sparrow (13 cm), and with a round head with short bill, short body, slightly forked tail and narrow, not very long wings. Adults (1) are brown above and white on the underside, with a brown band across the breast; ♂ = ♀. Juv. birds have the feathers on the upperside edged with white. ✛: It flies rapidly and expertly, alternating rapid wingbeats with intervals of gliding in shallow undulations. It generally flies close above water. It perches on shrubs or wires alongside water and roosts in large aggregations in reedbeds, often together with swallows. ☉: In flight it often utters a dry, rasping *cherrip, cherrip*, etc.; its song is a low, harsh twittering, reminiscent of the swallow's. ♋: In the mountains of southern Europe the similar Crag Martin (*Hirundo rupestris*). At a distance the House Martin (p. 155).

Ecology ◈: It is found in lowland and foothills near water where there are suitable vertical sand or earth banks; in the non-breeding season also at other larger bodies of water. ∞: It may be observed by water. Its numbers are more plentiful near and above the nesting grounds; nesting colonies may be readily found by searching brickworks, sandpits, clay banks, etc.

Bionomy ↔: It is migratory. In the non-breeding season it occurs in loose flocks. It is found at the nesting grounds in Apr.—Oct. ଓ: It nests in burrows which it digs in clay or sand banks (2); there are always feathers in the nest. The four to six white eggs (17.7×12.6 mm) are laid in May—July. It has one to two broods a year, nests in colonies, and incubates for 15 days. The young are cared for by both parents and fledge after 19 days. ◖: Small invertebrates captured in flight.

Conservation Locally it is endangered. Its numbers fluctuate according to changes in habitats suitable for nesting. It is possible to protect it by preserving banks for nesting and by halting excavation at sites of colonies during the nesting period.

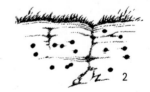

2

1

Barn Swallow
Hirundo rustica

Identification Appearance — voice — behaviour

✳ : As large as a sparrow (19 cm) but more slender, with typical sickle-shaped pointed wings and a rather long, forked tail (3, 4). Adults (1) have a deep red forehead and chin, but otherwise they are entirely blue-black above; the underparts are creamy, with a dark band on the breast below the chin. ♂ = ♀. Juv. birds are duller and their outer tail feathers are shorter. ✦ : It perches on wires, occasionally descending to the ground; it flies expertly and not very high up, often close above the ground, and in cold weather immediately above the surface of water. It roosts in large aggregations in reedbeds. ☉ : It often calls a *vit-vit-vit* or in alarm *slivit*; its song is a lengthier mix of twittering and chirping sounds ending in a broad *dzerzz*. ☞ : In parts of southern Europe the similar Red-rumped Swallow (*H. daurica*). At a greater distance or greater speed the House Martin (p. 155) may be mistaken for the Barn Swallow, but it has a short tail, white underparts and a conspicuous white rump (5). The Sand Martin (p. 153) is short-tailed and has a clear brown breast band (2).

Ecology ◈ : Open, mainly farm country from lowland to mountain elevations, often close to water. ∞ : It is readily located by observation and by its voice; to discover the location of the nests observe and check on adult birds.

Bionomy ↔ : It is migratory and is found at the nesting grounds in Apr.—Oct. ৩ : The nest is built by the ceiling inside buildings, rarely outside; it is an open cup-shaped structure of mud, usually lined with feathers. The three to six white eggs, thickly covered with dark markings (19.4×13.7 mm), are laid in Apr.—Aug. It has one to three broods a year, nests solitarily, and ♀ incubates for 16 days. The young are cared for by both parents and remain in the nest 22 days. ◖ : Small arthropods, mostly insects, captured in flight.

Conservation It is declining in some areas. It is necessary to ensure the birds' access to places suitable for building their nest; they will also accept a similarly shaped man-made nest.

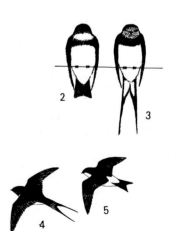

2

3

4

5

1

House Martin
Delichon urbica

Identification Appearance — voice — behaviour

✳: Smaller than a swallow (13 cm) and it also has shorter and broader wings and a short, shallowly forked tail. Adults (1) are blue-black above with a conspicuous white rump, and entirely white on the underside, including the short-feathered legs; ♂ = ♀. Juv. birds have the crown tinged with brown. ✦: It flies very expertly, often fluttering upward in a slanting line and then gliding downward in an arc. It perches on wires together with other martins and swallows; on the ground it generally occurs only by water when gathering mud for building its nest. ☉: Its call, a dry *brrit,* is heard very frequently; its alarm call is a high *siyer.* Its song consists of soft, inconspicuous twittering notes, less rich than the Barn Swallow's. ☺: In appearance the Sand Martin (p. 153), in coloration the Barn Swallow (p. 154), in southern Europe the Red-rumped Swallow (*Hirundo daurica*).

Ecology ◈: Mainly built-up areas, from lowland to mountain elevations; it flies long distances in search of food. ∞: It is readily found by observation and by its voice; the nest may be discovered by observing adult birds or by exploring suitable sites.

Bionomy ↔: It is migratory and is found at the nesting grounds in Apr.—Oct. In the non-breeding season it occurs in loose flocks. ☺: The nest is usually located on the outside of a building under a cornice, balcony, etc., rarely on rock faces; it is cemented to the building all the way to the upper edge except for the entrance. The three to five white eggs (18.3×13.1 mm) are laid in May—Aug. It has one to three broods a year, usually nests in colonies, and incubates for 15 days. The young are cared for by both parents and fledge after 26 days. ◐: Small arthropods, mainly insects, captured in flight.

Conservation It is necessary to tolerate the nests on buildings; the birds will also accept similar man-made nests. At present it is numerous.

Tawny Pipit
Anthus campestris

Identification Voice — appearance — behaviour

✴: The size of a sparrow (16 cm) and with a slender body, longer bill and quite long tail. Adults (1) are greyish-brown with darker wings and tail, the latter edged with white; the underparts are almost white, the breast tinged with pink and without dark markings; ♂ = ♀. Juv. birds are streaked dark brown above and on the breast. ✦: It runs about rapidly on the ground and holds its body erect whenever it stops; it is reminiscent of the Yellow Wagtail (p. 161). It flies short distances; the male's flight, accompanied by song, is generally undulating and ends with the bird's descending in a glide. It also perches on wires. ☉: Quite often heard is its call note *chirp;* the song is a repeated *zirluee-zirluee.* ☜: In the non-breeding season in similar localities other pipits, but all have markings on the underside and a different voice. Also Richard's Pipit (*A. novaeseelandiae*), rare in Europe and larger in size.

Ecology ◈: Fallow land with sparse, short grass cover, mainly sandy and stony soils at lower elevations; in the non-breeding season also fields. ∞: It may be identified by its voice and by observing birds at suitable sites; look for the nest by walking about suitable sites, also by watching the birds, especially when feeding.

Bionomy ↔: It is migratory and usually occurs singly. It is found at the nesting grounds in Apr.—Oct. ☙: The nest is located on the ground in short grass. The four to five greyish eggs with brown markings (21.5×15.7 mm) are laid in Apr.—July. It has one, occasionally two, broods a year, nests solitarily, and ♀ incubates for 14 days. The young are cared for by both parents and fledge after 14 days. ◖: Small terrestrial invertebrates.

Conservation This is a declining, rather scarce species. Effective methods of protection are not known at present.

Tree Pipit
Anthus trivialis

1

Identification Voice — behaviour — appearance

✳: As large as a sparrow (15 cm). Adults (1) are streaked brown and their tail is edged with white; ♂ = ♀. Juv. birds are browner and more heavily patterned. ✦: It perches in trees, often at the very top, also on wires, and runs with rapid steps on the ground and along thicker branches. Its flight is rapid and undulating. As he sings, ♂ flies up from the top of a tree in a slanting line, then, with partly spread wings and spread tail held upward at an angle, parachutes down again on to a branch or elevated spot. ☉: It is heard frequently; the call is a delicate, penetrating *pseeb*, the alarm note is *sit sit*. The song is resonant and consists of various trills ending in a descending *seea-seea-seea*. ⬡: The Meadow Pipit (p. 158), which, however, is more olive-coloured, more heavily patterned, has a sharp call and occurs in different habitats. In the mountains and on the coast of southern Europe the Water Pipit (p. 159), which, however, is greyer and with the breast practically unmarked in breeding plumage, has dark legs, and has a different voice.

Ecology ◆: Light woodlands, open glades, young plantations, as well as open areas with scattered trees, from lowland elevations to the upper forest limit; in the non-breeding season fields, etc. ∞: In the nesting period it is readily located by its song. The nest is generally discovered only by searching the site and flushing the sitting bird or by observing the behaviour of adult birds. In the non-breeding season it may be identified by its voice or by flushing the bird.

Bionomy ↔: It is migratory and is found at the nesting grounds in Apr.—Sept. ◔: The nest is hidden on the ground (in grass, under scrub, etc.). The four to six whitish eggs, heavily patterned dark (20.4×15.4 mm), are laid in Apr.—Aug. It has one to two broods a year, nests solitarily, and ♀ incubates for 13 days. The young are cared for by both parents and fledge after 12 days. ◑: Probably mostly small arthropods gathered on the ground.

Conservation This is an important open-woodland bird and very good songster that was formerly kept as a cagebird. No special protection is necessary.

1

Meadow Pipit
Anthus pratensis

Identification Voice — appearance — behaviour

✳: The same size as a sparrow (15 cm) and with a slender body and rather long tail. Adults (1) are olive-brown with darker markings, the underside being pale with conspicuous dark markings on the breast and flanks but with none on the rump (3); ♂ = ♀. In juv. birds the underparts are yellowish. ✦: It walks and runs about quickly on the ground. Its flight is rapid and jerky, with shallow downbeats. When flushed, it almost always calls and flies around the spot in circles. It generally sings in flight, gliding to the ground in a slanting line as it does so, but in the end dropping straight downward. ☉: It is heard frequently; its call is a sharp *ist-ist,* its alarm note a repeated *tirree.* The song is an increasingly rapid number of whistling notes terminated by a fluty trill. ☜: The Tree Pipit (p. 157), which, however, is yellower, has a softer call note, and inhabits a different environment; the Water Pipit (p. 159), which is grey to olive above, almost unmarked below in breeding plumage (mountain form), its call note is generally monosyllabic, and when it terminates its song it descends to the ground in a slanting line; and in northern Europe the very similar Red-throated Pipit (*A. cervinus*), which, however, has a different wing formula (4) from that of the Meadow Pipit (2) and is more heavily patterned, including on the rump (5).

Ecology ◈: Damp meadows, moorland, rough pasture with marshy places, from lowland to subalpine elevations; in the non-breeding season fields, marshes. ∞: Explore suitable sites and flush the birds; at the nesting grounds it may be recognised by its song. The nest may be discovered by observing the birds, especially when feeding, or by exploring the site and flushing a sitting bird.

Bionomy ↔: It is generally dispersive and migratory and occurs also in small loose flocks. It is found at the nesting grounds in Mar.—Oct. ☋: The nest is located on the ground, concealed in thick grass. The four to five brownish eggs, heavily patterned darker (19.5×14.5 mm), are laid in Apr.—July. It has one to two broods a year, nests solitarily, and ♀ incubates for 13 days. The young are tended by both parents and fledge after 14 days. ◖: Mostly small invertebrates gathered from the ground.

Conservation It is numerous. Protection consists primarily in preserving the nesting grounds.

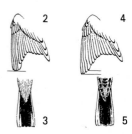

2   4

3   5

158

1

Water Pipit
Anthus spinoletta

Identification Appearance — voice — behaviour

✳: As large as a sparrow (16 cm). Adults of the mountain form (*A. s. spinoletta* — 1), distributed in central and southern Europe, are greyish-brown with dark markings above; during the breeding season the underparts are pinkish and practically unmarked, in the non-breeding season they are white and streaked brown; the tail is white at the edge, and the legs are blackish-brown. Birds of the coastal forms (*A. s. littoralis/petrosus/kleinschmidti*), distributed in northern Europe, are entirely very dark olive with underparts heavily patterned darker and tail edged with grey. ♂ = ♀. Juv. birds are more heavily patterned. ✦: It walks and runs about quickly on the ground, nodding its head, and perches on elevated boulders. Its flight is rapid and undulating. As he sings, ♂ flies up from an elevated spot and descends all the way to the ground in a slanting line. ☉: The call note is generally a monosyllabic *weest;* the song is an increasingly rapid number of whistling notes ending in a fluty trill. ♋: The Meadow Pipit (p. 158), which is olive-brown, with conspicuously patterned underside and pinkish-brown legs, and has a generally multisyllabic call; the Tree Pipit (p. 157), which has markings on the underside, pinkish legs, and hoarser call.

Ecology ◈: Stony mountain meadows above the forest limit (mountain form) and rocky sea coasts (coastal form). In the non-breeding season birds of both forms are found by water. ∞: It is readily recognised at the nesting grounds by its voice and song; the nest may be

discovered by observing the behaviour of the birds, generally when feeding, or making a thorough search of the site and flushing a sitting bird. In the non-breeding season it may be located by its voice and by chance observation.

Bionomy ↔: It is generally migratory and is found at the nesting grounds in Mar.—Oct. ∽: The nest is located on the ground, generally by a stone. The three to five grey eggs, heavily patterned darker (21.4×15.7 mm), are laid in Apr.—July. It has one to two broods a year, nests solitarily, and ♀ incubates for 14 days. The young are cared for by both parents and fledge after 14 days. ◗: Mostly small arthropods gathered from the ground.

Conservation It is widespread and common only in some areas. No special protective measures are necessary, apart from protection of its habitat (especially for the mountain form).

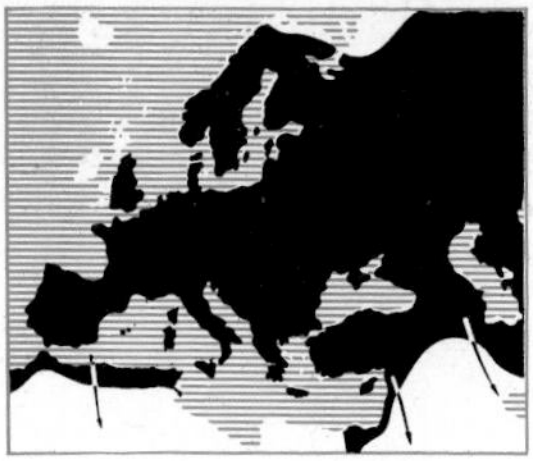

Yellow Wagtail
Motacilla flava

Identification Appearance — voice — behaviour
✱: The size of a sparrow (16 cm) and with a long, narrow tail. Adults are olive-green above, yellow on the underside; ♂ is a brilliant yellow in the breeding season, while ♀ is always dingy yellow with the markings on the head plainer. Juv. birds are even paler than ♀, brownish, with dark markings on the neck. The many subspecies in Europe differ mainly in the head coloration of the ♂♂, whereas ♀♀ and juv. birds are often indistinguishable. ♂ *M. f. flavissima* (2), distributed in western Europe and Great Britain, has a bright yellow forehead, throat and stripe over eye. ♂♂ of the following subspecies have a white stripe over the eye: *M. f. flava* (1, 3) of central Europe, with blue-grey crown, dark ear region and yellow chin; *M. f. iberiae* (4) of the Iberian Peninsula, with dark grey crown, black ear region and white chin; and *M. f. beema* (6) of the European USSR, with pale grey crown and ear region and white chin. The pale stripe above the eye is absent in ♂♂ of *M. f. thunbergi* (7) of northern Europe, with dark grey crown, black ear region and yellow chin; *M. f. cinereocapilla* (5) of southern Europe, with grey crown, blackish ear region and white chin; and *M. f. feldegg* (8) of southeastern Europe, with black crown and ear region and yellow chin. Hybrids often cannot be distinguished from one another. ✦: It walks and runs about quickly on the ground, nodding its head, and often perches on tall stems. Its flight is rapid and undulating. ⊙: It frequently utters its loud call, *pseeyih;* the song is a short and simple *sip-sip-sip-sipsi.* ♋: In eastern Europe the Citrine Wagtail (*M. citreola*): the two have different wing formulae (9 — Yellow Wagtail, 10 — Citrine Wagtail). Watch out also for the Grey Wagtail (p. 162), which has a very long tail and dark chin, but which breeds in different habitats.
Ecology ◆: Open spaces, mainly wet meadows, damp moors, etc., mostly in lowland and hilly country. ∞: It may be readily recognised by observation and by the voice and behaviour of the birds; the nest is very well concealed and may be discovered by observing the behaviour of the birds, mainly when feeding, or by exploring the site; a sitting bird, however, flies off long before you come close.
Bionomy ↔: It is migratory and is found at the nesting grounds in Mar.—Sept. In the non-breeding season it occurs in small loose-knit groups. ◡: The nest is located on the ground in grass. The four to six greyish-yellow darkly patterned eggs (17.8×14.4 mm) are laid in Apr.—July. It has one to two broods a year, nests solitarily, and ♀ incubates for 14 days. The young are tended by both parents and fledge after 11 days. ◑: Small invertebrates, gathered from the ground and from grass.
Conservation Though still common, it is greatly declining in numbers in some areas. We do not know the exact reasons for its disappearance or effective means of protecting it. Preserving the nesting grounds is a must.

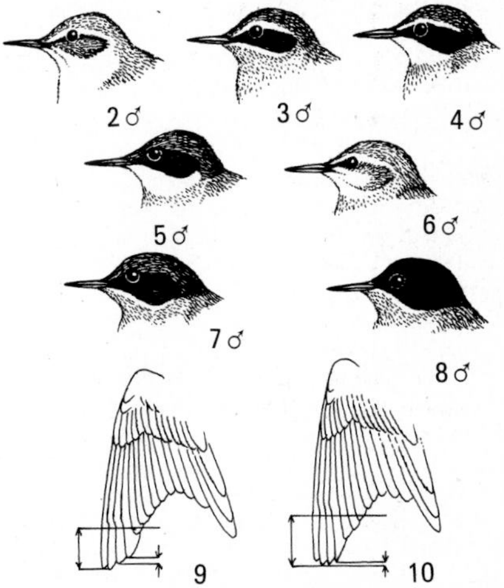

1

Grey Wagtail
Motacilla cinerea

Identification Voice — appearance — behaviour — habitat

✳: Larger than a sparrow (18 cm), it has a slender body and very long tail. Adults have a grey head and back, a dark tail edged with white, and yellow rump and underparts. ♂ in breeding plumage (1) has a black chin, ♀ has a white chin. The non-breeding plumage of both is the same except that the breast of ♂ is a more brilliant yellow. Juv. birds resemble the adults in non-breeding plumage but are paler, brownish, with markings on the throat and breast. ✦: It runs about quickly and perches on shores by water, mainly on stones, pumping its tail up and down. It flies rapidly, in deep undulations, generally above the water, occasionally hovering in one spot. ☉: It is heard frequently: the call is a sharp metallic *tsizik,* the alarm *seeit,* and the song twittering and fluty notes. ♋: The similar Yellow Wagtail (p. 161), which never has a black chin, has a more mellow call, and occurs in different habitats. Also possibly the rare, vagrant, Citrine Wagtail from Asia.

Ecology ◈: Shores, mainly the stony banks of streams. ∞: It may be readily observed and heard on smaller watercourses; the nest may be discovered by exploring suitable sites and observing feeding birds. In the non-breeding season it may also be seen by the edge of larger bodies of still water.

Bionomy ↔: It is partly migratory, is a solitary bird, and is found at the nesting grounds in Mar.—Oct. ♒: The relatively large nest (up to 18 cm across) is located in a semi-cavity in a rock face, gully, under a bridge, etc., beside water. The four to six creamy eggs with reddish-brown markings (18.7×14.3 mm) are laid in Apr.—July. It has one to two broods a year, nests solitarily, and incubates for 12 days. The young are tended by both parents, 14 days in the nest and a further ten days outside the nest. ◖: Aquatic insects and their larvae which it gathers on the shore.

Conservation Apart from preserving natural riverbeds, no special protective measures are necessary. On banks that are less suitable it is possible to put out semi-enclosed nestboxes.

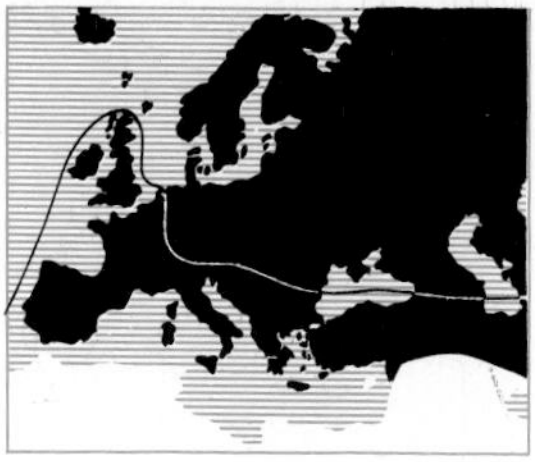

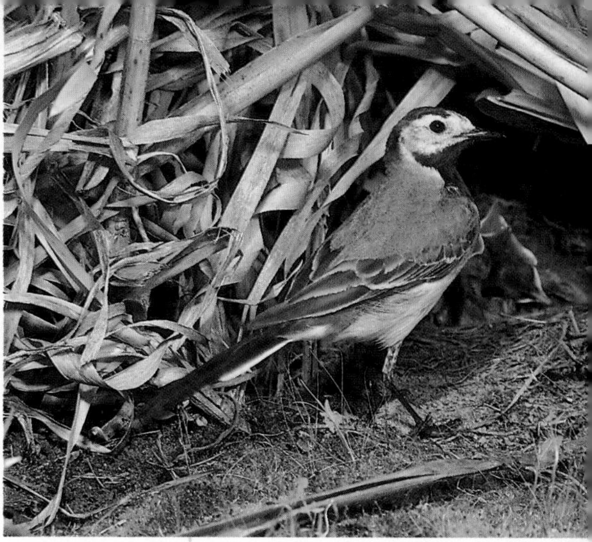

1

Pied or White Wagtail
Motacilla alba

Identification Appearance — voice — behaviour
✱: About the same size as the Grey Wagtail (18 cm) and with a slender body and very long tail. Adults are black, grey and white. In breeding plumage ♂ (1) has a black chin, throat and breast, while ♀ has less extensive black on the head and breast and the white forehead intermingled with grey. In the non-breeding plumage ♂ has only a black band across the breast, the chin and throat being white; ♀ is coloured the same as in the breeding season. Birds of the subspecies *M. a. yarrellii* (2) of the British Isles have a black back (♀ dark grey) in breeding plumage, and in non-breeding plumage a rather broad black breast-band. Juv. birds have a white breast tinted greyish-yellow. ✦: It walks and runs about rapidly on the ground, continuously pumping its tail. Its flight is rapid, undulating; occasionally it hovers in one spot. It roosts in large numbers in reeds, trees and on buildings. ⊙: Its call — a loud penetrating *tsivlik* or *tsleewee* — is heard frequently; the song, of weak, twittering notes, is heard less often. ♋: It is unmistakable.
Ecology ◆: Open locations, even small expanses with bare muddy and sandy soil, flat shores, lawns, parks, from lowland elevations to the upper forest limit. ∞: It is readily observed and heard; the nest may be discovered by examining suitable cavities or observing the behaviour of the birds, especially young birds.
Bionomy ↔: It is partly migratory and is found at the nesting grounds in Mar.—Oct. ☋: The nest is located in a semi-cavity, not very high up, usually in a rock crevice or on a building. The four to six grey-blue eggs (20.0×15.1 mm), heavily patterned darker, are laid in Apr.—July. It has one to three broods a year, nests solitarily, and incubates for 13 days. The young are cared for by both parents and stay in the nest 14 days. ◑: Small invertebrates gathered from the ground or captured in low flight.
Conservation No special protection is necessary.

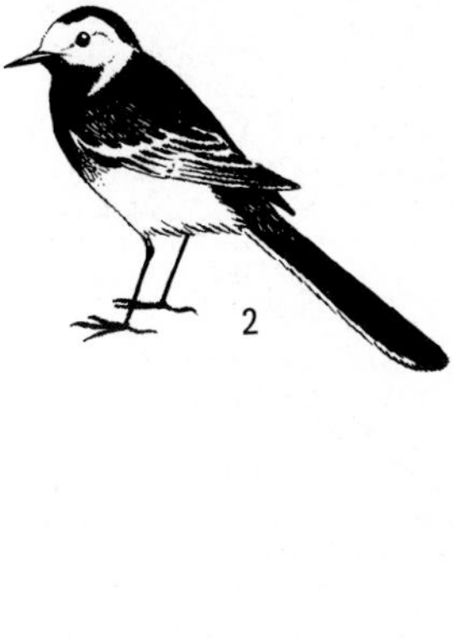

2

1

Waxwing
Bombycilla garrulus

Identification Voice — appearance — behaviour

✳: Larger than a sparrow (18 cm) and with robust body, a crest laid back on the nape, and a short tail. Adults are pinkish-brown with conspicuous coloured markings — red, yellow, white — on the wings and tip of the tail. The dark area on the chin of ♀ is smaller than that of ♂ (1) and not sharply demarcated. Juv. = adults. ✚: It perches on trees feeding acrobatically, occasionally hovering around the outer branches and flying down to water. In flight it resembles a Starling, the wings being triangular; it flies in flocks in closed formation. ☉: A soft, frequently uttered *sirr*... ☞: It is unmistakable; in flight it differs from the Starling (p. 228) in its coloration and voice.

Ecology ◈: Northern taiga; in the non-breeding season forests, parklands as well as built-up areas. ∞: At the nesting grounds it may be located by the voices of the birds and by observing their flights from one spot to another; the nest is hard to find, even from watching the behaviour of the birds. In the non-breeding season it may be seen when flying from one spot to another or on trees eating berries, mainly rowan and mistletoe berries.

Bionomy ↔: It is migratory and is found at the nesting grounds in Apr.—Sept. In the non-breeding season it often forms very large flocks. ᱦ: The nest is a large structure in the top of conifers. The three to six bluish, faintly dark-spotted eggs (23.8×15.5 mm) are laid in May —June. It has one brood a year, nests solitarily, and ♀ incubates for 14 days. The young are

cared for by both parents, it is not known for how long. ◐: In summer small invertebrates, otherwise the berries of various trees and shrubs.

Conservation It is numerous and at its wintering grounds an invasional bird. No special protective measures are necessary.

164

1

Dipper
Cinclus cinclus

Identification Habitat — appearance — behaviour — voice
✳: Larger than a sparrow (18 cm), it has a robust body and short neck and tail. Adults are black-brown above, the chin, throat and breast are white, and the belly is blackish-brown (in the north European race *C. c. cinclus*) or reddish-brown (race *C. c. aquaticus* — 1, found mainly in central and southern Europe, and *C. c. gularis* of Britain); ♂ = ♀. Juv. birds are grey, the white feathers on the underside edged a dark grey. ✦: It perches on stones in the water or on the shore, constantly bobbing. It swims very well, even underwater. It generally flies close above the water. ☉: Its sharp *zit zit* call is heard frequently, especially in flight; the song is short and fluty, and ♂ sings even in winter. ♋: It is unmistakable.
Ecology ◈: Fast-flowing streams with stony beds; in the non-breeding season also other watercourses. ∞: Look for it by walking alongside watercourses and observing boulders in the water farther ahead; its presence is also revealed by the tops of rocks in the water soiled with its droppings. When flushed, it flies fast and in a straight line low above the water, and returns from the boundaries of its territory flying higher, generally uttering its call all the while. Look for the nest in suitable sites in the nesting territory or by noting feeding birds.
Bionomy ↔: It is a resident, solitary bird, sometimes moving to ice-free waters for the winter. ౿: The nest, a large domed structure with entrance at the front, moss on the outside and leaves on the inside, is located close to the

water in a semi-cavity in a rock, under a bridge, between tree roots, etc. The four to six white eggs (25.6×18.6 mm) are laid in Mar.—Apr. It has one or two broods a year, nests solitarily, and ♀ incubates for 17 days. The young are cared for by both parents, remain in the nest 24 days, from the 14th day they leave the nest when disturbed, and at 42 days are independent. ◐: Small aquatic animals gathered on the bottom as well as on stones above the water's surface.
Conservation In places where there are insufficient nesting sites it is possible to put out open-fronted nestboxes close to water. Other means from protecting its habitats.

1

Wren
Troglodytes troglodytes

Identification Voice — size — appearance — behaviour
✴: A very small bird (10 cm), much smaller than a sparrow. It has a rounded body and short neck, legs and tail. Adults (1) are brown with dark markings and paler on the underside; ♂ = ♀. Juv. birds are more mottled above and on throat. ✦: It moves expertly through brushwood and thick undergrowth, from which it flies out only infrequently. It perches with characteristically cocked tail, crouching down frequently. It flies only short distances, very rapidly and in a straight line. ☉: It often utters its loud call *tek tek*; its alarm is a harsh *terr terr,* and its song a rapid sequence of loud fluty and trilling notes. ♋: It is unmistakable.
Ecology ◈: Woods, scrub, farmland, gardens, reeds, from lowland districts to the upper forest limit. In the non-breeding season often gardens and built-up areas, etc. ∞: It may be recognised by its voice, heard throughout the year; the nest may be discovered by the behaviour of the birds, best during the period of feeding the young, and by exploring suitable sites.
Bionomy ↔: It is generally resident and dispersive; only extreme northern populations migrate a little southward. It is found at the nesting grounds in Mar.—Oct. It lives solitarily. ꙩ: The nest is a spherical structure, with entrance hole at the front, made of leaves, grasses and moss and located in the dense ground tangle of roots of uprooted trees, in earth banks, as well as on buildings or beside tree trunks. The six to seven white eggs, speckled reddish-brown (16.6×12.6 mm), are laid in

Apr.—July. It has one to two broods a year, nests solitarily, and ♀ incubates for 16 days. The young are tended by both parents, 16 days in the nest and as many as 18 days more outside the nest. ◑: Almost exclusively small insects gathered from the ground.
Conservation It is numerous. No special protective measures are necessary.

166

1

**Dunnock or
Hedge Sparrow**
Prunella modularis

Identification Voice — behaviour — appearance

✳: As large as a sparrow (15 cm), it has a slender body and slightly forked tail. Adults (1) are brown with dark markings above, and with the sides of the head and entire underparts bluegrey; ♂ = ♀. Juv. birds are paler, virtually without a hint of blue tones, and more heavily streaked. ✦: It is a solitary bird, living concealed in the thick ground layer of vegetation; it flies rapidly, in a straight line and only short distances. It often sings perched at the top of a bush or tree, dropping to the ground and out of sight when alarmed. ☉: Its call is a very sharp and piercing, albeit not very loud *tseeit tseet*. The song is a rapid sequence of high-pitched to sharp and fluty warbling notes, perhaps somewhat monotonous and repetitive. ♋: If adequately visible it is unmistakable. The song slightly resembles the Wren's, Treecreeper's, as well as the Rock Bunting's.

Ecology ◈: Woods from lowlands to the dwarf pine belt, where it is a typical inhabitant; also gardens, shrubby field boundaries, as well as built-up areas. ∞: Locate it by its voice, which is heard throughout the day in Mar.—July. The nest is usually close to the singing ♂, but is hard to find; it is most often discovered by accidentally flushing the sitting bird when searching the site or by observing the behaviour of the birds. In the non-breeding season it may be recognised by its call or by examining birds moving about secretively in thickets and undergrowth.

Bionomy ↔: It is partly migratory and is found at the nesting grounds in Mar.—Oct. ᵥ: The nest is located at a relatively low height in dense undergrowth or in a tree, also on the ground; the building material includes moss. The four to five dark blue-green eggs (19.5×14.5 mm) are laid in Apr.—July. It has one to three broods a year, nests solitarily, and ♀ incubates for 13 days. The young are cared for by both parents. They remain in the nest 13 days, leaving it while still incapable of flight. ◕: Mostly small invertebrates captured on the ground; in winter plant seeds gathered from the ground or in the ground layer of undergrowth.

Conservation No special protective measures are necessary.

1

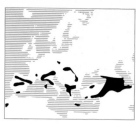

Alpine Accentor
Prunella collaris

Identification Appearance — behaviour — voice

✳: Larger than a sparrow (18 cm) and with robust body and short neck, bill and tail. Adults (1) have the upperside streaked grey-brown, the head and underside are blue-grey, the flanks streaked chestnut, and the chin white with dark markings; ♂ = ♀. In juv. birds the upperside is browner, and the entire underparts are duller and streaked with brown. ✦: It hops about on the ground in a crouched posture and perches on the tops of boulders. Its flight is quite rapid and undulating; as a rule it flies at a relatively low height and short distances. ☉: Its call note *trui trui* is not heard very frequently; its song is fluty and reminiscent of the Dunnock's. ⅌: It is unmistakable.

Ecology ◪: Rocky areas with grassy and scree slopes above the dwarf pine belt. In the non-breeding season it occurs at lower elevations on rocks, often by mountain chalets. ∞: At or above the upper forest limit either observe birds perching on boulders and flying from one spot to another or note their whereabouts by their calls. The nest may be located by the behaviour of the birds, particularly when feeding, or by a detailed search of the site. In the non-breeding season it may be seen by chance in suitable habitats.

Bionomy ↔: In winter it descends to lower elevations, sometimes even quite far from the nesting grounds. It is found at the nesting grounds in Mar.—Oct. ☽: The nest is generally located in a rock crevice, less often beneath a boulder or on a building. The three to six vivid blue-green eggs (20.0×16.6 mm) are laid in Apr.—July. It has one or two broods a year, nests solitarily, and incubates for 14 days. The young are cared for by both parents and leave the nest after 16 days, as yet not fully fledged. ◉: Smaller invertebrates and seeds gathered and captured on the ground or in refuse.

Conservation It is quite plentiful at its nesting grounds, otherwise it is only locally distributed. It should be provided with full protection, special protective measures being determined by the local conditions.

1

European Robin
Erithacus rubecula

Identification Voice — appearance — behaviour

✳: Smaller than a sparrow (14 cm) and with a large round head and characteristic large eyes. Adults (1) have brown upperparts and reddish-orange forehead and underside as far as the lower breast; ♂ = ♀. Juv. birds are very different, dark above and light brown below with pale scale-like markings. ✦: It hops about on the ground with slightly drooping wings and half-cocked tail, frequently stopping and crouching down. It flies short distances in undulating flight, perches and also sings on trees. ☉: Its loud *tic-tic-tic* call is often heard; the alarm note is a thin penetrating *seehs*. The song is short, with melancholy fluty whistles; it sings practically the whole year long, in spring frequently in the evening. ♋: It is unmistakable.

Ecology ◈: Woods of all kinds, gardens, from lowland elevations to the upper forest limit. It occurs mainly in places with shrubby undergrowth, in the non-breeding season often in waterside vegetation. ∞: It is readily recognised throughout the year by its voice as well as its appearance. The nest and newly fledged young may be located by observing the behaviour of the adult birds, mainly when feeding, the nest also by exploring suitable sites.

Bionomy ↔: It is partly migratory and occurs singly throughout the year. ∾: The nest is placed in a semi-cavity in the ground, mainly in earth banks, occasionally also in grass, on the ground, on a tree, or on a building. The five to seven creamy eggs, speckled reddish-brown (19.8×15.1 mm), are laid in Apr.—July. It has one to four broods a year, nests solitarily, and ♀ incubates for 14 days. The young are tended by both parents, 14 days in the nest and a further eight days outside the nest. ◑: Small invertebrates, mainly insects and their larvae, even bees, less often plant seeds and fruits. Animals are gathered mainly from the ground but also on branches in thickets and even in water; fruits and seeds are gathered mainly on shrubs and trees.

Conservation It is numerous. No special protective measures are necessary.

1

Identification Voice — appearance — behaviour

✳: Larger than a sparrow (17 cm). Adults (1) are brown with a russet-tinged tail. ♂ = ♀. Juv. birds are darker, with scale-like markings. ✦: It leads a secretive life in thickets and is seldom seen. It hops about quickly on the ground with partly drooping wings and half-cocked tail, which it wags and spreads slightly. ☉: It often utters its muffled call note *tak-tak*; when nervous, e.g. beside the nest and the young nestlings, it utters a loud *weep* or *weep-krr-krr*. Its well-known song is very musical and varied, differing among individual birds and regions: it begins with whistling notes *tee-tee-tee,* that gradually become increasingly louder, then change into clear mellow *tiu-tiu-tiu-tiu* and fast, deep *chook* notes and are followed by various melodies. ♂ sings perched on a branch throughout the day, even at noon, but is heard mostly at night. ♋: In northeastern Europe from the Elbe-Odra-Tisa-Danube line the very similar Thrush Nightingale (*L. luscinia*), which differs from the Nightingale (2) in its wing formula (3). The night song of the Woodlark (p. 151) may be mistaken for that of the Nightingale.

Ecology ◈: Deciduous woods including small woods with shrubby undergrowth, often near water, from lowland to hilly country. ∞: It is easily recognised by its song (Apr.—July), near the nest and its offspring by its agitated alarm note. (NB: A singing ♂ is not necessarily an indication of nesting, particularly at a later date.)

The nest is hard to find: it is necessary to search the undergrowth at the site where the bird sings with great thoroughness, also note the adult birds, especially when feeding.

Bionomy ↔: It is migratory and is found at the nesting grounds in Apr.—Sept. ♒: The nest is located in thick undergrowth on the ground; dry leaves are used in its construction. The three to five olive-green eggs, heavily spotted brown (21.0×16.1 mm), are laid in Apr.—June. It has one, exceptionally perhaps two, broods a year, nests solitarily, and ♀ incubates for 13 days. The young are cared for by both parents, 11 days in the nest and a further ten days outside the nest. ◗: Small arthropods, in autumn also juicy fruits, all gathered from the ground or in the thick ground layer of herbaceous vegetation.

Conservation It is locally numerous. Apart from restricting the clearing of thickets at the nesting grounds, no other protective measures are necessary.

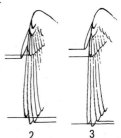

2   3

1

Bluethroat
Luscinia svecica

Identification Appearance — voice — behaviour

✲: Smaller than a sparrow (14 cm). ♂ in breeding plumage is brown above, with russet at the base of the tail, and pale on the underside with a brilliant blue expanse from the chin to the breast in the centre of which is a small patch coloured russet (race *L. s. svecica* — 1 — of northern Europe) or white (*L. s. cyanecula* of central Europe). Some individuals, however, do not have this patch. In the non-breeding plumage the throat is paler with dark markings. ♀ ♀ of both subspecies have a variably whitish throat edged with a band of black-brown spots in both plumages. Juv. birds are brown with heavy pale spotting, but soon moult and then resemble ♀. ✦: It leads a secretive, solitary life in dense vegetation, mainly alongside water. ⊙: It does not sing very often. Its song is conspicuously articulated, beginning with a *deep-deep-deep* and continuing with a mixture of fluty and sharp notes. When singing, it perches on the top of taller plants, occasionally flying up and descending again in fluttering flight. Its call is a distinctive *tac tac* and a soft *feet*, the alarm a throaty *turrk*. ♋: It is unmistakable.

Ecology ◆: Damp marshy places or dense shoreline vegetation, from lowland to subalpine elevations. ∞: In the breeding season it reveals its presence by its song or may be seen by chance. The nest is hard to find, requiring a thorough search of the site; an easier way is to observe feeding birds. In the non-breeding season they may be seen by chance; their occur-

rence is more often determined by capturing the birds.

Bionomy ↔: It is migratory and is found at the nesting grounds in Mar.—Oct. It occurs singly. ♒: The nest is hidden on the ground or in the ground layer of vegetation. The four to six dark olive-brown eggs, heavily patterned blackish-brown (18.8×14.2 mm), are laid in Apr.—July. It has one to two broods a year, nests solitarily, and ♀ incubates for 14 days. The young are tended by both parents, 14 days in the nest and a further 14 days outside the nest. ◗: Small invertebrates, towards autumn also plant fruits, gathered on the ground.

Conservation It is not very plentiful and is declining in numbers. In the case of lowland populations, it is necessary to protect the nesting grounds.

1

Black Redstart
Phoenicurus ochruros

Identification Voice — appearance — behaviour

∗: Smaller than a sparrow (14 cm), and with a large head, relatively long tail and longer legs. Adult ♂ (1) is mostly black, but has a white patch on the wings and a rusty-red tail; ♀ is always dark grey-brown without the white wing patch. Juv. birds resemble ♀, but their underside is darkly patterned. ✦: It perches on the tops of buildings or stones, continually quivers its tail, often crouches, and flies down to the ground, where it runs and hops about very quickly. Its flight is rapid, skilful, with occasional abrupt turns in pursuit of flying insects. ☉: It is heard often. Its call is a sharp *feet*, when alarmed *feet-tek-tek*; its song (Mar.—Sept.) is a fast, loud, brief rising and descending warble, interrupted with a quiet crackling hiss. ♂ sings from wires or the tops of buildings or rocks. ∽: It is unmistakable; only juv. birds resemble the young of the European Redstart (p. 173), which, however, have paler yellow-brown underparts and are always more markedly patterned on the upperside. The wing formulae are different (Black Redstart — 3, European Redstart — 2).

Ecology ◈: Rocky places from lowland to subalpine elevations and built-up areas. ∞: It is readily identified by its song and other calls, otherwise it is often seen on stones or buildings. Look for the nest close to where a bird is singing or locate it by observing adult birds, which are not readily alarmed as a rule.

Bionomy ↔: It is partly migratory and is found at the nesting grounds in Mar.—Oct. It occurs singly. ∞: The nest is located in semi-cavities in rocks and buildings, not very high up. The four to six white eggs, sometimes with reddish-brown markings (19.5×14.5 mm), are laid in Apr.—July. It has one to three broods a year, nests solitarily, and ♀ incubates for 14 days. The young are cared for by both parents, 16 days in the nest and a further 14 days outside the nest. ◑: In spring almost exclusively insects, spiders, molluscs and worms; in autumn also berries. Food is gathered on the ground or caught on the wing.

Conservation It is plentiful. No special protective measures are necessary. Nesting may be promoted by putting out nestboxes.

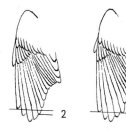

2   3

1

European Redstart
Phoenicurus phoenicurus

Identification Voice — appearance — behaviour
✴: The same size as the Black Redstart (14 cm), and with a slender body and long thin legs. Adult ♂ (1) is grey above, has a white forehead, black mask, chin and throat, and a rusty-red breast and tail; ♀ is grey-brown above, whitish on the underside, with buff-brown breast. Juv. birds resemble ♀ but have darker markings, especially on the upperparts.
✦: It perches on branches, often crouches, quivers its tail, flits about and flies down to the ground. Its flight is undulating, light and rapid; it expertly pursues flying insects. ☉: It often utters its call *wheet-tuc-tuc* or a fluty *hueet*; the song is soft and short and composed of a high-pitched note followed by two short deeper notes and then several higher-pitched trills. ♋: It is unmistakable. ♀ and juv. birds resemble those of the Black Redstart (p. 172), which, however, are darker, slate-grey, and without markings on the upperside.
Ecology ◗: Open, mainly broad-leaved, woods, gardens and parks in built-up areas, from lowland to mountain elevations. ∞: It is easily recognised by its song; in the non-breeding season by its call and behaviour. Look for the nest by observing the behaviour of the birds, mainly when feeding, and by examining suitable cavities.
Bionomy ↔: It is migratory and is found at the nesting grounds in Apr.—Sept. It is a solitary bird. ᴗ: The nest is located in tree cavities or semi-cavities, very occasionally also in the open, on buildings or on the ground, as well as in man-made nestboxes. The five to seven vivid blue-green eggs (18.7×13.9 mm) are laid in Apr.—June. It has one or two broods a year, nests solitarily, and ♀ incubates for 13 days. The young are cared for by both parents, 14 days in the nest and a further 13 days outside the nest. ◑: Small arthropods, mostly insects; towards autumn also plant fruits. Food is gathered on the ground, less often also on branches.
Conservation It is a declining species. Effective methods of protection are not known as yet, but putting out nestboxes may help.

1

Whinchat
Saxicola rubetra

Identification Voice — behaviour — appearance

∗: Smaller than a sparrow (13 cm), it has a large head, short tail and relatively long legs. Adults have darkly patterned upperparts, a white stripe over the eye, and a dark tail with white patches at the base. ♂ (1, at left) has dark cheeks and the upperwings are blackish-brown with a white patch; ♀ (1, at right) is duller and has the markings on the upperparts and upperwings paler. Juv. birds resemble ♀, but lack the white wing patch and have brown markings on the breast. ✦: It perches on elevated spots, mainly on taller herbaceous plants, flies down to the ground, often crouches, and jerks its wings as well as its tail. Its flight is brief, undulating; occasionally it hovers in a single spot. ☉: It frequently calls a loud *yu*, when alarmed *yu-tic-tic*. The song is short and fast, and composed of fluty, rasping and chirping sounds; ♂ sings from elevated spots. ♋: The Stonechat (p. 175), especially ♀ and juv. birds, but their head is darker and the tail is dark at the base.

Ecology ◈: Damp meadows and commons, from lowland to subalpine elevations; in the non-breeding season also fields and coasts. ∞: It is readily located by its voice. The nest is very well concealed, its location being best discovered by observing the behaviour of the birds; the sitting ♀ flies off in the evening in search of food and then returns to the nest. Another means is to walk through suitable sites and flush the sitting bird.

Bionomy ↔: It is migratory and is found at the nesting grounds in Apr.—Sept. ᗑ: The nest is located on the ground, concealed in thick grass. The five to six dark blue-green eggs, sometimes with reddish-brown markings (19.1×14.6 mm), are laid in Apr.—July. It has one, possibly two, broods a year, nests solitarily, and ♀ incubates for 13 days. The young are tended by both parents, 14 days in the nest and a further 12 days outside the nest. ◑: Mainly insects and other invertebrates gathered or caught on the ground or in the air.

Conservation It is quite plentiful but declining in places. It is necessary to preserve its nesting environment.

1

Stonechat
Saxicola torquata

Identification Voice — behaviour — appearance

✳: Smaller than a sparrow (14 cm), it has a round head and short tail. Adult ♂ (1) has the head, throat, upperparts and tail black, the rump white with black and buff markings, the sides of the neck white and the breast orange. In the duller ♀, the black of the upperparts is replaced by pale brown with darker markings and the throat is pale. Juv. birds have the upperparts dark brown with pale markings and underparts light brown with dark markings. ✦: It perches on elevated places with body held very erect, often jerking its wings and tail, and flies down to the ground. Its flight is low, brief, jerky and undulating. ☉: It frequently utters its brusque call *wheet* or *wheet-tsack-tsack*; the intense alarm note is *wheet-kr-kr.* Its song is delivered from an elevated spot, sometimes in flight, and is short, nondescript, and composed of grating and chirping notes. ♋: The similar Whinchat (p. 174) is paler, and its tail is white at the base; its song is louder and more melodious.

Ecology ◑: Fallow land, dry meadows, pastureland, moors, glades, hedgerows alongside field paths in lowland and hilly country, in the non-breeding season also fields and coasts. ∞: Its voice is readily identified, as are birds perched on elevated places, especially alongside country paths. The nest is well hidden and it is necessary to make a thorough search of the site, when you may flush the sitting ♀; it may also be found by observing adult birds, especially when feeding the young (these, however, leave the nest when they are still incompletely feathered).

Bionomy ↔: It is generally dispersive or migratory and is found at the nesting grounds in Mar.—Oct. ᴗ: The nest is concealed on the ground in thick grass. The four to six dark blue-green eggs, speckled reddish-brown (18.4×14.2 mm), are laid in Mar.—July. It has one to four broods a year, nests solitarily, and ♀ incubates for 14 days. The young are cared for by both parents, 16 days in the nest and several days more outside the nest. ◓: Small insects and other invertebrates gathered on the ground or caught on the wing.

Conservation This is a declining species. Effective methods of protection are not known, apart from protection of the nesting grounds.

1

Wheatear
Oenanthe oenanthe

Identification Appearance — voice — behaviour

✳: As large as a sparrow (15 cm), and with a larger round head, short tail and longer legs. Adults are grey, with blackish-brown wings and gleaming white rump and sides of uppertail. ♂ (1, 2) has a grey back, a black mask and a sandy breast; ♀ is greyish-brown above, buff on the underside and has a white stripe above the eye. Juv. birds resemble ♀ but have dark mottling.

✦: A solitary bird, it hops about on the ground, bobbing up and down and flirting its outspread tail, and perches on elevated stones, fences, etc. It flies short distances, at low level, and flutters up in pursuit of flying insects. ☉: Its call *weet weet* is uttered infrequently, when alarmed *tek-tek-weet*; the song is short and composed of fluty tones intermingled with grating and twittering sounds. ☙: In southern Europe other members of the genus *Oenanthe*, mainly the Black-eared Wheatear (*O. hispanica* — 5), Isabelline Wheatear (*O. isabellina* — 3), and Pied Wheatear (*O. pleschanka* — 4); in southwestern Europe the Black Wheatear (*O. leucura* — 6).

Ecology ◈: Stony and sandy areas with sparse vegetation, from lowland to subalpine elevations; in some areas construction sites; in the non-breeding season also fields and coasts. ∞: It may be identified by its voice and by examining birds perched on fences, walls and boulders. The nest may be discovered only by watching adult birds, particularly when feeding.

Bionomy ↔: It is migratory and is found at the nesting grounds in Mar.—Oct. ᴡ: The nest is a hole in the ground or in a wall. The five to six pale blue eggs (20.6×15.6 mm) are laid in Apr.—June. It has one to two broods a year, nests solitarily, and ♀ incubates for 13 days. The young are cared for by both parents, 15 days in the nest and several more outside the nest. ◑: Small arthropods, mainly insects, caught on the ground or in low flight.

Conservation This is a greatly declining species. Methods of protection are not known as yet.

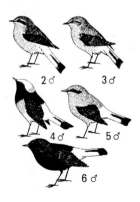

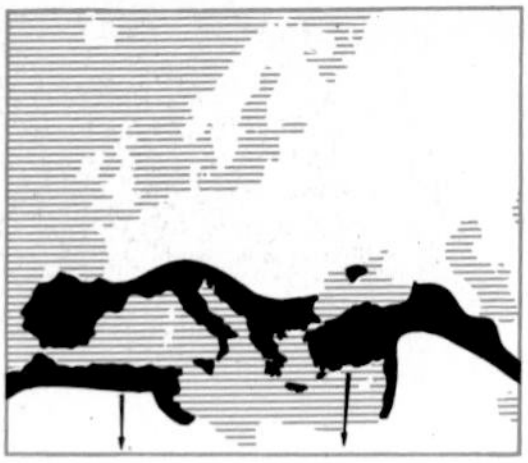

1

Rock Thrush
Monticola saxatilis

Identification Behaviour — size — voice — appearance
✱: Smaller than the Blackbird (19 cm), it resembles a Song Thrush with a shorter tail. Adult ♂ (1) has the head and upper back greyish-blue, the underparts and tail orange, and the lower back white; ♀ is greyish-brown above, the underparts are buff with dark and pale markings and the throat is white. Juv. birds resemble ♀ but are conspicuously spotted white. ✦: A very shy bird, it perches upright on elevated places, mainly on boulders, from where it flies down to the ground to catch insects; it hops about rapidly with partly drooping wings, jerking them and spreading its tail as it bobs up and down. It flies lightly and rapidly in shallow undulating flight at a low height. ⊙: The song, delivered from elevated places as well as on the wing, is strong, melodious and variable and not very long. The call note is a *yu yu*; when alarmed it gives a *check check.* ♋: In southern Europe the Blue Rock Thrush (*M. solitarius*), which, however, lacks rusty-orange in its plumage.
Ecology ◈: Rather dry rocky areas with short grass cover, from lowland to subalpine elevations, sometimes even in places frequented by humans (quarries, built-up areas). In the non-breeding season also fields. ∞: Listen for its call and from a distance inspect with binoculars birds perched on rocks in possible nesting areas. As a rule it is necessary to remain a lengthier while in the given spot. Discover the nest by observing the behaviour of the birds, particularly when feeding, also by investigating suitable crevices. In the non-breeding season it may be encountered by chance observation.
Bionomy ↔: It is migratory and is found at the nesting grounds in Apr.—Sept. ⊌: The nest is located in a rock crevice. The four to five blue-green eggs (25.7×19.3 mm) are laid in Apr.—June. It has one or two broods a year, nests solitarily, and ♀ incubates for 14 days. The young are tended by both parents, 15 days in the nest and several more outside the nest. ◑: Mainly insects, caught in low flight or on the ground, also spiders, molluscs and worms. In summer and autumn also fruits gathered on the ground as well as on plants.
Conservation This is a declining species with only a patchy distribution. Birds must be protected from being caught at the nesting sites, but otherwise no effective means of protection are known.

1

Ring Ouzel
Turdus torquatus

Identification Appearance — voice — behaviour

∗: Smaller than the Blackbird (23 cm) but looks very much the same. Adult ♂ is black with a patch the shape of a half-moon on the breast, coloured white (race *T. t. torquatus* of northern Europe) or dingy brownish (race *T. t. alpestris* of central Europe), and with a pale area on the wings. ♀ (1) is brownish-black above, the underparts are patterned with pale scale-like markings, and the pale half-moon patch is mottled a dingy brown. Juv. birds do not have the half-moon patch on the breast and have bold whitish markings. ✦: It leads a secretive life. It hops about on the ground and flies rapidly over short distances. ☉: The alarm note *tak-tak-tak* is like the Blackbird's. The song is fluty, rather short, and composed of distinct segments *tchere-tcheevee-titcho-o* repeated in succession. ♋: Its appearance is unmistakable; only its alarm note may be confused with that of the Blackbird.

Ecology ◈: In northern Europe rocky moorland vegetation with scattered trees and shrubs, in central Europe coniferous mountain forests. ∞: At the nesting grounds it may be identified by its song and other calls, in open areas also by the coloration and behaviour of the birds. The nest may be discovered mainly when the young are being fed or by a detailed search of the site. In the non-breeding season it is seen occasionally by chance.

Bionomy ↔: It is migratory and is found at the nesting grounds in Apr.—Sept. ʊ: The nest is sited not very high up in a tree by the trunk, in northern Europe in clumps of vegetation on the ground. The three to five green eggs, heavily spotted reddish-brown (29.8×21.6 mm), are laid in Apr.—June. It has one or two broods a year, nests solitarily, and ♀ incubates for 14 days. The young are cared for by both parents, 15 days in the nest and several days also outside the nest. ◐: Small arthropods, in season also fruits, gathered on the ground or on trees.

Conservation Locally it is quite plentiful. No special protective measures are necessary.

178

1

Blackbird
Turdus merula

Identification Appearance — voice — behaviour

∗: A well-known medium-sized bird (25 cm). Adult ♂ (1) is black, with a yellow-orange bill; ♀ is blackish-brown with paler, variably patterned underparts. Juv. birds are brown and darkly patterned; in their 2nd year their primaries are still brown, discernible even when the wings are folded. ✦: This is mainly a solitary bird. It hops about on the ground; its flight is rather slow, the wingbeats interspersed with brief intervals of gliding. In the non-breeding season it roosts at communal roosting sites, where the birds converge in the evening. In spring there are frequent combats over territories. ☉: Its call is frequently heard; the alarm note is *tchick-tchick*, the warning note is a piercing cry. The song is well known — loud and melodious, and delivered by the ♂ from an elevated spot, mainly early in the morning and at dusk. ♋: It is unmistakable. In mountain forests and upland moors watch out for the Ring Ouzel (p. 178), which has a white patch the shape of a half-moon on the breast.

Ecology ◈: Woods and forests, from lowland to mountain elevations; nowadays mostly built-up areas. ∞: In built-up areas it may be found without any trouble; in woods by its song (Feb.—July). The nest is readily located, in woods by observing the behaviour of the birds, especially when feeding the young.

Bionomy ↔: It is only partly migratory, many birds remaining to winter throughout most of range. It occurs usually singly all the year round. ᴥ: The nest is located in thickets, in low trees, on buildings. The three to five extremely variable eggs, usually green with dense reddish-brown markings (29.4×21.6 mm), are laid in Mar.—Aug. It has one to five broods a year, and ♀ incubates for 13 days. The young are tended by both parents, 14 days in the nest and a further 18 days outside the nest. ◑: The composition of the diet depends on the season. Smaller invertebrates are the staple food in spring, the fruits of trees and shrubs in summer and autumn, with additional household scraps in winter. Food is gathered on the ground and on branches.

Conservation It is very plentiful. In gardens it may damage fruits and vegetables. Protection is not necessary.

1

Fieldfare
Turdus pilaris

Identification Voice — appearance — behaviour

✳: As large as the Blackbird (25 cm) and with the typical appearance of a thrush. Adults (1) have the top of the head and rump grey, the back brown, and the underparts brownish with prominent brownish-black markings. ♂ has conspicuous black markings on the grey crown and a black tail; ♀ has smaller brownish-black markings on the crown and is duller, with a blackish-brown tail. Juv. birds are more heavily patterned below as well as above. ✦: It runs and hops about on the ground, pausing often, and frequently perches on trees. Its flight consists of leisurely wingbeats interspersed with intervals of gliding with wings pressed to the body. ☉: It frequently utters its typical harsh *shak-shak* call, often in flight, and also gives a faint *seeh*. The song is a mix of twittering, whistling and squeaky sounds; ♂ sings while perched, as well as in flight. ♋: It is unmistakable.

Ecology ◀: Small woods, edges of forests as well as groups of trees by damp meadows and pastureland, from lowland elevations to the upper forest limit. In the non-breeding season also open country in fields, gardens, tree avenues, etc. ∞: Breeding birds are best located by their voices; they often breed in small colonies. At the nesting grounds they fly only short distances from the nests, which are sometimes not concealed at all; with the birds uttering their warning cries beside them, they are found with relative ease. In the non-breeding season flocks of birds are easily observed on the ground or

perching in trees and flying from one spot to another; they fly in relatively tight and protracted formations.

Bionomy ↔: It is partly migratory, generally occurring and nesting in some numbers. ☼: The nests are located on the branches of trees by the trunk. The four to six greenish eggs, heavily patterned russet-brown (30.6×22.1 mm), are laid in Apr.—June. It has one or two broods a year, and ♀ incubates for 14 days. The young are cared for by both parents, 14 days in the nest and another 14 days outside the nest. ◖: Small molluscs, annelids, insects and fruits, gathered on the ground as well as on trees.

Conservation This is a plentiful species and increasing in number in places. No special protective measures are necessary.

1

Redwing
Turdus iliacus

Identification Voice — appearance — behaviour

✳: Smaller than the Blackbird (20 cm) and resembles the Song Thrush. Adults (1) have a conspicuous white stripe over the eye, the cheeks bordered below by a pale stripe, and rusty-red flanks and underwing-coverts; ♂ = ♀. Juv. birds are darkly patterned above and below and the red colouring is not so vivid. ✦: An extremely shy bird. It perches on branches, hops about on the ground and flies in the evening to communal roosting sites in the woods. ☉: At the nesting grounds individual birds sing from the tops of trees; a common phenomenon in spring is the joint singing of flocks of birds at the roosting site. The song is twittering with fluty tones, is fainter than that of the Song Thrush and sounds like *tree-tree-tree-trz-tri*. The contact call is a sharp *ceezr* or fainter *eeeih* (it may be heard when the birds are on the wing at night), the alarm note *tchi-tak*. ☺: Primarily the Song Thrush (p. 183), which, however, does not have a white stripe over the eye, has pale-coloured flanks and underside of the wings, and a different voice.

Ecology ◈: More open woods as well as parklands with tree avenues, water and meadows, from lowland elevations to the upper forest limit. ∞: At the nesting grounds it may be recognised mainly by its song; the nest may be discovered by the behaviour of the birds, especially when feeding, and by exploring suitable sites (the Redwing often nests in Fieldfare colonies). In spring even non-breeding birds sing. In the non-breeding season it may often be found in fields and thickets with berries, often in large flocks. Listening to the birds' calls is the best way to locate them.

Bionomy ↔: It is migratory and generally occurs in flocks. It is found at the nesting grounds in Apr.—Oct. ꙮ: The nest is usually low down in a tree or in thickets and is generally made of slender twigs, grass stems and mud. The five to seven blue-green eggs, heavily patterned reddish-brown (25.1×19.0 mm), are laid in May—July. It has one or two broods a year, nests solitarily, and ♀ incubates for 12 days. The young are tended by both parents, ten days in the nest and several more outside the nest. ◑: The same as for other thrushes.

Conservation It is plentiful and is expanding its range. No special protective measures are necessary.

Identification Voice — appearance — behaviour

✳: Smaller than the Blackbird (23 cm) and has the typical appearance of a thrush: robust body, stout bill and legs, large eyes, long tail and long pointed wings. Adults (1) are brown above and buff with brown markings below; ♂ = ♀. Juv. birds have pale scale-like markings on the upperside. ✦: It perches on trees, the male usually at the very top when singing, and hops about on the ground. It flies with leisurely wingbeats interspersed with brief intervals of gliding with wings pressed to the body. ☉: It is heard quite often. The call is a penetrating *sip sip*. The song is loud and persistent, like the Blackbird's but with varied phrases; typical is the repeating of the separate phrases, e. g. *huidip huidip kredit kredit...* ☊: Most similar is the Redwing (p. 181), distributed throughout Europe, which, however, has a white stripe above the eye, reddish-brown flanks and underside of the wings, and a different voice. Very occasionally some thrushes from western Asia occur in Europe in Aug.—Dec., e. g. the Dusky Thrush (*T. naumanni eunomus* — 2), Naumann's Thrush (*T. naumanni naumanni* — 3), Black-throated Thrush (*T. ruficollis atrogularis* — 4) with a black throat, and the extremely rare Red-throated Thrush (*T. ruficollis ruficollis*); these thrushes, however, differ more markedly from the Song Thrush in coloration but they are the same size.

Ecology ◆: Woods of various kinds from lowland elevations to the upper forest limit, parklands, as well as gardens and parks in built-up areas. ∞: At the nesting grounds in Mar.—July it is readily recognised by its song; the nest may be found without difficulty in the bottom layer of vegetation by examining dense growths of small trees and shrubs. In the non-breeding season it may be recognised also at night by its call, in the daytime by chance observation.

Bionomy ↔: It is mostly resident but also migratory and is found at the nesting grounds in Mar.—Sept. In the non-breeding season it occurs also in loose groups. ಐ: The nest is located in dense thickets or low down in trees. It can be recognised by its typical construction (5). The outside is woven of twigs, dry plant stems and grasses, and the interior is of rotting wood, leaves and mud cemented together to form a smooth layer; the cavity is provided with no further lining. The four to five blue-green, black-speckled eggs (27.2×20.5 mm) are laid in Apr.—July. It has one to three broods a year, nests solitarily, and ♀ incubates for 13 days. The young are cared for by both parents, 13 days in the nest and a further 18 days outside the nest. ◖: Small invertebrates, in season also the fruits of trees and shrubs; food is gathered on the ground and on branches.

Conservation Not necessary; this is a plentiful bird.

1

1

Mistle Thrush
Turdus viscivorus

Identification Voice — appearance — size — behaviour

✳: The largest European thrush, larger than the Blackbird (28 cm). Adults (1) have the upperparts brown, the underparts patterned with very prominent dark round markings, and the underside of the wings white; ♂ = ♀. Juv. birds are patterned above. ✦: It perches in treetops as a rule; in winter often in trees where mistletoe grows. Its flight is rapid and sustained, with long shallow undulations. On the ground it hops about. ☉: Very often, including in flight, it utters a rattling alarm *tserrr*; its call is a soft *seei*. The song is loud, melodious and fluty, similar to the Blackbird's but with short phrases. ♋: The similar Song Thrush (p. 183) is much smaller and has a different voice.

Ecology ◈: Mature woodland of various kinds from lowland elevations to the upper forest limit, generally close to open country with meadows and pastures; locally also in built-up areas. ∞: It is easily recognised by its voice; it sings from the end of winter, often while there is still snow on the ground. The nest may be discovered by exploring probable nesting sites and by the behaviour of the birds, mainly when bringing food to the nest.

Bionomy ↔: It is partly migratory and is found at the nesting grounds in Feb.—Sept. It is a solitary bird. ୰: The nest is located high up in a tree by the trunk or on marginal branches; mud is used in its construction. The four to five yellow-green eggs with russet-brown markings (30.8×22.3 mm) are laid in Mar.—June. It has one or two broods a year, nests solitarily, and

♀ incubates for 14 days. The young are tended by both parents, 15 days in the nest and a further 20 days outside the nest. ◑: Invertebrates and berries of trees, gathered on the ground and on branches. In winter mistletoe berries form an important part of the diet.

Conservation It is a relatively plentiful bird; no special protection is necessary.

1

Grasshopper Warbler
Locustella naevia

Identification Voice — behaviour
∗: Smaller than a sparrow (13 cm), it has a slender head and body and a short, rounded tail. Adults (1) are olive-brown above with dark streaks, and buffish-white below often with a few spots on the breast; ♂ = ♀. Juv. birds are warmer brown above and buffer below. ✦: It leads a secretive life, moving about in dense thickets or herbaceous vegetation and running about in thick undergrowth as well as on the ground. It flies only very short distances, as a rule dropping down out of sight in vegetation when disturbed. ⊙: ♂ sings often, generally at night and towards morning, perched rather low down in a shrub or on a raised stem while doing so. The song is a monotonous *se-errrr*, like a fishing reel, often very lengthy. The call note is a soft *tuck-tuck*, the alarm note a sharp *sitt.* ♋: Savi's Warbler (p. 186) has a very similar but deeper voice. The River Warbler (*L. fluviatilis*) is similar in appearance but lacks the dark markings above, and its song is different.
Ecology ◈: Damp meadows with dense herbaceous undergrowth and solitary shrubs, less often also overgrown woodland clearings, from lowland to mountain elevations. In the non-breeding season also reedbeds, fields, etc. ∞: It is readily located by its song in Apr.—July; in the non-breeding season, however, its presence may be proved only by chance observation or by capturing the bird. The nest is hard to find, and even the behaviour of the birds by the nest is very inconspicuous. When bringing food to the young, they drop down into the vegetation some distance from the nest and clamber the rest of the way through the undergrowth; only in wet conditions do they fly directly to the nest.
Bionomy ↔: It is migratory and is found at the nesting grounds in Apr.—Sept. It lives solitarily in the breeding as well as the non-breeding season. ꙍ: The nest, made of broader grass blades on the outside and finer blades on the inside, is located in a dense tangle of vegetation at ground level. The five to six reddish eggs with darker markings (17.6×13.6 mm) are laid in May—July. It has one to two, occasionally three broods a year, and incubates for 13 days. The young are cared for by both parents, ten days in the nest and several more outside the nest. ◑: Small, less mobile arthropods, mainly insects, gathered mostly on the ground or in the ground layer of herbaceous vegetation.
Conservation It is relatively numerous; no special protective measures are necessary.

1

Savi's Warbler
Locustella luscinioides

Identification Voice — habitat — behaviour
✳: Smaller than a sparrow (14 cm), it has a slender body and short, rounded tail. Adults (1) are entirely brown, paler below; ♂ = ♀. Juv. birds are slightly darker. ✦: It leads a very secretive life. It perches on reed stalks, flying down into the vegetation when disturbed; it flies only a short distance from one spot to another. It clambers through the dense bottom herbaceous layer of reedbeds, sedges, etc. ☉: It is often heard, even at night. When singing, ♂ perches slantwise on the reed stem but not at the very top. The song is a monotonous lengthy *chirr*, preceded by deeper sounds *pt-pt-urrrrr* audible from close range. The call is a soft *tsik*, the alarm note a sharp explosive *pit*. ☜: Its song resembles the Grasshopper Warbler's (p. 185), but the latter's is higher-pitched, more ringing, and rarely delivered directly from reedbeds. The song of the River Warbler (*L. fluviatilis*) is different.
Ecology ◈: Reedbeds and other similar marshland vegetation, in lowland and hilly country. In the non-breeding season also bushes. ∞: It is readily identified by its voice, mainly by its song; in the non-breeding season its presence may generally be determined only by capturing the bird. The nest is hard to find, even by the behaviour of the birds, which feed the young in a very secretive manner; it is most likely to be discovered by inspecting the thick bottom layers of vegetation and flushing a sitting bird.
Bionomy ↔: It is migratory and is found at the nesting grounds in Apr.—Sept. It is a solitary bird. ᴥ: The nest, made of flat dry leaves, is lo-

cated low down in the thick layer of vegetation by the water's surface. The four to five white, brown-patterned eggs (19.7×14.6 mm) are laid in Apr.—Aug. It has one to two broods a year, nests solitarily, and incubates for 13 days. The young are cared for by both parents, ten days in the nest and several more outside the nest. ◐: Small, less mobile invertebrates, mainly insects, gathered from leaves, from the ground, or from the water's surface.
Conservation It is numerous only in places. Apart from protecting the nesting grounds, no other protective measures are necessary.

1

Sedge Warbler
Acrocephalus
schoenobaenus

Identification Voice — appearance — behaviour
*: Smaller than a sparrow (12 cm), it has a large head. Adults (1) have brown upperparts streaked a darker colour, and yellowish-white underparts; there is a conspicuous white stripe over the eye and the crown is streaked ochre and brown (2). ♂ = ♀. Juv. birds have the sides of the throat and the crop speckled brown. ✛: It climbs jerkily on reed stems and often flies from one spot to another in rapid, slightly undulating flight close above the reedbeds.
♂ perches on the tip of a reed stem as he sings, frequently flying up in the air and dropping back down again. ☉: It frequently sings its song composed of a mix of fluty whistling, grating and chirping notes and rapid harsh trills. The call note is a harsh *tek tek*, the alarm note *trrr*. ♋: Other smaller, streaked members of the genus *Acrocephalus*: mainly the Aquatic Warbler (*A. paludicola*), which has different markings on the head (3), and in southern Europe the Moustached Warbler (*A. melanopogon*), which, however, has a very dark crown and ear-coverts.
Ecology ◆: Thick marshland vegetation, mainly reedbeds and tangled shrubbery. ∞: It is easily recognised by its song (Apr.—July); in the non-breeding season only by chance encounter or by catching the bird. Try and find the nest by making a thorough search of the thick bottom layer of herbaceous vegetation, often nettles, or by observing the behaviour of the birds, mainly when feeding.
Bionomy ↔: It is migratory and is found at the nesting grounds in Apr.—Sept. It is a solitary bird. ⌇: The nest is placed low down in thick vegetation and the lining often contains feathers. The four to six yellowish, brown-patterned eggs (18.0×13.5 mm) are laid in May—July. It has one or two broods a year, nests solitarily, and ♀ incubates for 13 days. The young are cared for by both parents, 15 days in the nest and several more outside the nest. ●: Small arthropods, mainly insects, gathered on plants or caught on the wing.
Conservation It is plentiful in places. Apart from preserving wetland habitats, no other protection is necessary.

2

3

1

Reed Warbler
Acrocephalus scirpaceus

Identification Voice — habitat — appearance — behaviour
∗: Smaller than a sparrow (13 cm), it has a slender head and rounded tail. Adults (1) are dark brown above with a rusty rump, and whitish tinged with buff below; ♂ = ♀ = juv. ✦: It leads a secretive life in reedbeds, moves about on the reed stems, and flies rapidly and with shallow undulations close above the reedbeds with partly spread and slightly drooping tail. When singing, ♂ perches on a stem in the middle of the reedbed, ☉: It often sings; its song, not a particularly loud one, is composed of several repeated phrases *tyrri-tyrri-cherk-cherk-cheehy-cheehy*, etc. The call note is a deeper *tsharr*, the alarm a loud *shkarrr*. ♋: The song is similar to the Great Reed Warbler's (p. 189), but is not nearly so loud, and differs from that of the Moustached Warbler (*A. melanopogon*) in that it does not include rising whistling notes. In appearance it is very similar to the common Marsh Warbler (*A. palustris*), in eastern Europe also to the Blyth's Reed Warbler (*A. dumetorum*) and Paddyfield Warbler (*A. agricola*); these species are best differentiated in the hand by the wing formula (Reed Warbler — 2, Blyth's Reed Warbler — 3, Marsh Warbler — 4, Paddyfield Warbler — 5).
Ecology ◈: Mostly reedbeds, even small ones. ∞: At the nesting grounds it is easily recognised by its voice; in the non-breeding season its presence may be proved by chance observation or by catching the bird. The nest is readily found by walking through the reeds, for nesting birds regularly utter their alarm by the nest.

Bionomy ↔: It is migratory and leads a solitary life. It is found at the nesting grounds in Apr.—Sept. ∽: The nest is woven around several reed stems not very high up. The three to five greenish, brown-patterned eggs (17.9×13.1 mm) are laid in May—Aug. It has one or two broods a year, nests solitarily, or in loose colonies, and incubates for 12 days. The young are tended by both parents, 11 days in the nest and a further 12 days outside the nest. ◖: Predominantly small insects gathered in the bottom layer of reedbeds, on trees, and also caught on the wing.
Conservation It is plentiful in places. No special protective measures are necessary, apart from protection of its habitats.

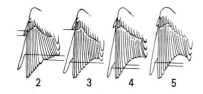

2   3   4   5

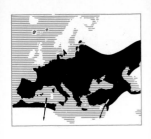

1

Great Reed Warbler
Acrocephalus arundinaceus

Identification — Voice — habitat — appearance — behaviour

∗: Smaller than the Blackbird (19 cm), it has a narrow head, stout bill and strong legs. Adults (1) are olive-brown above, with underparts shading to white, and have a pale stripe over the eye; ♂ = ♀. In juv. birds the upperparts have a rusty tone and the underparts are more buff without any white. ✦: It perches in reedbeds and clambers over the stems, frequently perches also in trees, wanders away from the reedbeds, and flies from one spot to another close above the reeds with partly spread and slightly drooping tail. ♂ generally perches on a reed stem as he sings, but also out in the open on branches. ⊙: It is often heard. The song is very loud to piercing, a strident *karre-karre-kit-kit-kurr-kurr*, etc. The call is a harsh *tuck tuck*, the alarm a churring *krrr.* ♋: It is distinctly larger than all other members of the genus *Acrocephalus*. The song is similar to the Reed Warbler's (p. 188), which may be heard in the same places, but is much louder. The Great Reed Warbler's song may also be confused with the song of some warblers of the genus *Hippolais*, namely the Olive-tree Warbler (*H. olivetorum*) and Booted Warbler (*H. caligata*).

Ecology ◈: Reedbeds with permanent water, mainly old beds; it also visits neighbouring fields. ∞: At the nesting grounds it is readily identified by its voice; the nest may be discovered by walking through the reedbed — adult birds generally utter their alarm by the nest. In the non-breeding season its presence may be determined by chance observation or by catching the bird.

Bionomy ↔: It is migratory and is found at the nesting grounds in Apr.—Sept. It is a solitary bird. ᴡ: The nest is woven around the stems of reeds, reedmace, etc. The three to six blue-greenish eggs with prominent brown markings (22.5×16.1 mm) are laid in May—July. It has one or two broods a year, nests solitarily, and ♀ incubates for 14 days. The young are cared for by both parents, 12 days in the nest and a further 11 days outside the nest. ●: Insects gathered on plants or at the water's surface.

Conservation This is a greatly declining species. However, no realistic means of protection are known as yet.

1

Icterine Warbler
Hippolais icterina

Identification Voice — behaviour — appearance

∗: Smaller than a sparrow (13 cm), it has a slender body and large, broad bill. Adults (1) are olive-green above; the stripe over the eye and entire underside are pale yellow; ♂ = ♀ = juv. ✦: It moves about mostly in tree-tops, where ♂ often delivers his song on outer branches with head raised upward, its feathers greatly ruffled and the gaping beak revealing the orange inside of the throat. It flies rapidly from one tree to another with shallow undulations. ☉: It often sings its loud and pleasant song composed of fluty notes and grating and creaky sounds in short, usually twice-repeated phrases, e.g. *chitudeeh-chitudeeh-dyerr-dyerr*, etc. The call note sounds like *chochoveekh* or *hueed*; the alarm is a distinctive *tek-tek-errr*. ☜: In western Europe the very similar Melodious Warbler (*H. polyglotta*), which, however, has a different wing formula (2) from that of the Icterine Warbler (3).

Ecology ◈: Parkland, mainly gardens, parks, forest edges, dry-land and shoreline vegetation, from lowland to submontane elevations. ∞: At the nesting grounds it is readily identified by its song (May—June); in the non-breeding season catching the bird or encountering it by chance is the only possibility. The nest may be located by a thorough search of the probable nesting site or by observing the behaviour of the birds, mainly when feeding.

Bionomy ↔: It is migratory and is found at the nesting grounds in May—Aug. It is a solitary bird. ❀: The nest, a small, very deep structure woven of grasses, bits of bark, paper, spider webs etc., is located on the branches of a bush or tree at a low height. The four to six pink eggs, lightly patterned with dark spots (18.4×13.5 mm), are laid in May—July. It has one, possibly two, broods a year and incubates for 13 days. The young are cared for by both parents, 13 days in the nest. ◐: Small invertebrates, mainly insects, and towards autumn also fruits of woody plants; food is gathered on branches and on leaves.

Conservation It is relatively plentiful. No special protective measures are necessary.

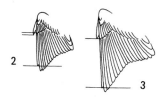

2

3

190

1

Barred Warbler
Sylvia nisoria

Identification Voice — behaviour — coloration ✳: The size of a sparrow (15 cm) and with a larger round head and a short tail. The adult ♂ (1) is grey above, whitish below with dark grey crescentic barring, and has yellow eyes; in ♀ the barring is less distinct. Juv. birds are almost a uniform grey-brown above, the underparts are creamy, without barring, and the eyes are brown. ✦: It clambers through thickets, less often in treetops, and is very shy. It flies only short distances, rapidly and low down, swerving abruptly as it alights. ♂ sings perched in thickets or else rising briefly above the thickets and then dropping down again. ☉: It sings often; the song is loud and composed of relatively long phrases with fluty and scratchy sounds interspersed with the rattling call note *tcherrr*. The alarm is *tek tek*. ♋: The song is very similar to the Garden Warbler's (p. 194), which, however, is mellower and lacks the rattling *tcherr*.
Ecology ◈: Warm hedgerows, clearings, forest edges, often together with the Red-backed Shrike. ∞: At the nesting grounds it is readily pinpointed by its song (May—June) and alarm note; in the non-breeding season by catching the bird or by chance. Look for the nest by searching the thickets in the nesting grounds.
Bionomy ↔: It is migratory, occurs singly, and is found at the nesting grounds in Apr.—Sept. ∾: The nest is placed in dense, often thorny thickets near the ground; it is strikingly thin-walled. The four to five yellowish, grey-patterned eggs (20.9×15.5 mm) are laid in May—June. It has one brood a year, nests solitarily,

and incubates for 14 days. The young are tended by both parents, 14 days in the nest and several more outside the nest. ◑: Insects gathered on twigs and leaves, towards autumn also fruits of woody plants.
Conservation It is a declining species, even though still relatively plentiful in places. Apart from preserving shrubby habitats, no realistic means of protection are known as yet.

1

Lesser Whitethroat
Sylvia curruca

Identification Voice — coloration — size — behaviour

✳: Smaller than a sparrow (13 cm) and very slender. Adults (1) have the top of the head grey and darker ear-coverts contrasting with the white throat; ♂ = ♀. Juv. birds have the top of the head a darker colour, the underparts buffish, and the wing-coverts edged paler ✦: It keeps in dense low thickets where it moves about very actively, occasionally flying rapidly a short distance close above the thickets. It sings while moving about, often on the edge of a bush. ☉: It sings very often; the song starts with very soft and delicate notes, audible only at close quarters, followed by a very loud trill *lilililil*. The call note is an abrupt *tak, tak*, the alarm *terrtek*. Quite similar in appearance is the Whitethroat (p. 193), which, however, does not have darker ear-coverts, has rufous colouring on the wings and has a different voice.

Ecology ◈: Thickets in gardens, woodland clearings, from lowland districts to the dwarf pine belt. ∞: At the nesting grounds it is easily located by its song (Apr.—July); the nest by making a thorough search of the thickets, or (with greater difficulty) by the behaviour of the adult birds. In the non-breeding season it may be recognised by its call note or its presence may be determined by chance observation.

Bionomy ↔: It is migratory and is found at the nesting grounds in Apr.—Sept. It is a solitary bird. ಞ: The nest is a very delicate structure placed low down in thickets or in a thick low tree. The four to five bluish, dark-spotted eggs (17.0×12.8 mm) are laid in Apr.—June. It has one or two broods a year, nests solitarily, and incubates for 12 days. The young are tended by both parents, 13 days in the nest and several more outside the nest. ◑: Mostly insects, their larvae and pupae; in summer and autumn also fruits. It gathers its food and plucks it from slender branches and from the leaves of trees and shrubs.

Conservation It is relatively plentiful. No special protective measures are necessary.

1

Whitethroat
Sylvia communis

Identification Voice — behaviour — appearance

✳: Slightly smaller than a sparrow (14 cm) and with a relatively long tail. Adults (1) are grey-brown above, the tail edged with white, and with pale patches in the wings formed by the rusty margins of the secondaries; the throat and belly are white. ♂ has the crown and ear-coverts grey; in ♀ they are brown. Juv. birds are duller, the throat and edges of the tail tinted buff. ✦: It keeps mostly in thickets and dense herbaceous vegetation, perching on branches in a crouching position with body bent slightly forward. It flies only short distances, rapidly and with shallow undulations. When singing, ♂ generally flies up above the thickets and then drops down again. ☉: It sings very often; the song is short and scratchy and ends with a questioning *herrot.* The call note is *wit wit* or *tak,* the alarm *charr.* ♋: Most like it in appearance is the Lesser Whitethroat (p. 192), which lacks rusty colour on the wings, has darker ear-coverts and has a different song. Another is the Spectacled Warbler (*S. conspicillata*) of southwestern Europe, which, however, has the eyes ringed with white and is smaller.

Ecology ◈: Hedgerows, thickets in fields, in clearings, from lowland districts to the dwarf pine belt. ∞: At the nesting grounds it is easily identified by its song. Try and find the nest by making a thorough search of the thickets at the site of its song. In the non-breeding season it may be located by its call note and by chance observation.

Bionomy ↔: It is migratory and is found at the nesting grounds in Apr.—Sept. ♥: The nest is a thin-walled structure located close to the ground in a dense tangle of herbaceous vegetation or thickets. The four to five greenish-grey eggs with large dark grey spots (18.1×14.0 mm) are laid in Apr.—July. It has one or two broods a year, nests solitarily, and incubates for 12 days. The young are tended by both parents, 11 days in the nest and several more outside the nest. ◑: Mostly insects and their developmental stages; in summer and autumn also fleshy fruits. Food is gathered on twigs and leaves.

Conservation It is quite numerous. No special protective measures are necessary.

1

Garden Warbler
Sylvia borin

Identification Voice — behaviour — appearance

∗: Slightly smaller than a sparrow (14 cm), slender, with a relatively stout bill and rather long tail. Adults (1) are an unobtrusive greyish-brown above, white tinged with brown below, without any conspicuous colour markings; ♂ = ♀. Juv. birds are tinged greenish above, yellowish below. ✦: It moves about secretively in thickets and treetops, and flies only short distances, rapidly, and low down. ♂ sings as he clambers through the undergrowth. ☉: It is heard very often. The song is loud and melodious with lengthy phrases, no marked differences in pitch and no disharmonious sounds. The call note is *chek-chek*, the alarm a deep *char*. ♋: The song is similar to the Barred Warbler's (p. 191) but is less harsh and without the rattling *tcherr*.

Ecology ◈: Thickets, scrub, and young growth in damp coniferous woods, alongside rivers and streams, less often neglected, overgrown cemeteries and parks. ∞: At the nesting grounds it is easily recognised by its song (Apr.—July). To find the nest make a thorough search of the thickets at the site. In the non-breeding season its presence may be discovered by chance observation or when catching birds.

Bionomy ↔: It is migratory, occurs singly, and is found at the nesting grounds in Apr.—Oct. ◡: The nest is a thin-walled structure located low down in dense thickets and herbaceous vegetation. The four to five yellowish, grey-spotted eggs (19.9×14.7 mm) are laid in Apr.—July. It has one or two broods a year, nests solitarily, and incubates for 12 days. The young are cared for by both parents, 11 days in the nest and several more outside the nest. ◖: Mostly insects and their developmental stages; in summer and autumn also fleshy fruits. Food is gathered on twigs and leaves.

Conservation It is quite numerous. No special protective measures are necessary.

194

1

Blackcap
Sylvia atricapilla

Identification Voice — coloration — behaviour
✳: Smaller than a sparrow (14 cm), slender,
with larger head. Adults are greyish-brown
above, pale below, and the tail lacks white
edges. ♂ (1) has a black cap, ♀ a reddish-
brown cap. Juv. birds resemble ♀ but are duller. ✦: It clambers rapidly through thickets and
treetops; it flies from tree to tree with shallow
undulations. ♂ sings in treetops. ☉: It is often
heard. The song is very loud, varied and melodious with lengthy phrases and ending with
characteristic clear fluty notes. The call note is
an emphatic abrupt *tek tek*, the alarm a soft
churr. ♋: It is practically unmistakable. (NB:
The song of some individuals is atypical.) In
southern Europe there is the possibility that it
may be confused with other black-headed warblers of the genus *Sylvia*, namely the Orphean
Warbler (*S. hortensis*), which, however, has
a different song, larger cap and pale eyes, the
Sardinian Warbler (*S. melanocephala*), Rüp-
pell's Warbler (*S. rueppellii*), and Ménétries's
Warbler (*S. mystacea*).
Ecology ◈: Light, open woods with shrubby
undergrowth, parks as well as gardens, from
lowland districts to the dwarf pine belt. ∞: At
the nesting grounds it is easily recognised by its
song (Apr.—July), and by its call even in the
non-breeding season. The nest may generally be
found with ease by searching through the vegetation at the nesting site.
Bionomy ↔: It is mostly migratory, usually occurs singly, and is found at the nesting grounds
in Apr.—Oct. ᴗ: The nest, a thin-walled structure, is placed low down in young trees or

thickets. The four to six yellowish brown-
speckled eggs (19.6×14.7 mm) are laid in
Apr.—June. It has one or two broods a year,
nests solitarily, and incubates for 12 days. The
young are cared for by both parents, 14 days in
the nest and several more outside the nest.
◑: Mostly insects in all developmental stages,
gathered on trees and shrubs; towards autumn
often the fleshy fruits of various woody plants,
especially elder.
Conservation It is a plentiful species. No special
protective measures are necessary.

1

Wood Warbler
Phylloscopus sibilatrix

Identification Voice — appearance — behaviour — coloration

∗: Smaller than a sparrow (12 cm), it has a slender body and a short tail. Adults (1) are olive-green with darker wings and tail, with a sulphur-yellow stripe over the eye, sulphur-yellow throat, and white belly. ♂ = ♀. Juv. birds are slightly duller. ✦: It generally moves about in treetops among the branches at the base of the crown and often flies down to the ground. ♂ sings perching on a branch conspicuously fluttering his partly drooping wings and tail, and continuing his song as he moves from branch to branch. ☉: It is often heard. The song is a sequence of chattering increasingly faster notes *zip-zip-zip-zip-zip-zirrrrr.* The call is a very loud, mellow *deeu* and *zip zip.* ☜: It is larger than other warblers of the genus *Phylloscopus* and differs both in appearance and in its voice. In southern Europe one may hear the slightly similar song of Bonelli's Warbler (*P. bonelli*).

Ecology ◈: Mature forests, mainly broadleaved woods (beechwoods) with sparse undergrowth, from lowland to mountain elevations, less often also parks, old gardens, etc. ∞: At the nesting grounds it is easily recognised by its song (Apr.—July), in the non-breeding season by chance sighting. The nest may be located by watching the behaviour of the birds, mainly when feeding, or by making a thorough search of the site.

Bionomy ↔: It is migratory and is found at the nesting grounds in Apr.—Sept. It is a solitary bird. ꕤ: The nest is generally placed on a slant-ing slope directly on the ground in grass; it is spherical and the lining is devoid of feathers. The five to seven white, brown-spotted eggs (16.0×12.5 mm) are laid in Apr.—June. It has one, occasionally two, broods a year, nests solitarily, and ♀ incubates for 13 days. The young are cared for by both parents, 12 days in the nest and several more outside the nest. ◖: Small invertebrates, gathered on leaves in treetops; in autumn also berries.

Conservation It is plentiful and is expanding its range. No special protective measures are necessary.

1↑

Chiffchaff
Phylloscopus collybita

Identification Voice — appearance — behaviour — coloration
✴: Markedly smaller than a sparrow (11 cm) and very slender. Adults (1) are olive greenish-brown above, the underparts are whitish, the stripe above the eye is yellowish, and the legs are blackish-brown; ♂ = ♀ = juv. ✦: It flits about very actively in treetops, often fluttering its wings at the tip of a branch, and flies rapidly from tree to tree. It sings as it moves about on the branches. ☉: It often sings, even in the non-breeding season. The song is a simple, loud, continually repeated *zilp-zalp-zilp-zalp*. The call note is *hweet* or a louder *tuee*, the alarm *uheet*; in spring it utters a soft *trrt-trrt*. ♋: In appearance mainly the Willow Warbler (*P. trochilus*), widespread throughout Europe; other warblers of the genus *Phylloscopus* are more rare. A reliable means of identification is the wing formula (2 — Greenish Warbler, *P. trochiloides*; 3 — Arctic Warbler, *P. borealis*; 4 — Willow Warbler; 5 — Chiffchaff; 6 — Wood Warbler, p. 196). Its song is unmistakable.

Ecology ◈: Lighter woods, clearings, also old gardens and parks, from lowland elevations to the upper forest limit; in the non-breeding season also scrub, reedbeds, etc. At the nesting grounds as well as in the non-breeding season it is readily identified by its song; the nest may be discovered by making a thorough search of the site or by the behaviour of the birds, particularly when constructing the nest and feeding the young.

Bionomy ↔: It is mostly migratory and is found at the nesting grounds in Mar.—Oct. ◡: The nest is placed in thin vegetation on the ground or close above the ground in a bush; it is spherical and the lining is almost always of feathers. The four to six white eggs, thinly speckled brown (15.2×11.9 mm), are laid in Apr.—July. It has one or two broods a year, nests solitarily, and ♀ incubates for 13 days. The young are tended by both parents, 15 days in the nest and a further 16 days outside the nest. ◑: Small insects and other arthropods gathered mainly on leaves; in summer and autumn also fleshy fruits.

Conservation It is very numerous. No special protective measures are necessary.

1

Goldcrest
Regulus regulus

Identification Voice — size — appearance — behaviour

✳: The smallest European bird (9 cm) and with a large round head and small bill. Adults are olive grey-green above, white below; ♂ has a black stripe each side of the yellow-orange crown, while in ♀ (1) the crown is yellow. In juv. birds the head lacks any colour pattern. ✦: It climbs and flits about very actively in the tops of trees, mainly conifers, often perches fluttering its wings on terminal twigs, and rarely comes down to the ground. Its flight is rapid. In winter it occurs in small flocks together with tits. ☉: It utters its delicate but high, piercing call note *si-si-si see-zi-zi* almost without cease. The song begins with very high-pitched notes, followed by more grating sounds, then rises in pitch and ends with a short descending trill. ♋: In appearance and call the Firecrest (p. 199), which, however, has a prominent white stripe above and a black line through the eye.

Ecology ◈: Mature, mainly coniferous woods, from lowland elevations to the upper forest limit. In the non-breeding season also parks, gardens, etc. ∞: Throughout the year it is easily recognised by its call; at the nesting grounds by its song, delivered the whole summer long and in fine weather even in winter. The nest is hard to find; the best way is to watch the birds when they build the nest and ♀ flies down to the ground for material, or during incubation when ♂ brings food to ♀.

Bionomy ↔: Except for north European populations it is a resident bird, roaming in small flocks also away from the nesting grounds in the non-breeding season. ꖰ: The nest is a thick-walled, almost spherical structure, woven around drooping branches (mainly on coniferous trees), generally high up; it is lined with feathers. The six to ten yellowish eggs with grey-brown markings (13.5×10.4 mm) are laid in Apr.—June. It has one or two broods a year, nests solitarily, and ♀ incubates for 15 days. The young are cared for by both parents, 17 days in the nest and eight days more outside the nest. ◑: Insects and spiders, gathered on branches.

Conservation: It is numerous, and no special protective measures are necessary.

1

Firecrest
Regulus ignicapillus

Identification Voice — size — appearance — behaviour

✳: Along with the Goldcrest, this is the smallest European bird (9 cm). Adults are greenish, with striking head markings: a black line through the eye, a white stripe over the eye, above that a black stripe, and the crown a brilliant orange in ♂ (1) and yellow in ♀. Juv. birds lack the black stripe above the eye and the crown is greenish like the back. ✦: It climbs and flits about very actively in the treetops, often perching and fluttering its wings at the tip of a branch. Its flight is rapid, undulating, and it usually flies only short distances. ☉: It utters its delicate but high, piercing call note *see-see-si see-zi-zi* almost incessantly. The song is a simple sequence of descending notes *see see si si sisisi*, increasing in speed towards the end. ♋: The Goldcrest (p. 198) is very similar but has a different head pattern; its call is identical, but its song is quite different, more complex.

Ecology ◆: Mature mixed forests from lowland elevations to the upper forest limit, as well as parkland vegetation; in the non-breeding season also bushes and scrub. ∞: It is easily recognised by its song (Mar.—July); when you hear the call you must check on the bird by observation. The nest is very hard to find; look for it in the same manner as for the Goldcrest's nest.

Bionomy ↔: It is generally migratory and is found at the nesting grounds in Mar.—Oct. ᵜ: The nest is a sturdy deep structure generally woven high around drooping branches of trees; the cup is usually covered by several feathers inserted into the edge. The seven to eleven yellowish eggs with reddish-brown markings (13.5×10.3 mm) are laid in Apr.—July. It has one or two broods a year, nests solitarily, and ♀ incubates for 15 days. The young are tended by both parents for 20 days in the nest. ◗: Small arthropods gathered on the branches of trees.

Conservation It is quite numerous. No special protective measures are necessary.

1

Spotted Flycatcher
Muscicapa striata

Identification Behaviour — voice — appearance
✳: Slightly smaller than a sparrow (14 cm).
The head is large, the wings broad and
rounded, and the tail relatively long. Adults (1)
are pale brown with dark markings; ♂ = ♀.
Juv. birds have scale-like markings on the upperparts. ✦: It perches upright in the open on
a high vantage point, such as a bare tree
branch, fence post, railing, telephone wire,
flicking its wings and tail as it utters its call. It
darts out suddenly to catch an insect, which it
seizes in expert hovering flight, returning in
a glide to its original perch or some other spot.
☉: It often utters its call, a sharp *tzee* or *sreet*;
the alarm is *tzee tek*. It does not sing very often;
the song is nondescript, a short, quiet *sip-sip-
sih-sitti-sih-sih.* ☺: The Brown Flycatcher
(*M. latirostris*) of Asia is very similar but is
very rare in Europe.
Ecology ◈: Light, open woods, parks and gardens, from lowland elevations to the upper forest limit. ∞: At the nesting grounds it is easily
recognised by its voice, mainly its call; otherwise it may be seen perched on an elevated spot
or in pursuit of prey. The nest may be discovered by watching adult birds, sometimes by
exploring suitable sites.
Bionomy ↔: It is migratory and is found at the
nesting grounds in Apr.—Sept. It occurs singly.
ʊ: The nest is placed on a firm foundation not
very high up in a tree or on a building, generally in a semi-cavity or slightly covered from
above. The four to five greyish, brown-patterned eggs (18.7×14.1 mm) are laid in May—
July. It has one or two broods a year, nests soli-

tarily, and ♀ incubates for 14 days. The young
are cared for by both parents, 14 days in the
nest and several more outside the nest.
◉: Mostly flying insects caught on the wing, in
cold weather gathered also from the ground.
Conservation This is a declining species, even
though quite numerous. No realistic means of
protection are known as yet.

1

Red-breasted Flycatcher
Ficedula parva

Identification Voice — behaviour — appearance — coloration
✻: Smaller than other flycatchers (11 cm), it has a large head, short tail and short wings. Adults are greyish-brown above, greyish-white below, and the tail has white edges at the base (2). ♂ (1) has a red throat; ♀ and young ♂ ♂ have a buff throat. Juv. birds resemble ♀ but have darker markings on the upperparts and throat. ✦: It keeps mostly in the lower parts of treetops, darting out expertly from the branches in pursuit of insects; in cold weather it also flies down to the ground. ☉: It is often heard. The song is very loud and monotonous, beginning with a repeated introductory motif and ending with a descending *zee-zr-zee-zr-zee-zrzrzr*. The call note is a fluty *ziluyee* or explosive *tik*, the alarm a wren-like *crrr*. ☜: It is unmistakable; the similarly coloured European Robin (p. 169) does not have the white at the base of the tail and its behaviour is entirely different.

Ecology ◈: Mature forest stands with sparse undergrowth, mainly beechwoods, from hilly country to the upper forest limit. In the non-breeding season also scrub, parks and gardens. ∞: At the nesting grounds it is easily identified by its song but locating it by observation is difficult. The nest may be discovered by watching birds building shortly after their arrival or hunting food for their offspring, usually within 100 m of the nest. In the non-breeding season it is less shy and may be observed more readily.

Bionomy ↔: It is migratory and is found at the nesting grounds in May—Sept. ❧: The nest is usually quite high up in a semi-cavity in a tree;

moss and spiderwebs are used in its construction. The four to six yellowish eggs, heavily patterned reddish-brown (16.6×12.7 mm), are laid in May—June. It has one brood a year, nests solitarily, and ♀ incubates for 15 days. The young are cared for by both parents, 14 days in the nest and about 14 days outside the nest. ◖: Mainly insects, gathered on branches and trunks of trees, less often in flight and on the ground.

Conservation It has a patchy distribution and is not very numerous. The nesting grounds are endangered by the felling of old stands, which should be preserved.

2

1

Collared Flycatcher
Ficedula albicollis

Identification Voice — appearance — coloration — behaviour

✻: Slightly smaller than a sparrow (13 cm). The adult ♂ (1) is black above, white below, has a white forehead, a large white patch on the wing (3) and a white collar around the neck; ♀ is greyish-brown instead of black. Juv. birds resemble ♀, but have slight markings on the upperside and the white wing patch is less conspicuous. ✦: Apart from the nesting season it leads a very secretive life in the lower parts of treetops, where it perches on branches and darts out in pursuit of insects; it also alights on tree trunks. It flies between trees very rapidly. ☉: The song is loud and brief, with rising and falling fluty notes. The call is a loud *seeb-seeb*, and when uttering it the bird partly spreads its wings and its tail; at the nest ♀ gives a warning *sib-sib-sib*. ♋: In a large part of Europe it is replaced by the similar Pied Flycatcher (*F. hypoleuca*), which has a black hindneck (2) and smaller white wing patch (4); in the southeastern parts of the Balkan Peninsula by the Semicollared Flycatcher (*F. semitorquata*), in which the white collar is broken.

Ecology ◀▶: Broad-leaved or mixed light woods, parks and gardens, from lowland to mountain elevations. ∞: During the nesting season it is readily located by its voice, as well as by observation; in the non-breeding period only by chance. When looking for the nest, examine suitable cavities or watch the behaviour of the birds, especially when feeding.

Bionomy ↔: It is migratory and is found at the nesting grounds in Apr.—Sept. ⚭: The nest is in a tree hole and never has any feathers in the lining. The four to seven pale blue eggs (18.1×13.3 mm) are laid in Apr.—June. It has one brood a year, nests solitarily, and ♀ incubates for 14 days. The young are cared for by both parents and remain in the nest 17 days. ◖: Small insects captured in flight or gathered from the ground and in trees.

Conservation It is numerous. No special protective measures are necessary. Nesting may be encouraged by putting out nestboxes in woodlands.

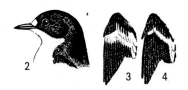

2

3

4

1

Bearded Tit
Panurus biarmicus

Identification Habitat — voice — appearance — behaviour

✳: As large as a sparrow (16 cm), it has a slender body, round head and striking, very long, graduated tail. The adult ♂ (1) has a pale grey head with black moustachial stripe and yellow eyes and bill; ♀ (2) has a brown head and no moustachial stripe. Juv. birds resemble ♀ but have a black area in the centre of the back: ♂ has a black stripe between the base of the bill and eye, and a yellow bill; ♀ lacks the black stripe at the base of the bill and has a darker bill. ✦: It moves about in reedbeds, climbing foot over foot up reed stems, often between two stems with legs spread wide apart. It flies from one spot to another in jerky, weak flight close above the vegetation, its long, slightly drooping tail clearly visible to the observer. ☉: It is heard very frequently, including when flying from one spot to another; its call note is a twanging *ping-ping* or *dzhing-dzhing*, its alarm *chirr*. ☺: It is unmistakable.

Ecology ◈: Reedbeds the whole year round, only very occasionally other habitats. ∞: It is easily recognised by its voice throughout the year. When looking for the nest either make a thorough search of the site (when the nest is approached, the birds often then stay close by and utter alarm calls) or watch the birds building their nest and feeding the young; however, they often fly quite far from the nest in search of food.

Bionomy ↔: Depending on the area, populations may be resident, dispersive, or migratory. The birds occur in rather large groups outside the nesting season. ဃ: The nest is placed in the thick bottom layer of reeds concealed in a clump of vegetation; it is small, made of reed blades and lined with reed panicles. The five to six white eggs with delicate reddish-brown markings (18.0×14.1 mm) are laid in Mar.—July. It has one to four broods a year, nests solitarily, and incubates for 12 days. The young are tended by both parents, occasionally even by other birds, 12 days in the nest and several more outside the nest. ◖: In summer mostly insects, in winter the seeds of reeds, all gathered on reeds.

Conservation It is locally plentiful but its numbers exhibit marked fluctuations. Apart from preserving old reedbeds, no special protective measures are necessary.

2 ♀

1

Long-tailed Tit
Aegithalos caudatus

Identification Voice — appearance — behaviour

✴: Smaller than a sparrow (14 cm). The head is round with a short bill, and the tail markedly long. Adults are white, brown, black and pink: north European populations of the *A. c. caudatus* group have a white head (3), central and west European populations of the *A. c. europaeus* group have a conspicuous black stripe above the eye (2), and south European birds of the *A. c. alpinus* group have a black stripe on the head and the back coloured grey (not black); birds in zones of overlap are of mixed coloration (1). ♂ = ♀. Juv. birds always have the sides of the head blackish-brown and are duller, with little pink colouring. ✦: It stays almost solely in trees and thickets, where it climbs and hangs skilfully on the branches in all positions. In flight, which is weak and undulating, a conspicuous feature is the long tail. ☉: It often calls loudly, *tsirrr-tsirrr* and *see-see-see*. ♋: It is unmistakable.

Ecology ◆: Younger, open woods, parkland including gardens, from lowland to mountain elevations. ∞: It may be readily heard and observed the whole year round. The nest is best discovered when it is being built (Feb.—Apr.) and when the young are being fed by watching the adult birds, or else by exploring suitable sites at places where it is continually present.

Bionomy ↔: It is resident. In the non-breeding season it roams in small flocks in the neighbourhood of the nest. ♡: The nest is a closed spherical structure with entrance just below the top; moss and lichens are used in its construction and there are always many feathers in the lining. The six to twelve yellowish, red-speckled eggs (14.2×11.1 mm) are laid in Mar.—June. It has one or two broods a year, nests solitarily, and incubates for 12 days. The young are cared for by both parents, occasionally also by other birds, 15 days in the nest and a longer while outside the nest. ◆: Mainly the larvae and eggs of insects and spiders gathered on branches, very occasionally also on the ground.

Conservation It is quite numerous. No special protective measures are necessary.

2   3

204

1

Willow Tit
Parus montanus

Identification Voice — appearance — behaviour

✳: Smaller than a sparrow (11 cm), it has a large head and rather short graduated tail (2). Adults (1) have brown upperparts, greyish-white underparts, a dull black cap on the head, a black patch on the chin, and the secondaries are edged paler, thus forming a pale patch on the wings; ♂ = ♀ = juv. ✦: It is quite shy and very active as it clambers amidst the thick branches of trees and shrubs. It flies only short distances, rapidly and expertly. The tits with which it is generally seen together include the Coal Tit (p. 207). Crested Tit (p. 206), and occasionally also the Marsh Tit. ☉: It often utters its deep harsh call *chay-chay* and high, thin *see-see*. The song varies locally, typical being *ti-tee-tee-ti* or *tsi-tsee-tsee-tsee* on the same pitch or slightly rising, or *pew-pew-pew*. ♋: Very similar is the Marsh Tit (*T. palustris*) with glossy black cap, but it does not have a pale wing patch and its tail is less graduated (3); in northern Europe the less similar Siberian Tit (*P. cinctus*), and in southeastern Europe the Sombre Tit (*P. lugubris*).

Ecology ◈: Various kinds of wooded areas from lowland to mountain elevations, mainly in damp places. ∞: It is quite easily identified the whole year round by its call note, and in spring at the nesting grounds (Feb.—May) by its song. The nest may be located by the behaviour of the birds when excavating a hole or when feeding the young, also by checking out suitable cavities at the given site.

Bionomy ↔: It is resident. In the non-breeding season it roams in groups around the nesting grounds. ♥: The nest is in a tree hole, always excavated anew (unlike other tits), mainly in rotting tree stumps. The six to ten eggs, sparsely patterned reddish-brown (16.1×12.3 mm), are laid in Apr.—June. It has one, occasionally two, broods a year, nests solitarily, and ♀ incubates for 15 days. The young are cared for by both parents and remain in the nest 18 days. ◕: Small arthropods as well as seeds, gathered in trees and on herbaceous plants.

Conservation It is quite numerous in places. No special protective measures are necessary.

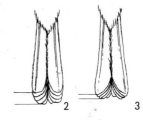

2   3

1

Crested Tit
Parus cristatus

Identification Voice — appearance — behaviour

∗ : Smaller than a sparrow (11 cm), it has short wings and tail and a pointed crest on the head. Adults (1) are brown above, whitish below, and have black and white markings on the head; ♀ has a slightly shorter crest. Juv. birds have an extremely short crest and the white colouring is tinted brown. ✦: It generally moves about on the branches in treetops, in winter often on the ground. It flies only briefly and rapidly; it is often very shy. When the young have fledged it joins other tits, treecreepers, Nuthatches and Goldcrests. ☉: It often utters its characteristic purring call *tzirrhyt* or *kurrrr*. The song is a soft, rarely heard twittering. ❦: It is unmistakable.

Ecology ◈: Mature coniferous forests, mainly spruce and pine woods, from lowland elevations to the upper forest limit; in the non-breeding season also broad-leaved stands, gardens, etc. ∞: It is easily identified by its call note the whole year round. The location of the nest is generally discovered by watching the behaviour of the birds, particularly when feeding the young, or by checking out suitable cavities at the site.

Bionomy ↔: It is resident. In the non-breeding season it roams in the vicinity of the nesting grounds, at most in small groups. ᴥ: The nest is usually not very high up in a tree hole, mainly an old cavity. The five to seven white eggs with reddish-brown markings (16.4×12.8 mm) are laid in Mar.—June. It has one or two broods a year, nests solitarily, and ♀ incubates

for 16 days. The young are tended by both parents and stay in the nest 20 days. ◕: Small insects in all their developmental stages and seeds, gathered on trees, in winter often on the ground.

Conservation It is quite plentiful. No special protective measures are necessary.

206

1

Coal Tit
Parus ater

Identification Voice — behaviour — appearance — coloration

✳: The size of the Blue Tit (11 cm), it has a large round head and short tail. The head of adults (1) is black with white cheeks and a white patch on the nape, the upperparts are olive-grey, and the underside is white tinged with buff; ♂ = ♀. Juv. birds are duller, the black areas are dark brown, the white areas tinted yellowish. ✦: It moves very briskly and expertly in all positions in treetops. It flies only short distances, very rapidly and in undulating flight. In the non-breeding season it forms small flocks together with other tits. ☉: Its soft call note *si-si* or *duee* may be heard almost continually. It often sings its loud monotonous song, *wee-tse-wee-tse-wee-tse.* ♋: The soft call note is very similar to and sometimes indistinguishable from that of birds of the genus *Regulus,* which it joins in winter. Its appearance and song are unmistakable.

Ecology ◈: Mainly older coniferous woods, from lowland elevations to the upper forest limit. In the non-breeding season also parks, gardens, mountain scrub. ∞: It is readily found by its voice (Jan.—June); it is not shy. The nest may be located by watching the behaviour of the adult birds.

Bionomy ↔: It is resident, dispersive, and only partly migratory, occasionally making invasional flights from northern Europe southward. In the non-breeding season it occurs in small flocks. ☡: The nest is in tree holes, ground holes, between stones, in stacks of wood, etc. The six to ten white eggs with reddish-brown markings (14.9×11.6 mm) are laid in Apr.—July. It has one or two broods a year, nests solitarily, and ♀ incubates for 15 days. The young are cared for by both parents and stay in the nest 19 days. ◑: Small insects and spiders, also seeds of trees and plants, gathered on trees and on the ground.

Conservation It is plentiful. No special protective measures are necessary; it will readily use man-made nestboxes.

1

Blue Tit
Parus caeruleus

Identification Voice — appearance — coloration — behaviour

✳: Conspicuously smaller than a sparrow (11 cm) and with a small head and short tail. Adults (1) have the crown pale blue edged with white and a narrow black stripe through the eye, otherwise the upperparts are brownish-green; the underside is pale yellow; ♀ is duller. Juv. birds are much duller and have the crown olive-grey and the sides of the head pale yellow.
✦: It is not shy and is very active, clambering over branches and hanging from them acrobatically in all positions. It flies only short distances, in undulating flight and not very rapidly. In the non-breeding season it forms small flocks with other tits. ☉: It often utters its delicate call *tsee-tsit,* also *tsit-tsit-heh-eh-heh;* the alarm is a churring *tserrretet.* The song sounds like *seeseesirr* and is delivered by ♂ even in flight. ♋: The call note resembles that of the Great Tit (p. 209). In eastern Europe the larger Azure Tit (*P. cyanus*) is rather similar in appearance.
Ecology ◆: Open, mainly broad-leaved woods from lowland to mountain forest elevations, parks, and gardens. ∞: It is readily identified the whole year round by its voice and by direct observation, in winter on bird-feeders. The nest may be located by watching the behaviour of the birds; it is often placed in a nestbox.
Bionomy ↔: It is mostly resident; northern populations sometimes make invasional movements to the southwest. In the non-breeding season it occurs in small flocks. ♡: The nest is in tree holes, woodpiles, wall crevices, often in

a nestbox, and is made of moss, hairs and feathers. The seven to twelve white eggs with reddish-brown markings (15.5×11.9 mm) are laid in Apr.—July. It has one or two broods a year, nests solitarily, and ♀ incubates for 14 days. The young are tended by both parents and stay in the nest 20 days. ◖: Small insects and spiders, fruits and seeds of flowers and trees, gathered on tree branches and on the ground.
Conservation It is plentiful and no special protective measures are necessary. It will nest in man-made nestboxes.

1

Great Tit
Parus major

Identification Voice — appearance — behaviour

✱: As large as a sparrow (14 cm) but slender, with a large round head. Adults (1) are greygreen above, yellow on the underside, the head is black with white cheeks, and there is a black longitudinal stripe down the breast; the head of ♀ is a duller black and the breast stripe is narrower and less prominent. In juv. birds the black is replaced by blackish-brown, the yellow is tinted green, and the breast band is inconspicuous. ✦: It is not shy. It hops about very restlessly on branches, often on the ground, and visits bird-feeders. Its flight is undulating, quite rapid and expert. In the non-breeding season it joins other tits to form small flocks. ☉: It sounds its penetrating call almost continually — *tvee-tuut* — also *pink-pink* (beware: the Chaffinch's is similar). The alarm note is *tcecerret*. The song is a loud *teeta, teeta, teeta* and a ringing *tsitsi-tu tsitsi-tu . . .* It often utters a variety of unusual sounds. ☜: Its voice sometimes resembles the Chaffinch's (p. 232) or the Blue Tit's (p. 208), but it may usually be identified after listening a while. In appearance it is unmistakable.

Ecology ◈: All types of woodlands, mainly sunny broad-leaved ones, from lowland to mountain elevations, also gardens and parks. ∞: It is easily heard as well as observed the whole year round. Locate the nest by observing the behaviour of the birds, especially when feeding, or check out suitable nesting sites, especially nestboxes.

Bionomy ↔: It is resident, and in most of Europe also partly migratory. During the nonbreeding season it occurs in groups. ☽: The nest is usually not very high up in tree holes, on buildings, in pipes of various kinds (even vertical and uncovered pipes), often in nestboxes; moss is used in its construction and there is animal hairs in the lining. The five to thirteen white, thinly spotted reddish-brown eggs (17.6×13.4 mm) are laid in Apr.—July. It has one or two broods a year, nests solitarily, and ♀ incubates for 14 days. The young are cared for by both parents, 19 days in the nest and a further 12 days outside the nest. ◖: Small insects, spiders and molluscs, various seeds and fruits; it gathers its food in trees as well as on the ground.

Conservation It is numerous and no special protective measures are necessary. It will nest readily in man-made nestboxes and visits birdfeeders in winter.

1

Nuthatch
Sitta europaea

Identification Voice — behaviour — appearance

✳: Slightly smaller than a sparrow (13 cm), it has a large head tapering into a long straight bill and short legs. Adults are blue-grey above with a black stripe across the eye; the belly in subspecies of the *S. e. europaea* group of northern Europe is white, while in subspecies of the *S. e. caesia* group from the other parts of Europe it is reddish-brown; ♂ has dark reddish-brown flanks, and in ♀ they are pale rusty-brown (1). Juv. birds have a brown tinge to the upperparts and brown lores. ✦: It climbs on tree trunks and branches in all directions, and occasionally hops about on the ground with partly raised head. It flies rapidly and expertly in shallow undulations. ☉: Often heard throughout the year is its loud whistling call note *tseet tseet,* a broad *chwet chwet* or a tit-like *sisi.* The song is composed of melodious whistles *teeh deeh,* a trilling *krikrikri,* in spring often *dew dew.* It is frequently heard tapping loudly on trees, and the sounds of its climbing on dry bark are sometimes audible. ♋: In southern Europe the similar Rock Nuthatch (*S. neumayer*) and in the woods of Corsica the Corsican Nuthatch (*S. whiteheadi*).

Ecology ◈: Broad-leaved and mixed woods, parks and gardens, from lowland to mountain elevations; in the non-breeding season also at bird-feeders in built-up areas. ∞: Throughout the year it may be readily heard and observed directly. Locate the nest by observing the behaviour of the birds, especially when preparing the nesting hollow and feeding.

Bionomy ↔: It is resident, in northeastern Europe also dispersive to invasional. In the non-breeding season it occurs singly or in pairs. It also joins flocks of tits. ʊ: The nest is located in tree holes, and often in nestboxes; the bird reduces the size of the entrance hole with mud, and bits of bark are used for the lining. The five to nine white eggs with reddish-brown markings (19.6×14.7 mm) are laid in Mar.—June. It has one, sometimes probably two broods a year, nests solitarily, and ♀ incubates for 16 days. The young are tended by both parents, 24 days in the nest and eight more days outside the nest. ◖: All insects of a size it can handle; from autumn onward the seeds and fruits of plants. It gathers its food on trees from cracks in the bark, as well as on the ground, and also visits bird-feeders.

Conservation It is plentiful. No special protective measures are necessary. It will nest in man-made nestboxes.

1

Wallcreeper
Tichodroma muraria

Identification Habitat — coloration — appearance — behaviour

∗: Larger than a sparrow (16 cm), it has a slender body, markedly long, slightly curved, awl-shaped bill, short tail and broad, rounded wings. Adults (1) are grey and blackish, and there is a conspicuous red patch and white markings on the wings; in breeding plumage ♂ has a black chin and throat, while in the ♀ the chin and throat are greyish-black. In the non-breeding plumage the chin and throat of both are white. Juv. birds have a brownish forehead and feathers on the upperside edged paler. ✦: It climbs rock faces from the bottom, working its way upward, then flies to another spot and climbs again; its movements are jerky, and it flicks and partly opens its wings. Its flight is fluttering, like a butterfly's. ☉: It is seldom heard. The call note is a thin, piping *zi-zi-zi-zui* or *diu,* the song a melodious, drawn-out, rising and descending fluty whistling. ♋: It is unmistakable.

Ecology ◈: Rock faces in mountains, mainly at alpine elevations. ∞: It is very difficult to determine its presence, usually by chance sighting of birds flying from one spot to another by the rock face. The nest may be located by the behaviour of the birds but is usually inaccessible, difficult to reach.

Bionomy ↔: It is a resident and solitary bird. In winter some birds descend to lower elevations and may then wander greater distances. At this time they may be seen on rocks, on the walls of old buildings, in quarries, etc. ᴡ: The nest is in a rock crevice. The three to five white eggs with reddish-brown markings (21.3×14.3 mm) are laid in May—June. It has one brood a year, nests solitarily, and ♀ incubates for 19 days. The young are cared for by both parents and stay in the nest for 29 days. ◖: Small arthropods gathered on rock faces and in rock crevices.

Conservation It is an important scarce and local bird. Even in places where it is a permanent inhabitant its numbers are few. It is essential to protect individual birds and above all their habitats and nests.

1

Treecreeper
Certhia familiaris

Identification Voice — appearance — behaviour — coloration

∗: Smaller than a sparrow (12 cm), it has a slender body, long, slightly curved bill and longer pointed tail (2). The bastard wing has a characteristic colour pattern (3). Adults (1) are streaked brown above, white on the underside, and have a darker band across the eye; ♂ = ♀. Juv. birds are sparsely streaked brown on the underparts. ✦: It climbs trees upwards and around the trunk in an irregular spiral, using its tail as a prop, and then flies to the base of another tree. In the non-breeding season it joins flocks of tits and Nuthatches. ☉: Its delicate, high call note *sirr, sisisirrr* or a softer *sri* may be heard the whole year long. The song is simple, composed of fluty notes, *sirr-suitirr-uit.* ♋: Short-toed Treecreeper (*C. brachydactyla*), a sibling species differing only slightly in the length of the bill, the claw on the hind toe, coloration (4), and colour pattern on the bastard wing (5).

Ecology ◑ *:* Woods, both coniferous and broadleaved; in the non-breeding season more often also gardens, parks, etc. ∞: It is readily identified throughout the year by its call; in Jan.—June by its song and direct observation. The nest may be located by the behaviour of the birds or by searching suitable sites.

Bionomy ↔: It is resident, at the most wandering in the immediate vicinity of the nesting grounds. ♲: The nest is not very high up in trees, in a cranny, under a piece of loose bark, in a semi-cavity, on the walls of buildings, often with a thick base layer of material; it will also use nestboxes. The four to seven whitish eggs with reddish-brown markings (15.7×12.1 mm) are laid in Apr.—June. It has one or two broods a year, nests solitarily, and ♀ incubates for 14 days. The young are cared for by both parents, 15 days in the nest and several more outside the nest. ◑: Small insects and spiders gathered in cracks in the bark of trees.

Conservation It is quite plentiful. No special protective measures are necessary. Nesting may be promoted by putting out nestboxes.

2 | 3 4 | 5

212

1

Penduline Tit
Remiz pendulinus

Identification Habitat — voice — nest — appearance
✱: Smaller than a sparrow (11 cm), it has a round head and very short bill. In breeding plumage (1) the head is grey with a conspicuous black band across the eye, and the body largely cinnamon-brown; ♀ has the back and breast a lighter brown. In the non-breeding plumage the black eye-mask is obscured by the grey-brown edges of the feathers, and the crown is greyish-brown; ♂ = ♀. Juv. birds (3) are paler and duller, with the crown greyish-white with rusty markings, and lack the black mask. ✦: It climbs the small thin branches of trees or the stems and panicles of reeds and reedmace. Its flight is brisk, undulating. ⊙: Often and all year round one may hear its delicate but penetrating, long, high-pitched call note *tseeih,* also a shorter *tsee* or soft *tsi-tsi-tsi.* The song, heard only infrequently, is a short sequence of rapid high-pitched fluty and grating notes, descending towards the end and terminated by a higher-pitched whistle. ♋: It is unmistakable. The call of the Reed Bunting (p. 248) is somewhat similar but lower-pitched.
Ecology ◆: Floodplain forests and shoreline vegetation in lowland and hilly country; in the non-breeding season mainly reedbeds. ∞: It is easily recognised throughout the year by its call note. The nest is likewise readily found by searching shoreline trees, mainly willows and poplars; the discovery of an incomplete nest need not be proof of nesting.
Bionomy ↔: It is partly migratory and is found at the nesting grounds in Mar.—Oct. In the non-breeding season it forms small flocks. ♉: The nest (2) is unique in shape: it is a pouch-shaped structure of plant wool suspended from the thin outer branches of a tree. ♂ generally builds several nests; the one in which the eggs are laid has a tubular entrance. The five to eight white eggs (16.2×10.5 mm) are laid in Apr.—June. It has one or two broods a year, nests solitarily, is polygamous, and ♀ incubates for 14 days and cares for the young alone for 19 days. ◕: Small invertebrates, in winter also seeds; all food is gathered on reeds and on the leaves of trees.
Conservation It is quite plentiful in places. No special protective measures are necessary.

2

3

Golden Oriole
Oriolus oriolus

Identification Voice — size — coloration
✻: The size of the Blackbird (24 cm), it has a slender body, rather short tail and broad wings. The adult ♂ (1) is a brilliant yellow, with blackish-brown wings and tail; ♀ has yellowish-green upperparts and the underparts whitish with dark streaks, except on the belly. Juv. birds have grey-green upperparts and the underparts white with dark longitudinal streaks (including the belly). ✦: It keeps mostly in tree-tops and flies rapidly with long shallow undulations. ☉: It is heard often. The song, a fluty *odeedli-weeo,* is striking and audible from a distance. The call and alarm note is a harsh croaking *ksherr;* at close range other sounds may also be heard. The young call *dyudit.* ♋: It is unmistakable.

Ecology ◈: Broad-leaved, sometimes mixed woods of various kinds, from lowland to hilly country; often also groves. ∞: It is readily identified by its voice throughout the entire nesting period. It is quite hard to find the nest, even though it is by no means concealed; it is best discovered from the behaviour of the birds.

Bionomy ↔: It is migratory and is found at the nesting grounds in Apr.—Sept. In the non-breeding season it leads a solitary life. ω: The nest is suspended between the forks of terminal branches usually in the top of a young tree, its upper edge firmly woven around boughs on either side. Bark fibre, strips of paper, etc. are used in its construction. The three to five white, sparsely brown-speckled eggs (30.5×21.3 mm) are laid in May—July. It has one brood a year, nests solitarily, and adults incubate for 16 days. The young are cared for by both parents, 14 days in the nest and several more outside the nest. ◕: Smaller invertebrates, mainly insects, spiders and molluscs, and fleshy fruits such as cherries and mulberries. It gathers its food in trees.

Conservation It is quite plentiful. No special protective measures are necessary.

1

Red-backed Shrike
Lanius collurio

Identification Voice — appearance — behaviour

✳: Larger than a sparrow (17 cm) and with a large head, black eye-mask, and stout, hooked bill. The adult ♂ (1) has a grey cap and rump, the remaining upperparts being chestnut-brown; the tail is white on either side at the base, and the underparts are pinkish-white. The outer tail feathers are bordered white at the tip (2) or lack white tips altogether. ♀ is entirely brown above, and the underparts are brownish-white with dark crescentic barring. Juv. birds resemble ♀, but with heavier barring both above and below. ✦: It perches on the tops or outer branches of shrubs, on tall posts, and on wires, from where it flies down to the ground in pursuit of prey, braking its landing with spread wings and tail. It also hovers briefly in one spot. Its flight is buoyant, skilful, and shallowly undulating. ☉: It often utters its sharp call *tsek-tsek* throughout the year. The song is rarely heard; it consists of soft chattering and grating sounds and often includes notes imitated from other birds. ♋: It is unmistakable. Juv. Red-backed Shrikes resemble those of the Woodchat Shrike (p. 217), but the latter are paler and show signs of a white wing bar and more black on the tail feathers (3).

Ecology ◈: Rather dry grassy areas with scattered bushes — pastureland, forest edges, clearings, hedgerows, from lowland to foothill districts. ∞: It is readily found throughout the nesting period by the call and by observing the birds. The nest is easily located by examining suitable shrubs at the site of the birds' occurrence.

Bionomy ↔: It is migratory and is found at the nesting grounds in Apr.—Sept. It leads a solitary life. ∾: The nest is a sturdy structure in thickets, mainly ones with thorny shrubs. The three to six pinkish, dark-spotted eggs (21.9×16.5 mm) are laid in May—July. It has one brood a year, nests solitarily, and ♀ incubates for 15 days. The young are cared for by both parents, 14 days in the nest and a further 25 days outside the nest. ◖: Insects, mainly beetles and hymenopterans, spiders and small vertebrates caught on the ground or on herbaceous plants. It impales its food on the spikes of thorny shrubs.

Conservation It is a greatly declining species. No realistic means of protection are known as yet.

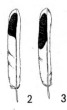

2   3

1

Great Grey Shrike
Lanius excubitor

Identification Appearance — size — behaviour — coloration

✳: The largest European shrike, as large as the Blackbird (24 cm). It has a large flat head with a stout hooked bill and a long tail. Adults (1) have a black eye-band and black wings and tail, a white wing bar, white edges to the tail, and white to creamy underparts; some ♀♀ are faintly patterned with brown scale-like markings on the breast. Juv. birds have dark scale-like markings on the entire underparts. ✦: It perches on the tops of trees, shrubs and poles, as well as on wires, often swinging its tail up and down or sideways; it flies to the ground for its food, and also hops about on the ground. Its flight is quite rapid and deeply undulating. Frequently it hovers in one spot with spread tail. ☉: It is heard only rarely. The call is a *shek shek,* the alarm note *aa-ech.* The song is a mix of chirping, whistling and twittering notes and is quite soft; ♂ generally sings from an elevated spot. ♋: In southern Europe the very similar Lesser Grey Shrike (*L. minor*) with a black forehead (2).

Ecology ◆: Open, damp, grassy country with scattered shrubs, trees or small woods, from lowland to submontane elevations; in winter also farm country. ∞: It is readily sighted throughout the year if you look for it in elevated spots, mainly on electricity wires; look for the nest in trees and shrubs at the site of the birds' occurrence.

Bionomy ↔: It is partly migratory and is found at the nesting grounds in Apr.—Oct. It leads a solitary life. ☙: The nest is a large structure

in the fork of a branch quite high up in a tree or shrub. The four to eight whitish, brown-spotted eggs (26.9×19.8 mm) are laid in Apr.—May. It has one brood a year, nests solitarily, and ♀ incubates for 15 days. The young are tended by both parents, 19 days in the nest and a longer while outside the nest. ◖: Smaller vertebrates and invertebrates captured on the ground, less often in treetops. It impales its prey on thorns or lodges it in the fork of a branch.

Conservation It is increasing in number in places. It is necessary to protect the nesting grounds.

2

216

1.

Woodchat Shrike
Lanius senator

Identification Appearance — coloration — behaviour

✳: Larger than a sparrow (17 cm) and with a large flat head and stout hooked bill. The adult ♂ is black and white with crown and nape reddish-brown, and has a large white patch on the wings and a white-edged tail (1); ♀ is duller. Juv. birds are pale brown with dark scale-like markings on the whole body. ✦: It is a very shy, solitary bird. It perches mainly in the tops of smaller trees, from where it flies down to the ground in pursuit of prey. Its flight is shallowly undulating. ☉: Its call, *tsek tsek,* is not very often heard. The song, consisting of twittering and rasping sounds with fluty whistles and imitations of the voices of other birds, is heard only infrequently. ♋: The juv. birds are similar to those of the Red-backed Shrike (p. 215); the latter, however, are darker, without any sign of a pale wing patch and without a pale rump.

Ecology ◈: Parkland, often larger parks and gardens, tree avenues, the edges of broad-leaved forests or smaller woods in lowland and hilly country. ∞: It is quite difficult to prove its presence, generally by direct observation, because its variegated coloration is very inconspicuous in the treetops. Look for the nest by making a thorough search of the treetops at the site of the birds' occurrence.

Bionomy ↔: It is migratory and is found at the nesting grounds in Apr.—Sept. ♥: The nest is a sturdy structure in the fork of a branch high up in a tree; sometimes it is made of very light-coloured material (the fluff of willow catkins, white feathers, etc.), with lining often of atypical material such as string, threads, bits of plastic, etc. The four to six greenish, brown-marked eggs (23.0×17.0 mm) are laid in May—July. It has one brood a year, nests solitarily, and ♀ incubates for 15 days. The young are tended by both parents, 14 days in the nest and for some time longer also outside the nest. ◕: Larger invertebrates, mainly insects, caught on the ground. Vertebrates are taken exceptionally.

Conservation This is a disappearing species. No realistic means of protection are known as yet.

1

Jay
Garrulus glandarius

Identification Voice — size — appearance — behaviour

✳: Smaller than a crow (35 cm). Adults (1) have a black moustachial streak and tail, black, white and blue wings, and white rump. The three groups of subspecies found in Europe differ in the coloration of the head: in birds of the *G. g. glandarius* type (distributed throughout most of Europe) it is a greyish wine-red with a black-streaked crown; in birds of the *G. g. brandtii* type (of northeastern Europe) the head and back are reddish-brown; in birds of the *G. g. atricapillus* type (of Crimea) the crown is black. ♀ is slightly smaller than ♂ and has a shorter crest. Juv. birds are duller and have fewer black bars on the blue wing-coverts. ✦: It stays in treetops, hopping about clumsily. Its flight is cumbersome, with irregular wingbeats; the broad rounded wings are striking. ☉: It often utters its distinctive harsh grating call, and frequently makes mewing sounds like the Common Buzzard. The song is rarely heard; it is soft and includes imitations of the voices of other birds and other sounds; in spring Jays also sing in chorus. ♋: It is unmistakable.

Ecology ◈: Forests and woods of all kinds, from lowland districts to the upper forest limit, also city parks and gardens. In the non-breeding season it also flies across unwooded regions. ∞: It is easily recognised by its call throughout the year. The nest is difficult to find, for the birds are extremely cautious and quiet in its vicinity. It is therefore necessary to observe the behaviour of the birds and explore suitable sites.

Bionomy ↔: It is mostly resident; birds from northern and northeastern Europe sometimes travel southwest. ཞ: The nest is generally high up in a tree or among dense branches. The four to eight grey-green, brown-speckled eggs (31.2×22.9 mm) are laid in Apr.—June. It has one brood a year, nests solitarily, and incubates for 17 days. The young are tended by both parents, 20 days in the nest and a further short period outside the nest. ◑: This is much varied: insects, spiders, woodland rodents, the young and eggs of birds, plant fruits and seeds. Food is gathered and hunted in trees, as well as on the ground.

Conservation From the game-management viewpoint it is considered a pest, but opinions vary. No special protective measures are necessary.

1

Magpie
Pica pica

Identification Appearance — voice — coloration

✳ : The size of a crow (45 cm, tail 23 cm). The very long graduated tail, rather short rounded wings, and contrasting glossy black and white coloration are characteristic (1); ♂ = ♀. Juv. birds are dull and have a shorter tail. ✦: It perches on trees and flies down to the ground, where it hops about. Its flight is cumbersome; the long tail and short rounded wings are conspicuous. ☉: It often utters a loud *kshak-kshak-kshak* or raucous *kshrak-kshrak.* The song is rarely heard; it is a mixture of chattering and raucous sounds. ⅏: It is unmistakable.

Ecology ◈: Cultivated, mainly farm country with small woods, waterside vegetation, also parks, and in some places close to human habitations so long as it is not persecuted by man; from lowland to mountain elevations. ∞: It may be heard as well as seen without difficulty the whole year round.

Bionomy ↔: It is resident. In the non-breeding season it occurs in small groups. ᴗ: The nest is in a treetop or in a shrub, usually high up among slender twigs; it is a large spherical structure of twigs roofed over with a sparse layer. The five to eight greenish eggs, densely patterned brown (33.7×23.6 mm), are laid in Mar.—June. It has one brood a year, nests solitarily, and incubates for 17 days. The young are cared for by both parents, 25 days in the nest and a further short period outside the nest. ◖: Smaller animals, birds' eggs, plant seeds and fruits. Food is gathered and hunted in trees, as well as on the ground.

Conservation It is considered a pest of small game and birds, and in some places is persecuted by man. Apart from regulating the hunting of small populations, no special protective measures are necessary.

Nutcracker
Nucifraga caryocatactes

Identification Voice — appearance — behaviour — coloration

✳: Smaller than a crow (33 cm) and with a large head, stout, straight bill, short tail, and broad rounded wings. Adults (1) are dark brown with white drop-shaped markings, a brown cap, and a white tail with a broad black band. The subspecies that breeds in central Europe (*N. c. caryocatactes* — 3, 5) differs from the invasional vagrant Siberian subspecies (*N. c. macrorhynchos* — 2, 4) in having a shorter, stouter bill and a narrow white terminal band on the tail. ♂ = ♀. Juv. birds are paler, with a whitish throat and smaller, fewer white markings. ✦: It perches upright at the top or on the outer branches of trees, and hops about on the ground. It generally occurs solitarily, even though several birds may be seen in one spot not far from each other. In flight it resembles the Jay, but its tail is shorter and the flight is more buoyant and skilful. The wings are conspicuously broad, and furthermore the white undertail-coverts and white tip to the dark tail stand out in sharp contrast to the body. ☉: It often utters its loud harsh *rrrek-rrrek;* the song is rarely heard and consists of creaky sounds. ♋: It is unmistakable.

Ecology ◈: Mostly coniferous forests from hilly country to the upper forest limit; in the non-breeding season also away from forests, including gardens in built-up areas. ∞: It is easily recognised the whole year round by its warning call, but at the nesting grounds it is very quiet and cautious. This makes it difficult to find the nest, which is located by chance or by persistent observation of the birds.

Bionomy ↔: It is dispersive and partly migratory; birds from northeastern Europe and Siberia sometimes make invasional migrations (July—Mar.) to the southwest. On such flights the birds are very tame, and for this reason the invasion is very conspicuous. Flocks of birds may include both subspecies together or else may consist almost entirely of just the one or other subspecies. It is found at the nesting grounds in Mar.—July. ∽: The nest is high up in a treetop; the outer layer is made of dry twigs. The three to five greenish eggs with minute greyish markings (33.9×24.1 mm) are laid in Mar.—June. It has one brood a year, nests solitarily, and ♀ incubates for 17 days. The young are tended by both parents, 23 days in the nest and a further short period outside the nest. ◑: Seeds and fruits of conifers, mainly cembra pine, hazelnuts, berries; less often insects, mainly beetles. Occasionally it captures small mammals, the young of birds, frogs, molluscs and earthworms. Food is obtained in trees, as well as on the ground.

Conservation Generally it is not very numerous but in some years, after the young have been reared, it is very plentiful. No special protective measures are necessary.

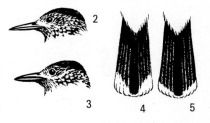

1

Alpine Chough
Pyrrhocorax graculus

Identification Habitat — appearance — voice — behaviour

∗: Smaller than a crow (38 cm) and with a small round head, long slender bill, and broad rounded wings. Adults (1) are entirely black, with a yellow bill and red legs; ♂ = ♀. Juv. birds are a dull colour, and the legs are brownish. ✦: It occurs on rocks, running and hopping about on the ground. Often it circles around the rocks; its flight is buoyant, skilful, with frequent twists and turns and intervals of gliding. ☉: It often utters a metallic *shirrik,* or *krree,* and a brief *chyup.* ☜: In parts of western and southern Europe the very similar Chough (*P. pyrrhocorax*), differing in having a longer, red bill (2).

Ecology ◈: Rock faces and grassy alpine slopes in mountains up to the snow line; in winter it moves to valleys and cultivated country at lower elevations. ∞: It is readily observed, as well as identified by its voice, the whole year round. The location of the nest may be determined with ease by the behaviour of the birds, but it is difficult to get to.

Bionomy ↔: It descends to lower elevations for the winter, occasionally wandering greater distances. It is found at the nesting grounds in Mar.—Oct. It nests solitarily as well as in colonies, and likewise occurs singly or in flocks in the non-breeding season. ♋: The nest is in a rock cavity or crevice; its foundation is of twigs. The four to five yellowish, brown-patterned eggs (38.3×26.4 mm) are laid in Apr.—May. It has one brood a year, and incubates for 20 days. The young are tended by both parents, 35 days in the nest and a further short period outside the nest. ◑: Small animals, plant fruits and seeds, caught and gathered on the ground.

Conservation In suitable conditions it is quite numerous. No special protective measures are necessary.

2

1

Jackdaw
Corvus monedula

Identification Voice — appearance — behaviour — coloration

✳: The size of the Collared Dove (33 cm), with a rather small head, thick neck and short stout bill. Adults (1) are black with a grey neck. In the east European ssp. *C. m. soemmeringii*, the grey of the neck is bordered below by white patches the shape of half-moons; ♂ = ♀. The plumage of juv. birds is tinged brown. ✦: It is not shy. It perches on buildings, on trees, and often walks about on the ground. It flies lightly, expertly, often flying about and soaring around steeples. In the non-breeding season it flies at dusk to roost in large numbers on trees, often together with Rooks. ☉: Its characteristic loud *kya-kya* is very often heard. ☎: It is unmistakable. In flocks of Rooks it differs in its voice, smaller size, and more rapid wingbeats.

Ecology ◑: Woods with old trees, parks, built-up areas, quarries, cliffs, castle ruins and rock walls in the vicinity of farm country; from lowland to submontane elevations. In the non-breeding season it generally roams the countryside away from the nesting grounds. ∞: It is readily located throughout the year by its voice or by direct observation. The nesting sites are conspicuous by virtue of the presence as well as the behaviour of the birds, but are usually hard to get to.

Bionomy ↔: It is partly migratory; in the non-breeding season it generally occurs in groups or flocks, often together with Rooks. It is found at the nesting grounds in Mar.—July. ∽: It nests solitarily as well as in colonies, sometimes very large ones, in tree holes, rock cavities, and in cavities in buildings; the foundation of the nest is made of twigs, often below the level of the entrance to the cavity. The three to six greenish-blue eggs with brown markings (35.1×25.1 mm) are laid in Apr.—May. It has one brood a year, and ♀ incubates for 17 days. The young are cared for by both parents, remaining in the nest 35 days. ◑: Mostly plant seeds and fruits; animal food consists mainly of beetles. Food is gathered and captured on the ground.

Conservation It is plentiful but greatly declining in number. In places it is of economic importance. Neither the reasons for its decline nor any realistic means of protection are known as yet.

223

1

Rook
Corvus frugilegus

Identification Voice — behaviour — appearance — coloration

∗ : As large as a crow (46 cm), it has a small angular head and relatively slender bill; the legs above the 'knee' are feathered, appearing 'trousered'. Adults (1) are black with a violet metallic sheen, and with bare skin at the base of the bill; ♂ = ♀. In juv. birds the area at the base of the bill is feathered. ✦: It is not shy. It flies skilfully and lightly, flocks of birds often availing themselves of thermal updrafts to soar in circles. In the non-breeding season the birds roost together at night in huge communities along with Jackdaws; their departure and return to the roosting site are quite regular. ☉: Very often heard, even in flight, is its harsh *kaa-kaa*, also *kro* or a deeper *gege*; it also makes other sounds. ♋: In western Europe the Carrion Crow (p. 225), which has a larger round head, a stouter, slightly downcurved bill, and unfeathered legs (without 'trousers'), and occurs singly or in small flocks.

Ecology ◈: Open countryside, mainly farm country, with small woods, from lowland to submontane elevations; it often nests and moves about in cities. ∞: It is easily recognised the whole year round by its voice and appearance; nesting colonies are conspicuous from a distance by the presence of the birds, and the nests are readily seen, though not easy to get to.

Bionomy ↔: It is resident in Britain but otherwise mostly migratory, and occurs in large flocks. Birds from northeastern Europe winter in central Europe, whereas birds from central Europe journey for the winter to southeastern Europe. It is found at the nesting grounds in Mar.—July. ♒: The nests are in trees, high up, usually several in a single tree; the foundation of the nest consists of dry twigs. The three to five blue-green, brown-spotted eggs (39.1×27.9 mm) are laid in Mar.—Apr. It has one brood a year, nests in colonies, and ♀ incubates for 17 days. The young are cared for by both parents, remaining in the nest for 30 days. ◖: Plant seeds, mainly cereal grains, smaller animals, and various food remnants. Food is gathered on the ground.

Conservation It is very numerous, though its numbers fluctuate in places. It is essential to protect the nesting colonies.

1

Carrion Crow
Corvus corone corone

Identification Appearance — behaviour — voice

✳: It measures 46 cm, has a stout, slightly arched bill, and legs devoid of feathers to the belly. Adults (1) are black with a green and purplish sheen; hybrid offspring of the Hooded and Carrion Crow exhibit varying expanses of grey. ♂ = ♀. Juv. birds are browner and nonglossy. ✦: It is rather shy. Its flight is less smooth and gliding than the Rook's; it seldom soars, and then only briefly. ☉: It often utters a harsh two- to three-syllabic *krrah-krrrah* or *krreh*, and a long-drawn-out *kraah*; in spring during courtship a rich *klong-klong*. ♋: Most similar is the Rook (p. 224), which has a slimmer body, straighter bill, bare at the base in adult birds, the upper part of the legs covered with feathered 'trousers', and generally occurs in flocks. The Raven (p. 227) is much larger, has a wedge-shaped tail, and a different voice.

Ecology ◈: Open farm country, woods, parks and cliffs, from lowland districts to the upper forest limit. ∞: It can be located by its voice and by direct observation the whole year long. In the vicinity of the nest, however, crows are very cautious and thus it is not easy to find the nest. As a rule its location may be determined by watching the birds as they fly from one spot to another and by checking out large nests at the site.

Bionomy ↔: It is resident, but some birds travel from central Europe to the southwest. In the non-breeding season several birds generally occur together or else it forms small flocks. ♥: The nest is high up in a tree or on a cliff; the basic construction is of dry twigs. The four to five blue-green, brown-spotted eggs (41.2×29.7 mm) are laid in Mar.—May. It has one brood a year, nests solitarily, and ♀ incubates for 18 days. The young are tended by both parents, remaining in the nest 33 days. ◕: Various plant seeds and smaller animals, gathered and caught on the ground.

Conservation It is relatively numerous in places, and is persecuted by man mainly because of the damage it causes to wildlife. It is necessary to regulate shooting of the birds.

1

Hooded Crow
Corvus corone cornix

Identification Appearance — behaviour — voice — coloration
∗: It attains a size of 46 cm and has a large, somewhat flattened head, stout, slightly curved bill, and rounded wings. Adults (1) have the head, throat, wings and tail black, the remaining parts grey; in hybrid offspring of this and the Carrion Crow black predominates over grey. ♂ = ♀. Juv. birds are duller. ✦: In places where it is persecuted it is wary. It perches on trees, walks about and makes short hops on the ground. It flies well but its flight is somewhat cumbersome, very occasionally interspersed with brief intervals of gliding. In the non-breeding season it flies in flocks to a common roosting site, such evening assemblies being very conspicuous. ⊙: It often utters its harsh *krrah-krrah-krrah* or a long-drawn-out *kraaah*; in spring during courtship a rich *klong-klong.* ♋: It is unmistakable.
Ecology ◆: Open, mainly farm country with woods, often near water, from lowland districts to the upper forest limit. ∞: It is easy to locate by its calls and by direct observation the whole year round. In the vicinity of the nest the birds are cautious, and in places where they are heavily persecuted the nests are usually very well concealed; watch them as they fly from one place to another and check on large nests at the site.
Bionomy ↔: It is generally resident, but populations from northeastern Europe travel to the southwest. ⊗: The nest is high up in a tree; it is made primarily of dry twigs. The four to five blue-green, brown-spotted eggs (41.5×29.2 mm) are laid in Mar.—May. It has one brood a year, nests solitarily, and ♀ incubates for 18 days. The young are tended by both parents, remaining in the nest 33 days. ◑: The same as that of the Carrion Crow (p. 225).
Conservation Its numbers depend on the extent to which it is persecuted by man. Protection is the same as for the Carrion Crow.

1

Raven
Corvus corax

Identification Voice — size — appearance — coloration
✳: The largest corvid bird in Europe (65 cm). Typical features are the very stout, straight bill with down-curved upper mandible, large head, long rounded wings, and a long, wedge-shaped tail (2). Adults (1) are entirely black; ♂ = ♀. Juv. birds are duller, with a brownish tone. ✦: It is very shy. It perches on trees, cliffs and walls; in this position the feathers on the throat stand out. It walks on the ground. It flies enduringly with powerful swings of its long wings, circling and frequently soaring; the courtship performance in spring includes aerial acrobatics. ☉: Often heard, even in flight, is its striking, far-carrying *krok-krok* or *kruk-kruk*, less often also other sounds. ♋: It is unmistakable.
Ecology ◈: Wooded regions with pastures, fields and water, rocky areas, sea coasts, from lowland districts to the alpine belt in mountains. ∞: The Raven is readily located throughout the year by its voice, and identified in flight by its silhouette. Finding the nest is difficult, even by observing the behaviour of the birds, for their hunting territory is large; more conspicuous are nests located on cliff ledges or trees.
Bionomy ↔: It is a resident and dispersive bird, found at the nesting grounds from Jan. In the non-breeding season it occurs in small groups, as well as in larger flocks. ♒: The nest is located on a cliff ledge or high up in a treetop; its basic construction is made of dry twigs. The four to six blue-green, brown-patterned eggs (49.2×33.7 mm) are laid in Feb.—Apr. It has one brood a year, nests solitarily, and ♀ incu-

bates for 20 days. The young are cared for by both parents, 40 days in the nest and a short period further outside the nest. ◕: Mainly carrion, even in advanced stages of decay, also smaller animals, varied refuse, gathered and caught on the ground.
Conservation It is quite numerous in places; its numbers are on the increase and its range is expanding. It is necessary to enact protective legislation.

2

227

1

Starling
Sturnus vulgaris

Identification Appearance — size — behaviour — voice — coloration

✳: Slightly smaller than the Blackbird (21 cm). The breeding plumage (1) is black with a metallic green and purple sheen, and the non-breeding plumage is browner, markedly speckled buff and white; ♂ = ♀. The juv. plumage is coffee-brown with a whitish throat. ✦: It is not shy. It perches on trees, buildings and telegraph wires, and walks about on the ground nodding its head. It flies rapidly, in a straight line, with fast wingbeats. In the non-breeding season huge flocks often perform striking manoeuvres in the air and at night roost together in reedbeds, in trees, or on buildings. ☉: It frequently utters its loud call *sheerr sheerr,* young birds *tshirr.* The song consists of smacking, rasping and whistling notes, often also imitations of the voices of other birds. ♂ generally sings beside the nesting cavity, fluttering his partly drooping wings and fluffing out the feathers on his head. ♋: In southwestern Europe the Spotless Starling (*S. unicolor*), and in eastern Europe the young of the Rose-coloured Starling (*S. roseus*). Adult Rose-coloured Starlings (2) differ in coloration.

Ecology ◈: Light broad-leaved woods, gardens, parks and urban areas, from lowland to mountain forest elevations. In the non-breeding season also farm country at lower elevations. ∞: It is readily identified by its voice and by direct observation the whole year round. The nest can be discovered without difficulty by the behaviour of the birds and by searching the site.

Bionomy ↔: It is mostly migratory and forms flocks comprising enormous numbers of birds. It is found at the nesting grounds in Feb.—July. ᴗ: It nests in tree holes, in holes in the ground or in buildings, very often in nestboxes prepared for other birds. The four to six greenish-blue eggs (29.4×21.1 mm) are laid in Apr.—June. It nests solitarily or in loose groups, has one or two broods a year, and incubates for 13 days. The young are cared for by both parents, 21 days in the nest and several more days outside the nest. ◑: Small invertebrates, plant fruits and seeds, depending on the season of the year. Food is gathered on the ground, as well as in trees.

Conservation The birds may cause damage in crops, as well as in gardens and orchards. Excessive encouragement of the birds is not advisable.

2

1

House Sparrow
Passer domesticus

Identification Appearance — behaviour — voice — coloration

✳: It attains a size of 14.5 cm, has a rather large head, a stout conical bill, and short wings and tail. Adults are grey and brown: ♂ (1) has a chestnut nape, a grey crown (in ssp. *P. d. italiae* it is chestnut-brown) and black chin and throat; in ♀ the entire underside is pale grey, the top of the head greyish-brown, and there is a pale stripe through/above the eye. Juv. birds resemble ♀, but have the corners of the bill yellow. ✦: It is not shy. It perches on trees, buildings and wires, and hops about on the ground. Its flight is undulating or straight, and rapid. In the non-breeding season large numbers of birds often roost together in trees. ☉: Its familiar call *chip-chip-charara*, etc., which is also part of its inconspicuous song, is heard practically all the time; as he sings, ♂ perches or hops about with partly drooping wings. ☙: The similar Eurasian Tree Sparrow (p. 230) has the entire top of the head chestnut-brown and a black patch on its white cheeks. In southern Europe the Spanish Sparrow (*P. hispaniolensis*) is similar, but black prevails in its plumage coloration.

Ecology ◈: Cultivated farm country as well as built-up areas, from lowland to submontane elevations. ∞: It is readily identified by its voice and by direct observation throughout the year. The nest may be found without difficulty by looking under eaves or by observing birds in trees.

Bionomy ↔: It is a resident bird that generally nests and occurs in small to large flocks.

♾: The nest is an untidy structure of plant material and feathers located in various holes, under eaves, behind drainpipes, in nestboxes; in trees it builds a spherical nest. The three to six eggs of widely diverse coloration but mostly greenish or white with dense dark markings (22.2×15.6 mm) are laid in Apr.—Aug. It has one to five broods a year and incubates for 14 days. The young are tended by both parents, 14 days in the nest and a further ten days outside the nest. ◑: Plant seeds, insects and varied scraps; when the young are being raised mostly small arthropods. Food is gathered on the ground as well as in trees.

Conservation An abundant species. Protection is not necessary.

1

Eurasian Tree Sparrow
Passer montanus

Identification Appearance — voice — coloration

∗: Slightly smaller than the House Sparrow (13 cm) and with a small round head, small bill, and short wings and tail. Adults (1) are grey and brown, the crown is chestnut-brown, the chin is black, and there is a small black patch on the white cheek. ♂ = ♀. Juv. birds are duller and have the corners of the bill yellow.
✦: It perches on trees and shrubs and hops about on the ground. Its flight is undulating or straight, and rapid. When the young have fledged the birds form flocks, often together with House Sparrows, Greenfinches, Goldfinches and other birds. ☉: It often utters its call *liplik,* also *chip chik;* in flight *tek tek.* The song, a combination of these notes, is infrequently heard. ♋: The ♂ House Sparrow (p. 229), which is somewhat larger, has a grey crown (in ssp. *P. d. italiae* this is chestnut-brown) and has a black area extending from beneath the bill to the breast.

Ecology ◗: Parkland, built-up areas with scattered greenery, also light woods, in lowland and hilly country. ∞: It is readily identified throughout the year by its voice and by direct observation. Look for the nest from the calls and behaviour of the birds or by checking on suitable holes as well as nestboxes in the locality.

Bionomy ↔: It is mostly resident, even though individual populations as well as individual birds travel to southwestern and southern Europe. After the young have fledged the birds form flocks. ♡: The nest is in tree holes, rocks,

mud-banks, walls of buildings, often in nestboxes; lots of feathers are used in its construction. The four to six white eggs, heavily patterned greyish-brown (19.1 × 14.2 mm), are laid in Apr.—July. It has one to three broods a year, nests solitarily or in small colonies, and incubates for 13 days. The young are cared for by both parents, 16 days in the nest and a further eight days outside the nest. ◖: Plant seeds and small invertebrates. It gathers its food on the ground, as well as on herbaceous and woody plants, and also visits bird-feeders.

Conservation It is plentiful but its numbers are declining in places. Where it occurs in large numbers it causes damage to farm crops. Protection is not necessary.

1

Snow Finch
Montifringilla nivalis

Identification Size — appearance — coloration — voice
∗: Larger than a sparrow (18 cm) and with a large head, short stout bill, thickset body and quite long tail. The adult ♂ (1, 2) is black, white and brown with a grey head; the wings are white with black tips and with a black patch at the bend. ♀ is less contrastingly coloured and has less extensive white. Juv. birds lack the black chin, all their wing-coverts are black, and the patch on the secondaries is also black. ✦: It perches and moves about on the ground with body held upright, but it does not perch on trees; when agitated, it jerks its tail. Its flight is rapid and undulating; when flushed it often returns to the same spot, flying out and back in a curve. ⊙: Its call, *tsuih, kik,* and a whistling *titri* is heard quite often; the alarm is *shreh.* Its song — *sitytshe-sitytshe* — is delivered in flight, as well as when perched. ᴥ: In winter it may be confused with the Snow Bunting (p. 245) in some areas, but the latter has the head white or brown, never grey, a white band above the eye, and the black centre of the tail broader at the tip.
Ecology ◈: Stony and grassy places in the subalpine belt of high mountains, where it also occurs in the vicinity of human dwellings. ∞: It may be recognised by its behaviour and appearance. The nest may be pinpointed by the behaviour of the birds.
Bionomy ↔: It is resident, moving in winter to open country at lower elevations and then very occasionally wandering greater distances. At this time it occurs in smaller as well as larger

flocks. ᴗ: The nest is in rock crevices, also in masonry or beneath the roofs of buildings, generally quite high up; it is quite large. The four to five white eggs (23.4×17.0 mm) are laid in Apr.—June. It has one brood a year, often several pairs nest relatively close together, and it incubates for 14 days. The young are tended by both parents, 20 days in the nest and a short period further outside the nest. ◖: Throughout the year plant seeds, in summer also small insects and spiders. The birds gather food on the ground and also visit bird-feeders.
Conservation It is quite numerous in places. No special protective measures are necessary.

2

1

Chaffinch
Fringilla coelebs

Identification Voice — appearance — coloration — behaviour

✳: As large as a sparrow (15 cm), it has a slender body and round head. Adults have brownish-black wings with two white bars, a dark tail edged with white, and a moss-green rump. ♂ is otherwise chestnut-brown: in breeding dress (1) the crown and nape are grey-blue, paler in non-breeding plumage. ♀ is greenish-grey instead of chestnut-brown, and is darker above. Juv.= ♀. ✦: It is not shy. It perches in trees, generally on the lower branches of the crown; on the ground and on thicker branches it moves by walking, nodding its head while doing so, and also hopping. Its flight is rapid and undulating. It often joins the company of other finches such as Bramblings and Greenfinches. ☉: It frequently utters its call *pink pink,* and in flight also *yip;* in summer it often calls *hueet* (heralding rain). The song is a loud, simple and short rattle, *rrr-chitchit-chetchet chittyeedeea,* with individual variations. ☜: It is unmistakable.

Ecology ◆: All habitats with trees from lowland districts to the upper forest limit, including tree-lined city streets. ∞: It is easily recognised by its voice, and the birds may be observed throughout the year. When looking for the nest, explore suitable places in the nesting territory or watch the behaviour of the adult birds.

Bionomy ↔: It is partly migratory and in the non-breeding season forms small as well as large flocks. It is found at the nesting grounds in Mar.—Aug. ᴗ: The nest is in a tree by the trunk or in the fork of a branch, not too high up; moss and lichens are used in its construction. The four to five reddish eggs with brown markings (19.2×14.5 mm) are laid in Apr.—July. It has one or two broods a year, nests solitarily, and ♀ incubates for 13 days. The young are cared for by both parents, 14 days in the nest and several days more outside the nest. ◑: Varies according to the season; it consists of the fleshy fruits and buds of plants, and small arthropods, mainly insects and spiders. The birds gather food on the ground, as well as on trees, and also visit bird-feeders.

Conservation It is plentiful. No special protective measures are necessary.

1

Brambling
Fringilla montifringilla

Identification Voice — appearance — coloration

✳: In size and appearance it resembles the Chaffinch but has a white rump in all its plumages. Adults have orange-brown and black wings with two pale bars and a brownish-black tail. ♂ in breeding plumage has a black head and back, and the upper part of the underside orange; in the non-breeding plumage (1) the head and back are mottled black and brown. ♀ is much paler, with a greyish-brown head. Juv. birds resemble ♀, with the rump tinged yellow-brown. ✦: It is not shy. It perches on trees; on the ground it walks as well as hops. Its flight is rapid, undulating. It often forms mixed flocks together with other finches or buntings; the birds roost in large congregations in woods. ☉: It often utters a broad *twek* to *tveih*, also *jip*, including in flight. The song is nondescript, creaky, reminiscent of the repeated wheezy *zwee* of the Greenfinch; ♂ sings perched on a branch. ♋: It is unmistakable.

Ecology ◈: Northern forests of various types and age. In the non-breeding season often beechwoods, open country — fields, fallow land, also built-up areas. ∞: It is readily identified by its call, even in flight. When looking for the nest, explore suitable sites or pinpoint its location by watching the behaviour of the birds.

Bionomy ↔: It is migratory and in the non-breeding season generally forms flocks. It is found at the nesting grounds in May—Sept. ♡: The nest is not very high up in a tree, in the fork of a branch by the trunk; mosses and lichens are used in its construction. The five to seven reddish, dark-patterned eggs (19.5×14.6 mm) are laid in May—July. It has one brood a year, nests solitarily, and ♀ incubates for 14 days. The young are cared for by both parents, remaining in the nest 11 days. ◗: Plant seeds and small arthropods, gathered on the ground and in trees; it also visits bird-feeders.

Conservation In some years it occurs in huge numbers. No special protective measures are necessary.

233

1

Serin
Serinus serinus

Identification Voice — size — behaviour
✻: Markedly smaller than a sparrow (11 cm) and with a small head and short, stout, conical bill. Adults (1) always have a yellow rump, conspicuous mainly when they fly up in the air, two yellow bars on the wings and a dark tail. ♂ has the fore part of the body a brilliant yellow, but otherwise is streaked green and brown. ♀ is duller, yellow-green, and more heavily streaked. Juv. birds resemble ♀, but are conspicuously streaked and lack the yellow rump. ✦: It perches on telegraph wires and trees and hops about on the ground. Its flight is rapid, undulating; when singing, ♂ often flies in the manner of a bat or perches with outspread wings, swaying from side to side. ☉: It often utters its chirping call *girlik* or *grrlit;* when alarmed, *dzueet.* The song is lengthy, loud, and often includes a chirping *girrlik;* ♂ sings perched on a tree or on a telephone wire, as well as in flight. ♋: ♀ and juv. birds resemble the Siskin (p. 237), which, however, has a yellow-edged tail, longer bill and different voice.
Ecology ◈: Cultivated countryside, mainly farm country, with orchards, tree avenues, also parks and gardens, from lowland districts to the dwarf pine belt. ∞: It is easily recognised by its voice, as well as its behaviour. The nest may be found by exploring suitable sites and by watching the behaviour of adult birds.
Bionomy ↔: It is migratory and is found at the nesting grounds in Mar.—Oct. After the young have fledged it generally forms small flocks. ☙: The nest is usually sited not very high up on the outer branch of a tree or shrub. The three

to five bluish eggs with dark brown markings (16.5×12.2 mm) are laid in Apr.—July. It has one or two broods a year, nests solitarily, and incubates for 13 days. The young are tended by both parents, 15 days in the nest and several more outside the nest. ◖: Seeds of weeds, cultivated crops, grasses, as well as woody plants, gathered from the ground or directly on the plants.
Conservation It is plentiful and expanding its range. No special protective measures are necessary.

1

Greenfinch
Carduelis chloris

Identification Voice — appearance — behaviour — coloration
✳: The same size as a sparrow (14 cm), it has a large head, stout conical bill and robust body. Adults are greenish with darker wings and tail, the latter edged with yellow at the base: ♂ (1) has brilliant yellow-green underparts and wings edged with a broad yellow border; ♀ is a greenish-brown and the yellow border on the wings is narrower. Juv. birds resemble ♀, but are browner and have indistinct dark streaking.
✦: It is not shy. It perches on trees, often at the very tip, and on the ground it hops about. Its flight is rapid, undulating. When the young have fledged it occurs in flocks, often together with other finches, Linnets, Yellowhammers, Tree Sparrows, etc. ☉: It often utters its ringing cal *teu teu teu teu teu*, also *chuwee chuwee* and a penetrating nasal *zwee*. The song is quite a lengthy, loud series of ringing notes, *duldyul-dyul-girr-gigigi-zweer*; ♂ sings perched on a tree or in bat-like display flight. ♋: The call note sometimes resembles that of other finches, but the song and the bird's appearance are unmistakable.
Ecology ◆: Parkland from lowland districts to the upper forest limit, gardens and parks in cities; in the non-breeding season mostly open countryside. ∞: It is easily recognised by its voice and by its appearance; it may be observed throughout the year. Look for the nest by searching suitable sites or else by watching the behaviour of adult birds.
Bionomy ↔: It is resident as well as dispersive. In the non-breeding season it usually forms flocks, but generally not very large ones. It is found at the nesting grounds in Mar.—Sept.
♒: The nest is placed not very high up amidst the branches of a tree or shrub; the outer layer is of dry twigs. The three to six bluish, brown-speckled eggs (19.9×14.5 mm) are laid in Apr.—Aug. It has one to three broods a year, nests solitarily, and ♀ incubates for 14 days. The young are cared for by both parents, 14 days in the nest and several more outside the nest. ◑: Throughout the year mainly plant seeds and buds of trees. It gathers its food on the ground as well as on woody plants, and visits bird-feeders.
Conservation It is plentiful. No special protective measures are necessary.

1

Goldfinch
Carduelis carduelis

Identification Voice — coloration — appearance — behaviour

✳: Smaller than a sparrow (12 cm), it has a round head, red face mask, and slender pointed bill. Adults (1) are brownish-grey and whitish with the head patterned red, white and black, and have a white rump and a black tail with white markings; ♀ has a smaller red mask. Conspicuous in all plumages is the yellow band on the black wings. In juv. birds the head is pale brown with dark markings. ✚: It is not shy. It perches restlessly on trees, shrubs and taller herbaceous plants and constantly flies from one spot to another, hovering briefly in the air before alighting. It comes to the ground only infrequently. Its flight is rapid and undulating. Sometimes it occurs in flocks together with Greenfinches and Linnets. ☉: It constantly utters its sharp abrupt *shtiglits-shtiglits,* also *tsvit-vit-vit,* especially in flocks; the alarm note is a *ah-eeh.* The song is high-pitched, twittering and chirping with sharp notes, often including the call note. ♂ sings perched on the top of a tree, a telephone wire or a herbaceous plant. ♋: It is unmistakable.

Ecology ◆: Parkland, gardens and woodland edges, from lowland districts to the upper forest limit. In the non-breeding season it may be seen in open country in fields, fallow land, hedgerows, etc. ∞: It is readily identified by its voice throughout the year. The location of the nest must be discovered by observing the behaviour of the adult birds.

Bionomy ↔: It is resident, dispersive, and partly migratory. In the non-breeding season it generally occurs in small flocks. �™: The nest is placed high up in a tree or shrub in the fork of an outer branch; it is thick-walled and lined with the fluff of thistles. The four to five bluish, brown-speckled eggs (17.4×13.1 mm) are laid in Apr.—Aug. It has one to three broods a year, nests solitarily, and ♀ incubates for 13 days. The young are tended by both parents, 13 days in the nest and several more outside the nest. ◑: Seeds of plants, mainly thistles, in smaller measure small invertebrates, gathered on plants, less often on the ground.

Conservation It is plentiful. No special protective measures are necessary.

1

Siskin
Carduelis spinus

Identification Voice — appearance — behaviour — coloration
✳: Markedly smaller than a sparrow (11 cm). The adult is yellow-green with the base of the tail edged yellow and two yellow bars on the wings: ♂ has a black crown and usually a black chin too, and the underparts and rump are a bright yellow; ♀ (1) is brownish-green above, pale yellow below, with dark streaking all over. Juv. birds resemble ♀ but are very pale and conspicuously streaked. ✦: It perches on the branches of trees, and hangs in all positions from slender twigs. Its flight is undulating; during the courtship it flies in the manner of a bat. It forms flocks. ☉: Its call, heard almost constantly, is *cee-zee,* in flight *deu-eh,* also *ket-yet-et;* birds in a flock keep up a continual twittering. The song is a rasping twitter with long-drawn-out wheezing whistles. ♂ sings perched on a tree or in flight. ♋: It is slightly similar to the Serin (p. 234), especially ♀ and juv. birds; the Serin, however, has a shorter, stouter bill, its head is never black, and its voice is different.
Ecology ◈: Coniferous woods with glades and clearings and brooks, sometimes also broad-leaved woods with groups of conifers. In the non-breeding season birch and alder stands, especially near brooks and rivers. ∞: It is readily identified by its voice throughout the year. The nest is very hard to find, this being best achieved by keeping a careful watch on the adult birds when they are building the nest and feeding the young.
Bionomy ↔: It is partly migratory, forming

flocks that are sometimes enormous. It is found at the nesting grounds in Mar.—Aug. ♋: The nest is placed on an outer branch high up in the top of a coniferous tree. The four to five bluish eggs with reddish-brown markings (16.4×12.3 mm) are laid in Mar.—June. It has one to two broods a year, nests solitarily, and ♀ incubates for 13 days. The young are cared for by both parents, remaining in the nest 14 days. ◖: Mostly seeds, in winter mainly alder and birch seeds, in summer the seeds of conifers and various herbaceous plants, gathered in trees or on plants, occasionally also on the ground.
Conservation Its numbers exhibit marked fluctuations from year to year. No special protective measures are necessary.

1

Linnet
Carduelis cannabina

Identification Voice — appearance — coloration — behaviour
✳: Smaller than a sparrow (13 cm), it has a round head and short cone-shaped bill. The adult ♂ (1) has a grey head, reddish forehead, pinkish-red to crimson breast, whitish rump and edges of the tail at the base, and a pale wing patch; ♀ is duller and has pale brown upperparts, buff underside, dark streaking all over, and lacks pink and red in the plumage. Juv. birds resemble ♀ but are more heavily streaked. ✦: It is not particularly shy. It perches on trees, shrubs and telegraph wires; its flight is rapid and undulating. After the young have fledged it forms flocks, often together with Greenfinches, Goldfinches, and Bramblings. ☉: It frequently utters its call *chechechechek* to *chukeeyoo*. The song is loud, lengthy and composed of chirping and twittering notes as well as fluty trills. ♋: The Redpoll (p. 240), which, however, always has a black chin and a different call note. The Twite (p. 239) is only faintly reddish, with rump coloured pinkish in ♂ and greyish-brown and streaked in ♀, and lacks the pale wing patch.
Ecology ◈: Parkland with grassy tracts alternating with thickets, gorse commons and heaths, from lowland districts to the dwarf pine belt. ∞: It is readily identified by its voice throughout the year. Look for the nest by searching suitable sites and by observing the behaviour of adult birds.
Bionomy ↔: It is partly migratory; in the non-breeding season it generally forms small flocks. It is found at the nesting grounds in Mar.—Aug. ♡: The nest is placed not very high up in dense thickets, young coniferous trees, climbing plants, etc. The four to six pale blue, brown-speckled eggs (17.8 × 13.2 mm) are laid in Apr.—Aug. It has one to three broods a year, nests solitarily, and incubates for 11 days. The young are cared for by both parents, 11 days in the nest and several more outside the nest. ◐: Plant seeds, mainly of weeds and grasses, very occasionally small invertebrates, gathered on plants as well as on the ground.
Conservation It is plentiful. No special protective measures are necessary.

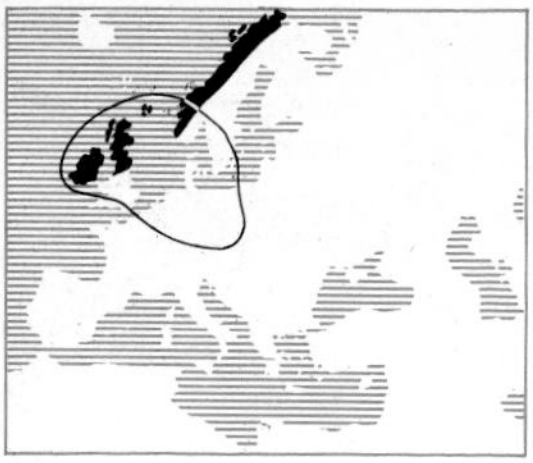

1

Twite
Carduelis flavirostris

Identification Voice — appearance — coloration
✳: Smaller than a sparrow (13 cm), it has a round head and small conical bill. Adults are brown above with dark streaks, the underparts, except the breast and flanks, are pale and unstreaked, the wings are dark with only one narrow pale bar, and the bill is yellow in winter and dark in summer; ♂ (1) has the rump coloured pinkish, while in ♀ it is greyish-brown with dark markings. Juv. birds resemble ♀ but the throat and breast are more conspicuously patterned. ✦: It perches and moves about mostly on the ground; its flight is rapid and undulating. It often joins flocks of Redpolls and Linnets. ⊙: Its striking call note *tweeik* and a softer *chek-chek-chek* is often heard, especially in flight. The song resembles that of the Linnet but is slower. ♋: It may be confused with the Linnet (p. 238), which, however, has a pale wing patch, pale-edged base of the tail, and paler rump, and ♂ of which has red on the forehead/crown and breast. The Redpoll (p. 240) has more red in the plumage and a black patch on the chin.
Ecology ◆: Unforested rocky places with low plant cover and thickets, e.g. moorlands, from lowland to subalpine elevations. In the non-breeding season it is often seen on the sea coast, inland on fallow land, often near water. ∞: If you know its call it can be identified fairly readily throughout the year, otherwise it is necessary to examine flocks of finches in open places. The nest may be discovered by the behaviour of the birds in suitable locations.

Bionomy ↔: It is migratory and is found at the nesting grounds in Apr.—Sept. In the non-breeding season it generally forms flocks. ◡: The nest in placed on a rock or cliff ledge. The five to six bluish eggs with reddish-brown markings (16.7×12.1 mm) are laid in Apr.—July. It has one or two broods a year, nests solitarily, and ♀ incubates for 13 days. The young are tended by both parents, remaining in the nest 15 days. ◑: Mostly plant seeds, mainly of weeds, gathered on the ground and, when there is snow cover, also on plants.
Conservation It is quite plentiful in places. No special protective measures are necessary.

1

Redpoll
Carduelis flammea

Identification Voice — appearance — behaviour — coloration

✳: Smaller than a sparrow (13 cm), it has a small round head, a short conical bill, and a forked tail. Adults have a red patch on the crown above the bill, and the chin is black. ♂ also has a red breast and paler red rump; ♀ (1) is more heavily streaked on the underside and has less red in her plumage. Juv. birds have a dark brown head and greyish-black chin and are heavily streaked. ✦: It is not particularly shy. It perches on trees and taller herbaceous plants and climbs along slender terminal branches, hanging in various positions. It forms flocks, occasionally together with other finches. ☉: It frequently utters its call note *chut chut-chut* or *dyuwee*, also a trilling *irrrr*; the alarm note is *tsooeet*. The song is a loud mix of short trills and call notes. ☍: In northern Europe the very similar Arctic Redpoll (*C. hornemanni*). The Linnet (p. 238) and Twite (p. 239) do not have a black patch on the chin and do not hang from twigs in trees.

Ecology ◈: It inhabits widely diverse environments depending on the region, from lowland districts to the dwarf pine belt; in winter it often occurs in areas of birch, alder or willow and in thickets in built-up areas, etc. ∞: It is easily recognised by its voice throughout the year. Sometimes the nest may be found by making a thorough search of suitable sites, otherwise it is rather difficult to spot by the behaviour of the adult birds.

Bionomy ↔: It is partly migratory. In the non-breeding season it forms flocks. It is found at the nesting grounds in Apr.—Aug. ❦: The nest is placed not very high up in a tree or thicket; often several pairs nest close to one another. The four to five bluish, brown-patterned eggs (15.9×12.2 mm) are laid in Apr.—July. It has one or two broods a year, and ♀ incubates for 11 days. The young are cared for by both parents, 12 days in the nest and several more days outside the nest. ◐: Plant seeds, less often also small insects. Food is gathered in trees, especially birches, on herbaceous plants and on the ground.

Conservation It is numerous, though its numbers exhibit marked fluctuations in individual years. No special protective measures are necessary.

1

Common Crossbill
Loxia curvirostra

Identification Voice — appearance — behaviour — coloration

*: The same size as a sparrow (16 cm), it has a large head and a stout bill with crossed tips. Adults have dark brown wings and tail; ♂ (1) is red, ♀ is yellow-green. Juv. birds are greyish olive-brown with heavy dark brown streaks. ♂ is sometimes yellow-green with a reddish rump. NB: Some individuals have two narrow white bars on the wings (var. *rubrifasciata*), similar to the Two-barred Crossbill (*L. leucoptera*). ✦: It perches on coniferous trees with cones, often on the top of the tree; it continually flies from one tree to another, also to the ground, or onto the roofs of mountain chalets. It flies very fast with shallow undulations, and flocks form loose formations. ☉: Frequently heard, including in flight, is its ringing abrupt call *glip glip*. The song is a mixture of trills and twittering and grating sounds, delivered from trees, often even in winter. ♋: The Parrot Crossbill (*L. pytyopsittacus*), which has a stouter bill (2), and the Two-barred Crossbill.

Ecology ◈: Almost exclusively spruce woods, mainly in the mountain forest belt, though it also nests in lowland districts. In the non-breeding season it also flies over unforested areas and even occurs in gardens. ∞: It is very easily recognised throughout the year by its voice; birds that are singing may be considered to be nesting birds no matter what time of the year if food is plentiful. The nest is very hard to find; the best way to learn its whereabouts is to observe the behaviour of the adult birds, particularly when they are building the nest, and to observe the ♂, who regularly brings food to the incubating ♀.

Bionomy ↔: It is nomadic and dispersive within its range in accordance with the available supply of spruce cones. It is an invasion species occurring irregularly in various regions and at various times, sometimes in great numbers. In the non-breeding season it occurs mostly in flocks. ᴥ: The nest is thick-walled and placed high up in a treetop by the trunk or amidst the branches. The three to four greenish eggs with reddish-brown markings (22.4×15.9 mm) are laid in Dec.—May, but also at other times. Incubation takes 14 days. The young are cared for by both parents, 17 days in the nest and a further lengthier period outside the nest. ◗: Seeds of coniferous trees, mostly spruces, extracted from cones on the trees.

Conservation No special protective measures are necessary, apart from preservation of its breeding habitat.

2

1

Scarlet Rosefinch
Carpodacus erythrinus

Identification Voice — appearance — behaviour — coloration
✷: As large as a sparrow (14 cm), it has a slender body, large head, stout bill, and slightly forked tail. The adult ♂ (1) is crimson with brown wings and tail; ♀ is grey-green above, and whitish below with dark streaking. Juv. birds resemble ♀ but are browner, with indistinct paler bands on the wings. In his first year ♂ is still greenish and often breeds in this plumage. ➔: It perches on the tops of trees and shrubs and on telegraph wires. Its flight is relatively rapid and undulating, but it does not fly particularly often. ☉: It often sings; the song is very loud, brief and monotonous, a melodious *teetitehteetiya*. The call note is *shayee* or a soft *tsvee*. ♋: It is unmistakable.
Ecology ◈: Meadows with sparse thickets from lowland districts to the dwarf pine belt — willow thickets by watercourses, dwarf pine, also gardens in residential areas, etc. ∞: It is readily identified by its song (May—July), otherwise it may be observed only by chance. Look for the nest in thickets near the spot where the bird sings; often you will flush a sitting bird. The presence of a singing ♂ need not necessarily be an indication of nesting.
Bionomy ↔: It is migratory and is found at the nesting grounds in May/June—Aug. It is a solitary bird. ᴥ: The loosely constructed nest is placed low down in dense short trees, thickets or herbaceous vegetation. The three to six bright blue eggs, lightly patterned a dark colour (20.1×14.3 mm), are laid in May—July. It has one brood a year, nests solitarily, in suitable places several pairs together, and incubates for 12 days. The young are tended by both parents, 12 days in the nest and several more outside the nest. ◑: Almost exclusively plant seeds, gathered on trees, herbaceous plants as well as on the ground.
Conservation It is quite plentiful locally and is expanding its range. Protection of the nesting grounds is sufficient, otherwise no special protective measures are necessary.

1

Bullfinch
Pyrrhula pyrrhula

Identification Voice — appearance — coloration
✳: As large as a sparrow (14 cm), it has a large, flat head, strikingly stout short bill and robust body. Adults have the top of the head, wings and tail black with a conspicuous white wing patch and white rump. ♂ (1) is vermilion-red below and grey above, ♀ greyish-pink below and darker above. Juv. birds lack the black cap, and their upperparts are brownish. ✦: It is often shy. It perches on slender terminal branches or on the tops of trees and shrubs. Its flight is quite rapid and undulating. ☉: It often utters its melancholy call note *peeu,* in flocks a soft *kit kit.* The song is not often heard and consists of quiet grating and wheezing notes. ♋: It is unmistakable.
Ecology ◈: Mainly coniferous and mixed woods, also orchards and parkland, from lowland districts to the mountain forest belt. In the non-breeding season it also occurs in unforested regions, in avenues of mountain ash, in gardens, etc. ∞: It is easily recognised by its call the whole year round. The nest may be discovered by observing the behaviour of the birds or investigating suitable sites in their respective nesting grounds.
Bionomy ↔: It is partly migratory, north European populations sometimes making invasional migrations to the other parts of Europe. It is found at the nesting grounds in Apr.—Aug. In the non-breeding season it generally occurs in pairs or small flocks; very occasionally it forms large flocks. ᴡ: The nest is placed not very high up, generally in a small, dense coniferous

tree, in a shrub, on the outer branches of trees, etc. The four to five grey-blue eggs with dark brown markings (20.5×14.9 mm) are laid in Apr.—July. It has one or two broods a year, nests solitarily, and incubates for 14 days. The young are cared for by both parents, 16 days in the nest and a further 10 days outside the nest. ◖: Seeds and buds of herbaceous and woody plants, in summer sometimes also small insects and spiders; food is gathered in trees, on herbaceous plants, as well as on the ground.
Conservation It is plentiful. No special protective measures are necessary.

1.

Hawfinch
Coccothraustes
coccothraustes

Identification Voice — appearance — behaviour
✳: Larger than a sparrow (18 cm) and with a markedly robust body, large flat head, enormous conical bill and unusually profiled primaries, making the wings seem as if they were full of holes when viewed from below in flight. The adult ♂ is pinkish-brown, darker above, with a grey neck and a broad white band on the dark wings; ♀ (1) is much duller, with a greyish crown and greyish-brown breast. Juv. birds have dark brown vermiculations on the head, neck and flanks. ✦: It is often very secretive. It perches in treetops, where it extracts seeds, often flying down to the ground for them. Its flight is rapid and shallowly undulating. ☉: It often utters its sharp explosive call *tsiks-tsiks-it,* as well as a more long-drawn-out *tseet,* including in flight. The song is rarely heard, even though in spring the birds sometimes sing in chorus; it is composed of low grating and twittering notes. On trees where Hawfinches congregate one can hear the cracking of seed husks and kernels. ♋: It is unmistakable.
Ecology ◆: Broad-leaved woods, parks, gardens and orchards, from lowland to mountain elevations. In the non-breeding season it occurs in larger numbers in beechwoods and stands of hornbeam when there is a rich yield of nuts. ∞: It is readily discovered throughout the year by its call. Locate the nest by observing the behaviour of the birds, mainly during the incubation period, when ♀ flies out of the nest and utters a loud *tsee-tsee-tsee-tsee* begging the ♂ to bring her food.

Bionomy ↔: It is partly migratory. In the non-breeding season it generally occurs in loose flocks. It is found at the nesting grounds in Mar.—Aug. ❀: The nest is usually in a tree, often by the trunk; the outer layer is of twigs and rootlets. The four to six pale blue-grey eggs with grey-brown markings (23.9×17.4 mm) are laid in Apr.—June. It has one or two, very occasionally three, broods a year, nests solitarily, and incubates for 12 days. The young are cared for by both parents, for 12 days in the nest and for a longer period outside the nest. ●: Mostly seeds and buds of trees and taller herbaceous plants, gathered in trees or on the ground.
Conservation It is quite numerous. No special protective measures are necessary.

1

Snow Bunting
Plectrophenax nivalis

Identification Voice — appearance — coloration — behaviour

✳: Larger than a sparrow (16 cm) and with a large, round head and short, stout bill. The adult plumage is extremely variable, brown-white-black, with a large white expanse on the wings standing out in sharp contrast (particularly in flight — 2) to the black primaries. In breeding plumage ♂ has a black back and white head; in the non-breeding plumage the crown and back are brown, the latter with black scale-like markings. ♀ (1) is similar to ♂ in his non-breeding plumage, but has the crown, cheeks and a patch on either side of the breast a vivid brown. Juv. birds resemble ♀, but have the throat and front part of the breast rusty-brown and the sides of the breast and flanks faintly streaked with grey. ✦: It is not shy, moves about on the ground, and its flight is rapid and shallowly undulating. ☉: It often utters its call, a bell-like *trrrling-tioo,* particularly in flight. At the nesting grounds it delivers its song, *tiuri-tiuri-tiuri-tetuee,* in descending flight or from a boulder. ♋: In winter in central Europe the Snow Finch (p. 231), which has a grey head and the tail white with only a narrow grey-black band down the centre.

Ecology ◈: Stony tundra from lowland to sub-alpine elevations. In the non-breeding season it occurs in fields, on coasts, in mountain meadows, and the like. ∞: It is readily identified by its voice and by direct observation throughout the year. The location of the nest may be discovered by observing the behaviour of the adult birds.

Bionomy ↔: It is migratory and in the non-breeding season forms small or larger flocks. It is found at the nesting grounds in Apr.—Sept. ◡: The nest is located in rock crevices, between boulders, in the walls of buildings; moss is used in its construction and feathers in the lining. The four to six greenish eggs with reddish-brown markings (22.0×16.1 mm) are laid in May—July. It has one, possibly two broods a year, nests solitarily, and incubates for 13 days. The young are cared for by both parents and stay in the nest for 12 days. ◕: In summer mostly insects; in autumn and winter, plant seeds. Food is gathered on the ground.

Conservation It is numerous. No special protective measures are necessary.

2

1

Yellowhammer
Emberiza citrinella

Identification Voice — appearance — coloration — behaviour

＊: More robust than a sparrow (16 cm). Adults have a cinnamon-brown rump and the tail is edged with white: ♂ (1) is yellow and reddish-brown; ♀ is much paler, with dark streaking and darker crown and cheeks. Juv. birds are pale yellow-brown with conspicuous markings on the front of the neck and breast. ✦: It often keeps to the ground, moving about with low hops. It also perches prominently on trees, bushes, buildings and haystacks and flies into farmyards. Its flight is rapid and undulating. ☉: It often utters its typical metallic call *tsik, tsik-tsik,* when taking to the air *tsik-tsirrr;* the alarm note is a high piercing *tseez.* The song is a simple *tsitsitsitsitsi-sweez* ending with an ascending note. ♂ sings from an elevated spot as early as late winter or in the autumn. ♋: In southern Europe the rare Cirl Bunting (*E. cirlus*). ♀♀ of most buntings are similar and cannot always be distinguished with certainty.

Ecology ◈: Light broad-leaved woods and their edges, scrub, farm country with trees and thickets, from lowland districts to the dwarf-pine belt. ∞: It is readily recognised by its voice, as well as by its appearance. The nest may be located by walking through the area where it is supposed to be and flushing the sitting bird, or by the behaviour of the adult birds.

Bionomy ↔: It is mostly resident and dispersive; only populations in the extreme northern parts of Europe are migratory. In the non-breeding season it generally forms flocks, often large ones. ♡: The nest is usually located on or near the ground in grass or low in a bush. The three to five whitish eggs, heavily patterned with brown spots and thread-like markings (21.1×16.2 mm), are laid in Apr.—Aug. It has one to three broods a year, nests solitarily, and incubates for 12 days. The young are tended by both parents, 13 days in the nest and several more outside the nest. ◖: Plant seeds, mostly grain and weed seeds, to a lesser degree small invertebrates. Food is gathered mainly on the ground.

Conservation It is numerous. No special protective measures are necessary.

1

Ortolan Bunting
Emberiza hortulana

Identification Voice — appearance — coloration

✳: As large as a sparrow (16 cm), it has a slender body and a rather long tail (1). The adult ♂ has a grey head and hindneck, yellow moustachial streak and chin, and reddish-brown belly and rump, the latter somewhat darker; ♀ is slightly paler. Juv. birds resemble ♀ but have prominent dark streaking on the upperparts and underparts. ✦: It is shy, perches on trees, less often also on telegraph wires, and moves about on the ground by hopping. Its flight is rapid and undulating. ☉: Its song, heard often, is a loud *tititi-ah* ending with a descending note is a delicate *tleeh* or *see-ip* and the like. ♋: The song resembles that of the Yellowhammer (p. 246); the latter, however, is faster, longer, and almost always ends with an ascending note. Distributed in southern Europe is the similar Rock Bunting (*E. cia*), in southeastern Europe Cretzschmar's Bunting (*E. caesia*) and very rarely and locally the Cinereous Bunting (*E. cineracea*).

Ecology ◆: Farm country with scattered trees, orchards, vineyards, tree avenues bordering roads, etc., in lowland and hilly regions. ∞: It is readily recognised by its song (Apr.—July); in the non-breeding season it may be encountered by chance. Locate the nest by observing the behaviour of the adult birds.

Bionomy ↔: It is migratory and occurs singly. It is found at the nesting grounds in Apr.—Sept. ᴗ: The nest is located on the ground in grass. The four to six eggs, grey-blue or reddish with dark spots and thread-like markings (19.9×15.6 mm), are laid in Apr.—June. It has one, possibly two broods a year, nests solitarily, and incubates for 13 days. The young are cared for by both parents, ten days in the nest and several days outside it. ◐: The type of food and manner in which it is obtained is comparable to that of the Yellowhammer.

Conservation It is not very plentiful and is declining in numbers. Neither the reasons for its decline nor any realistic means of protecting it are known.

1

Reed Bunting
Emberiza schoeniclus

Identification Habitat — voice — appearance — coloration

*: As large as a sparrow (15 cm). Adults are brown above, greyish-white below, with dark streaks all over. ♂ in breeding plumage (1) has a black head and throat and a white collar and moustachial streak; in the non-breeding plumage the head is blackish-brown. ♀ has a brown crown, cheeks edged with pale stripes, a dark moustachial streak and a white chin. Juv. birds resemble ♀ but have conspicuously streaked plumage. ✦: It perches on reed stems in reedbeds and hops about in the ground layer of vegetation as well as on the ground. Its flight is jerky and undulating, slower than that of other buntings. ☉: It frequently utters its long-drawn-out piercing call *tseeu;* the alarm note is *tsit.* The song is a short, loud *tseeu-ti-tay-tsis,* quickening in tempo; ♂ sings his melody perched on the top of a reed stem, bush, etc. ☙: The call resembles the Penduline Tit's (p. 213) but is slightly stronger.

Ecology ◀▶: Reedbeds and other wetlands from lowland to submontane elevations. In the non-breeding season it is not infrequently found far from water. ∞: It is readily identified by its song and is also easily observed. Look for the nest by carefully investigating likely spots, usually flushing a sitting ♀ at the same time, or else by observing the behaviour of the adult birds.

Bionomy ↔: It is mostly migratory; in the non-breeding season it also occurs in small groups. It is found at the nesting grounds in Apr.—Oct. ᴗ: The nest is located in the thick ground layer of herbaceous vegetation, generally on dry ground. The three to five brownish eggs with blackish-brown spots and thread-like markings (19.6×14.8 mm) are laid in Apr.—July. It has one or two broods a year, nests solitarily, and ♀ incubates for 13 days. The young are tended by both parents, for 12 days in the nest and several more days outside it. ◑: Mostly plant seeds; small invertebrates are fed mainly to the young. Food is gathered on the ground, as well as from taller plants.

Conservation It is necessary to protect the nesting sites. It is locally numerous.

Corn Bunting
Miliaria calandra

Identification Voice — appearance — behaviour

✳: Larger than a sparrow (18 cm), it has a large flat head, stout bill, and robust body. Adults (1) are darker above, paler below; ♂ = ♀. Juv. birds have the feathers on the back edged paler. ✦: It perches on elevated spots — the tops of trees, bushes, haystacks, electricity poles, telegraph wires — and hops about on the ground. Its flight is more cumbersome than that of other buntings but rapid; when flying a short distance from one spot to another, it leaves its legs dangling. The birds roost together in large numbers in reedbeds. ☉: It frequently utters a characteristic *zeerrp* when it flies up; the call note is an explosive *tik* or a rather drawn-out *seehp,* in the autumn also *tip-a-tip.* The song is a simple jingling *tsik-tsik-tsrissississ;* ♂ sings perched on an elevated spot, or on the wing just before alighting. ♋: It is unmistakable.

Ecology ◆: Open cultivated country with meadows, pastures, also downland; in the non-breeding season it also occurs by human habitations, from lowland to hilly regions. ∞: It is readily identified by its voice throughout the year. The nest is hard to find — either by making a thorough search of a possible site and flushing a sitting bird or by observing the behaviour of adult birds.

Bionomy ↔: It is partly migratory, wintering throughout practically the whole of its breeding range; in some districts it disappears in winter. In the non-breeding season it also forms large flocks. ᔒ: The nest is located on the ground in a thick growth of grass. The three to five yellowish or greyish-blue eggs with dark brown markings (24.9×18.3 mm) are laid in Apr.—July. It has one to two (three?) broods a year, nests solitarily, and ♀ incubates for 13 days. The young are cared for mostly or solely by ♀, ten days in the nest plus a further lengthier period outside the nest. ◑: Both plant and animal matter, seeds, plants, and small insects, gathered on the ground as well as from plants.

Conservation It is a rapidly and greatly declining species. No realistic means of protection are known as yet.

Birds of open country, cliffs and woodlands

This section includes all the other bird groups and species not included in the preceding three sections. They are relatively few in number, differ markedly in appearance, inhabit various environments, and their behaviour and way of life are likewise very diverse.

Fowl-like birds (Galliformes) are typified by the Pheasant (1). They include familiar, relatively large birds with characteristic coloration, the males generally markedly different from the females. They have short strong legs and a short stout bill. One group lives in woods (the grouse family — Tetraonidae), the other mainly in open country (the pheasant family — Phasianidae). In birds of both groups breeding is preceded by a distinctive courtship display, often accompanied by vocal expressions.

Large, long-legged birds of various systematic groups (the crane family — Gruidae, the bustard family — Otididae, the stone-curlew family — Burhinidae) are typified by the Common Crane (2). Some resemble storks in appearance, others large species of fowl-like birds. They generally inhabit open areas, from marshland to arid steppes.

The pigeons and their allies (Columbiformes), typified by the Rock Dove (3), are well known. They are medium-sized birds with legs adapted for walking, a short tarsus and well-developed toes, and a small head with characteristically shaped bill. Some (the sandgrouse family — Pteroclididae — living in dry scrub areas) also have other typical adaptations developed in response to their environment and way of life. All are superb fliers.

Smaller species of birds resembling songbirds are typified by the Common Kingfisher (4). Some are brightly coloured, for example the European Bee-eater, whereas the coloration of others is quite sober, e.g. the Common Cuckoo. They inhabit widely diverse environments to which they have accommodated through diverse adaptations.

Typical tree dwellers are the birds of the woodpecker family (Picidae), typified by the Black Woodpecker (5). The woodpeckers are a very distinctive group of medium-sized birds specially adapted to climbing the trunks of trees. Their legs are typically designed to this purpose, the bill is adapted to chisel wood, and the extraordinarily long, extensible tongue is adapted to extract food from the chiselled tunnels.

1

Hazel Hen
Bonasa bonasia

Identification Size — appearance — behaviour — voice

∗: A small gallinaceous bird the size of a partridge (36 cm) and with a robust body and small head. The adult ♂ (1) has a small crest, black chin and throat, dark and light markings all over, and the tail is grey with a black band near the tip. ♀ is duller, with a pale throat and a shorter crest. Juv. birds resemble ♀ but their plumage is even duller. ✦: It walks and runs about on the ground and flies up into trees. Its flight is rapid, accompanied by a loud whizzing sound made by the wings. ☉: During the courtship period ♂ utters a soft whistling, *tseeui tsi tsi tsitsitsi tseeyi,* which rises at the beginning and then drops again at the end; the alarm is *witwit;* young birds make piping sounds. ☜: At forest edges it may be confused with the Grey Partridge (p. 257), which, however, has a reddish-brown tail, and in woods with the ♀ Black Grouse (p. 254), which is darker and has a slightly forked tail.

Ecology ◗: Extensive damp woods with coniferous trees, hazels, birches, tangled undergrowth, blueberry bushes, etc. ∞: During the courtship period (Mar.—May, late Aug.—beginning of Nov.) it can be identified by its voice; it can also be called up with a bird whistle. Otherwise it may be flushed by chance when walking about the nesting grounds.

Bionomy ↔: This is a resident bird that nests solitarily, later forming families or occurring singly. ◡: The nest, made of leaves, is located on the ground, generally at the foot of a tree. The seven to twelve yellowish, brown-spotted eggs (40.6×29.1 mm) are laid in Apr.—June. It has one brood a year, and ♀ incubates for 25 days. The young are cared for only by ♀. They leave the nest on hatching, fly about at the age of 15 days, are fully grown at 35 days, and fully independent at 90 days. ◖: Buds, catkins and berries of trees, shrubs and herbaceous plants, in summer also small terrestrial invertebrates.

Conservation No longer numerous and it has disappeared in places. Nowadays it is a game bird only locally. Its numbers are declining owing to the changes in forest management. Where it does occur it should be provided with full protection.

Willow Grouse or Willow Ptarmigan
Lagopus lagopus

Identification Appearance — size — behaviour ✳: Slightly larger than a partridge (40 cm). The summer plumage of adults (3) is dark brown, the tail edged with black, and the wings are white; the winter plumage is white except for the sides of the tail (4); the intermediate plumage between these two periods is variously patterned (1, 2). ♀ is smaller and paler than ♂ and has discernible dark markings, particularly on the flanks, and the chin light-coloured to white. Juv. birds resemble ♀ but have brown markings on the white wings. In the subspecies *L. l. variegatus,* found on the coast of Norway, there are brown markings on the wings throughout the year and on the body even in winter; the subspecies *L. l. scoticus,* found in Britain, is dark (including the wings) throughout the year. ✦: It walks and runs about on the ground, flies up into the air low over the ground, and alternates rapid wingbeats with long intervals of gliding flight on partly drooping wings. ☉: Throughout the year it utters various barking and cackling sounds; the young make soft piping sounds. ♋: In some regions the very similar Ptarmigan (*L. mutus*), so much alike that it is difficult to distinguish between the two.

Ecology ◆: Tundra and moors, mainly at lower elevations, in some places also above the forest line. ∞: It may be discovered by its voice and by flushing the bird while walking about, also when looking for the nest and fully-grown young.

Bionomy ↔: It is resident; individual birds occasionally fly longer distances away from the nesting grounds. In the non-breeding season it generally forms flocks. ◡: The nest is located in dense low undergrowth. The six to nine yellowish eggs with brown markings (42.5×30.8 mm) are laid in Apr.—June. It has one brood a year, nests solitarily, and ♀ incubates for 22 days. The young leave the nest on hatching, are guided about by both parents, fly when 12 days old, are fully grown at 33 days and fully independent after two months. ◖: Almost exclusively young heather shoots nipped off the plants, also buds and fruits of plants taken from the ground as well as branches; in summer also invertebrates.

Conservation Locally this is an important game bird; its numbers are gradually declining. It is necessary to provide rational management of the bird populations along with the regulation of hunting. Birds are also being reared artificially and released into the wild.

1

Black Grouse
Tetrao tetrix

Identification Appearance — size — behaviour — voice

∗: About the size of a domestic hen (♂ 55 cm, ♀ 40 cm), it has a robust body and small head. The adult ♂ (1) is black and dark brown, with a white wingbar, underwing and undertail, and a lyre-shaped tail. ♀ is patterned dark brown and rufous with pale undertail-coverts. Juv. birds resemble ♀ but are duller, and the feathers on the upperside have a pale central streak; ♂ juveniles are more reddish. ✦: It generally remains concealed on the ground but also flies up into trees and even perches on slender branches. It flies rapidly, sometimes even quite high up, alternating rapid wingbeats with intervals of gliding flight with wings spread. ⊙: During the courtship ♂♂ utter hissing and bubbling sounds that carry a long distance; ♀♀ with young chicks cluck softly. ♋: ♂ is unmistakable; ♀ resembles ♀ of the Capercaillie (p. 255) but the latter is larger and lacks the white band on the underside of the wings.

Ecology ◗: Large forests and their edges, woodland clearings, moors, and even alpine meadows. ∞: In spring (Mar.—May) at the courting grounds about sunrise, locate the birds by their calls. Otherwise try to find them by walking through suitable sites, in winter also by their tracks and signs.

Bionomy ↔: It is resident, occasionally wandering away from the nesting grounds. In spring it appears at communal courting grounds; in the non-breeding season it occurs in groups. ♺: The nest is located on the ground, well concealed in the undergrowth. The six to twelve brownish eggs with dark brown markings (50.0×36.4 mm) are laid in May—June. It has one brood a year, and ♀ incubates for 25 days. The young leave the nest on hatching, are guided about only by ♀; after ten days they fly about a little, and are fully independent at the age of three months. ◑: Various seeds and berries, mainly blueberries, cranberries, and in winter the nuts of birch trees, gathered on the ground as well as from trees. A major part of the diet of young birds consists of insects.

Conservation Locally this is still an important game bird but its numbers are declining rapidly. It is essential to protect its habitats (mainly moors), and in the case of declining populations to provide full protection.

1

Capercaillie
Tetrao urogallus

Identification Appearance — size — behaviour — voice
∗ : The largest European gallinaceous bird, ♂ being as large as a Turkey (85 cm, ♀ 60 cm). The adult ♂ (1) is black and brown, the ♀ dark yellowish-brown with dark markings. Juv. birds resemble ♀ but are duller and smaller.
✦ : It lives a secretive life in woodlands, mainly on the ground but also in trees, where it also roosts. It flies up noisily; its flight is quick and close above the ground, rapid wingbeats being interspersed with brief intervals of gliding. In spring the males perform their courtship displays in trees or on the ground. ⊙ : During the courtship performance ♂ makes striking sounds (a knocking sound — trill — popping sound — grinding sound); ♀ with young chicks clucks softly. ⚇ : ♂ is unmistakable; ♀ resembles ♀ of the Black Grouse (p. 254), which, however, is smaller, has a forked tail and a white band on the underside of the wings.
Ecology ◈ : Extensive coniferous woods with old stands, blueberry bushes, ant nests; it occurs as a relict species chiefly in mountains. ∞ : In spring (Mar.—May) before sunrise, it may be identified by its voice at the courting grounds; its calls, however, do not carry far and for that reason it is essential to observe the hunting rules of approaching shy birds. Otherwise it may be flushed by chance when walking through the terrain where it is likely to be found.
Bionomy ↔ : It is resident. In spring at the courting grounds the birds occur close together, occasionally in some numbers, otherwise it is a solitary bird. ⚭ : The nest is located on the ground, usually by a tree stump, at the foot of a tree, bush, etc. The five to nine pale yellow-brown eggs with brown markings (56.3×41.7 mm) are laid in Apr.—May. It has one brood a year, and ♀ incubates for 25 days. The young leave the nest on hatching, and are guided about only by ♀ ; from the 15th day they fly about, and are fully grown after three months. ◕ : From late autumn until May conifer needles and leaf buds of trees; in the remaining months also blueberries, cranberries, beechnuts, also a few insects. The young feed exclusively on insects at first, mainly ants, later increasing the quantities of berries. Food is gathered on the ground as well as on trees.
Conservation It is not numerous and is greatly declining in number. Locally it is an important game bird; relict populations are endangered mainly by changes in the environment. It is essential to provide full protection or to regulate hunting strictly. Birds are also being reared artificially and released into the wild.

1

Chukar
Alectoris chukar

Identification Appearance — size — behaviour — voice

✳: The size of the Grey Partridge (33 cm), it has a robust body and small head. Adults (1) are greyish-brown above with prominent markings on the head and throat, dark bands on the flanks, the tail edged reddish-brown, and have a red bill and legs; ♂ > ♀. Juv. birds are buff, lack dark markings around the whitish throat, have occasional dark stripes on the flanks and yellowish bill and legs. ✦: It leads a secretive life in thick grassy and shrubby undergrowth. When disturbed it flies rapidly close above the ground, alternating rapid wingbeats with intervals of gliding flight on spread wings. ☉: Quite often it utters sounds resembling those of the domestic hen — *chak-chak-chak-per-chak-cha-kar chakar*. ♋: In southern Europe the very similar Rock Partridge (*A. graeca*), in western and southern Europe the less similar Red-legged Partridge (*A. rufa* — 2).

Ecology ◆: Dry scrub and grassy areas. ∞: It may be identified by its voice; you may flush the birds when walking through the terrain where they are likely to be found.

Bionomy ↔: It is a resident bird that leads a solitary life but after the nesting period also occurs in small flocks. ☽: The nest is located on the ground amidst vegetation and often near boulders. The eight to fifteen yellowish eggs with brown markings (39.8×29.8 mm) are laid in Mar.—June. It has one, possibly two broods a year, and ♀ incubates for 23 days. The young leave the nest on hatching, are guided about by both parents, fly about after seven days, and are fully grown at the age of 50 days. ◉: Mostly plant seeds, less often also bits of plants and small invertebrates, gathered on the ground.

Conservation It is locally numerous, but generally is declining in numbers or has even completely disappeared. Locally it is still a game bird; its decline is apparently due to excessive hunting. Rational measures should be taken to regulate hunting, and where its numbers exhibit a permanent decline hunting should be prohibited altogether.

2

1

Grey Partridge
Perdix perdix

Identification Appearance — size — behaviour — voice

✳: It has a small (30 cm) thickset body and a small head. Adults are grey and brown. ♂ has a conspicuous rusty-brown horseshoe-shaped mark on the breast; ♀ (1) often lacks this mark, is darker above and less rusty, and the orange cheeks are smaller and duller. Juv. birds are yellow-brown without the rusty-brown and grey markings, particularly on the head. ✦: It generally walks or runs about on the ground. When disturbed it flies up close above the ground and only a short distance; the loud rapid fluttering of the wings is interspersed with brief intervals of gliding on spread wings. ☉: During the courtship period it utters its familiar, very loud call *chirr-ik chirr-ik.* ♋: It is unmistakable.

Ecology ◈: Open country, mainly fields with hedgerows, permanent grassy areas, fallow land, etc., in lowland and hilly country. ∞: In spring (Mar. — May) it may be identified by the calls of the courting males. The birds utter their calls in the morning and evening. Look for the nest by walking through the area; ♀ sits very tightly. In the non-breeding season observe flocks in open places; in winter take note of tracks and bird droppings.

Bionomy ↔: This is a resident bird that forms pairs in spring and after the breeding period occurs in families and small flocks. ∞: The nest is concealed on the ground in grass or under bushes. The ten to twenty yellow-brown eggs (35.0×26.5 mm) are laid in Feb. — June. It has one brood a year, and ♀ incubates for 24 days.

The young leave the nest on hatching, are guided about by both parents, fly about at the age of 15 days, and are fully grown at three months. ◑: Adults feed mainly on seeds and the green parts of plants; small invertebrates form only a supplement. In young birds the reverse is true. Food is gathered on the ground.

Conservation This is an important game bird, even though its numbers have exhibited a marked decline. This is apparently due to changes in the landscape and methods of farming. The birds are being reared artificially and released into the wild.

1

Common Quail
Coturnix coturnix

Identification Voice — appearance — habitat
∗: Europe's smallest gallinaceous bird (17 cm). It resembles a partridge in shape but ♂ is only about half the size. Adults are yellowish- or rusty-brown with barring and streaking; compared with ♂ (1), ♀ has less prominent dark markings on the head, the cheeks and throat are always pale, and there is no dark stripe on the throat. Juv. birds resemble ♀ but lack the dark streaks on the lower cheeks and the markings on the flanks are not longitudinal. ✦: It leads a secretive life on the ground in thick low undergrowth. It flies up only rarely; its flight is rapid and straight, with regular rapid wingbeats. During migration it often utters its call at night. ☉: Its call is the familiar loud and repeated *pwit-pwiwic*. ♋: Its call is unmistakable. It may be confused with young partridges. In southern Spain the sparsely distributed, similar Andalusian Hemipode (*Turnix sylvatica*); locally Japanese Quails (*C. japonica*) are released into the wild.
Ecology ◈: Open country with fields and meadows; during migration also elsewhere. ∞: It is very easily identified by its voice and the constant presence of the birds (watch out for non-breeding birds and birds on passage). Otherwise it may be spotted only by chance flushing of the bird or in fields when the nest is exposed by mowing.
Bionomy ↔: This is a migratory, solitary bird, but sometimes also forms loose groups. ♈: The nest is located on the ground in thick vegetation. The eight to thirteen pale yellow-brown eggs with large brown markings

(30.1×22.5 mm) are laid in May—Aug. It has one, sometimes two broods a year, nests solitarily, and ♀ incubates for 18 days. The young leave the nest on hatching, fly about from the 10th day, and are fully independent at 60 days. ◗: Plant seeds and insects gathered on the ground and on plants.
Conservation Locally it is hunted. Its numbers have declined sharply; in some places it now occurs irregularly or has completely disappeared. Its decline is apparently due to changes in the environment. Apart from regulating hunting, there are few realistic means of protection.

1

Pheasant
Phasianus colchicus

Identification Appearance — voice

✳: As large as a domestic hen (♂ 85 cm, ♀ 55 cm), it has a thickset body, small head and wedge-shaped tail. The adult ♂ (1) has a very long tail, dark green head with red cheeks and small feathered 'horns', and the remaining parts of the body a dark bronze. There is marked variation in its coloration as a result of cross-breeding with various imported forms; some birds have a white collar, others are entirely a very dark colour (morph *tenebrosus*). ♀ is yellow-brown with dark markings. Juv. birds resemble ♀ but are duller, with less prominent markings and a shorter tail. ✦: It stays mostly on the ground, runs well, and during its period of activity comes out of the undergrowth into open spaces. It flies only when flushed, close above the ground, and rapidly with noisy wing-beats. It roosts on trees. ☉: Its alarm note, a loud repeated *keerk-kok,* is well known. When courting, ♂ utters a loud *kreey,* followed by noisy fluttering of the wings. ♋: It is unmistakable.

Ecology ◈: Open country with small woods, fields, reedbeds, etc., mainly at low elevations. ∞: During the courtship period (Apr.—June) it is readily identified by its calls, otherwise observe the birds in the morning and evening at the edges of woods, by reedbeds, etc.; they may also be seen by walking through the area and flushing the birds.

Bionomy ↔: This is a resident bird and generally occurs in groups. ᴗ: The nest is located on the ground in thick vegetation. The eight to sixteen yellow-brown eggs (45.0×35.4 mm) are laid in Mar.—July. It has one brood a year, is polygamous, and ♀ incubates for 25 days. The young leave the nest on hatching, are guided about solely by ♀, fly about from the 12th day, and are fully independent after 75 days. ◖: Various seeds, berries and bits of grass, moss, small invertebrates and vertebrates. Food is gathered on the ground or in the lowest layer of vegetation.

Conservation This is an important game bird to which particular care is devoted by gamekeepers and whose hunting is generally regulated. It is reared artificially and the birds then released into the wild.

Common Crane
Grus grus

Identification Appearance — size — voice — behaviour

✳: Larger than a stork (115 cm, wingspan 230 cm), it has a long neck, bill and legs, broad straight wings with rounded, finger-like tips, and a short tail concealed by a tuft of feathers (elongated inner secondaries) when the bird is standing. Adults (1) are grey and black, with a white band on either side of the neck (3) and a red crown; ♂ = ♀. Juv. birds have a brown head and neck, as well as brown feathers on the upperside, which gradually change colour during the 2nd—4th years. ✦: It leads a secretive life in marsh vegetation; in flight it holds the neck outstretched. When migrating, it travels in flocks in line formations (2). The courtship antics include special dances with leaps into the air, bowing, and loud calls. ☉: Its call is a loud *ü krrr ü krrr...* intermingled now and then with loud trumpeting. ☺: In flight with its extended neck it resembles storks, but the latter fly in a different manner and differ in plumage colour. In southern and eastern Europe the similar Demoiselle Crane (*Anthropoides virgo*), with a black neck and white ear tufts behind the eyes (4).

Ecology ◈: Marsh vegetation; in the non-breeding season also fields and pastureland. ∞: At the nesting grounds it may be located by its call; look for the nest by walking through the area. Parents with young come out from the vegetation in the morning and evening to forage for food in the vicinity. In the non-breeding season it may be identified by its call and by chance observation.

Bionomy ↔: It is migratory; migrating birds follow specific routes to specifically delimited wintering grounds. ౿: The nest is a mound of plant material built in marshes. The two brownish eggs with dark markings (94.0×62.0 mm) are laid in Mar.—June. It has one brood a year, nests solitarily, and incubates for 30 days. The young leave the nest on hatching, are guided about by both parents, sometimes separately, and are fully fledged at 70 days. ◑: Primarily the green parts of plants, seeds and fruits, some small animal life. Food is gathered on the ground, from plants and in shallow water.

Conservation It is disappearing in places. It should be provided with full protection and freedom from disturbance at the nesting sites. Preservation of the nesting grounds is also essential.

2

3   4

1

Stone-curlew
Burhinus oedicnemus

Identification Voice — habitat — appearance
∗: The size of a hen pheasant (42 cm) and with a slender body, large head, strikingly large eyes, and relatively long legs. Adults (1) are pale brown with dark markings above, paler and streaked below, and have a prominent broad white band on the wings; ♂ = ♀. Juv. birds have fewer markings and the greater wing-coverts are black in the centre and white at the tips. ✦: It is shy and leads a very secretive life. It runs about on the ground, alternating rapid running with stops when it strikes a rigid pose. It generally flies only when disturbed, close above the ground, with leisurely wingbeats. It is active mainly at night. ☉: During courtship it utters a loud hoarse *khrueei*, often repeatedly, at relatively frequent intervals. ♋: It is unmistakable; its voice is slightly reminiscent of the Curlew's.

Ecology ◈: Always open tracts of fallow land with sparse herbaceous vegetation or with small shrubs and trees, mainly on chalky, sandy or gravelly soils, pastureland, fields, woodland clearings. ∞: It may be recognised by the loud calls at the nesting grounds (Apr.—June), mainly at night. You may frequently flush a bird when walking through the terrain where it is likely to be found. The nest may be pinpointed by observing the adult birds. In the non-breeding season the Stone-curlew may be encountered only by chance.

Bionomy ◈: It is mostly migratory and is found at the nesting grounds in Apr.—Oct. ♆: The nest is a depression in the ground sparsely lined with material from the vicinity — bits of dry plants or stones. The two sandy-yellow brown-patterned eggs (53.5×38.5 mm) are laid in Apr.—July. It has one brood a year, nests solitarily, and incubates for 26 days. The young are cared for by both parents, leave the nest on hatching and fledge at the age of 40 days. ◖: Mainly terrestrial snails, insects and worms, very occasionally small vertebrates, gathered and hunted on the ground or on low plants.

Conservation This is an endangered species. Preserving suitable habitats is vital.

Identification Appearance — size — behaviour — habitat

✳: This is a robust bird the size of a domesticated Turkey (♂ 100 cm, ♀ 80 cm, wingspan 2—2.5 m). It has a large, thickset body (3), small head, and rather long neck. The adult ♂ (1) has a grey head with feathery moustache; the head turns white and the moustache becomes longer with increasing age. ♀ is smaller (2) with reddish-brown head, and lacks the moustache. Juv. birds resemble ♀ in appearance and size; from the first spring ♂ differs in size. ✦: In the non-breeding season the birds form segregated flocks comprising only the one sex or the other. The bustard is a shy bird, walking slowly with body held upright and flying only when disturbed, with leisurely wingbeats. The courtship display is very distinctive. It begins early in the morning or late afternoon. The cock struts about with tail laid on his back, slightly drooping wings and neck slightly inclined backward; then he inflates his throat pouch, lays his neck on his back, lowers his wings and turns them inside out so that he looks like a white fluffy ball. Only rarely do the males engage in combat. ☉: ♂ makes a soft hissing or barking sound. ♋: It is unmistakable. In southern Europe the sparsely distributed Little Bustard (*Tetrax tetrax* — 4).

Ecology ◀▶: Extensive meadows and fields, particularly ones with clover, young cereals and forage grasses, rape, very occasionally sugar beet and potato fields. ∞: At the courting grounds during the courtship period (Mar.—June), it may be observed with care from a distance in the morning and evening. The nest may be discovered by chance, mainly in the course of fieldwork. In the non-breeding season try to locate the birds by patient observation in suitable places.

Bionomy ↔: This is a resident bird, leaving its territory only in severe winters. ༀ: The nest is a shallow depression on the ground in herbaceous vegetation. The two olive brownish-green eggs with darker markings (79.5×56.9 mm) are laid in Apr.—May (Aug.). It has one brood a year, nests solitarily, and ♀ incubates for 24 days.

The young leave the nest on hatching, are guided about only by ♀, and are capable of flight after 30 days. ◕: Primarily plant food, mainly green plant parts, less often seeds. Animal food consists mainly of insects. The bird obtains its food on the ground or by nipping it off; from under snow by digging with its bill.

Conservation An endangered species. It occurs only in a few areas and in relatively small numbers. Birds are being reared artificially and then re-introduced into the wild. It is essential to preserve their environment and perhaps make some changes in the landscape, such as laying out small fields with rape.

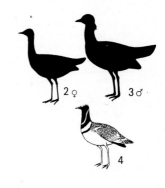

1

Black-bellied Sandgrouse
Pterocles orientalis

Identification Appearance — behaviour — voice
∗: As large as a dove (34 cm), it has a small head, short bill, plump body merging into a wedged tail, and extremely short legs. The wings are long, pointed, and arc-shaped in flight (2); on the underside the greyish-white coverts contrast strongly with the dark flight feathers. Adults are pale grey-brown with a black belly: ♂ (1) has the top of the head grey, the chin and sides of the head rusty-brown, and the crop grey; ♀ has the top of the head and crop brown with dark markings, and the chin and sides of the head yellow-brown. Juv. birds resemble ♀; their head and breast are dotted with black. ✦: This is a shy bird that stays mainly on the ground, flying in large numbers to water. Its flight is rapid, with regular wing-beats. ☉: Its call is a far-carrying, bubbling *charr-charr-rur*, repeated two or three times in succession and uttered mainly in flight. ♋: In southern Europe the very similar, sparsely distributed Pin-tailed Sandgrouse (*P. alchata*); on rare occasions the Pallas's Sandgrouse (*Syrrhaptes paradoxus*) of Asia makes invasional visits to Europe.
Ecology ◈: Dry flat regions with sparse herbaceous vegetation, such as the dry beds of salt lakes, but also stubble-land, pastureland, more frequently at higher elevations. ∞: The presence of the birds may be determined by observation and by searching through suitable sites, by their calls, and by their flights from one site to another.
Bionomy ↔: This is a resident bird occurring in

small groups in the non-breeding season. ༡: The nest is a hollow on the ground sparsely lined with dry stems. The two to three yellowish, brown-patterned eggs (47.5×32.4 mm) are laid in Apr.—July. It has one, possibly two broods a year, nests solitarily, and incubates for 25 days. The young leave the nest on hatching and are tended by both parents. It is not known how long they take to fledge. ◐: Seeds of various herbs gathered on the ground.
Conservation This is an endangered species and should be provided with full protection, including preservation of its nesting grounds.

2

1

Rock Dove
Columba livia

Identification Appearance — behaviour — voice
✳: The size of a medium-large variety of domestic pigeon (33 cm). It looks like a grey city pigeon with two dark wingbars, a white rump and dark-tipped tail (1). ♀ is duller than ♂, and the neck is less glossy; juv. birds are duller still, with a minimum of sheen on the neck, and are tinged brown. ✦: It perches on cliffs, and walks about on the ground; the courtship display of ♂ includes cooing sounds and posturing. It flies rapidly and expertly, flocks flying in irregular formations. ☉: The familiar cooing note may be heard throughout the year. ♋: Very similar are some varieties of domestic pigeons or escaped pigeons, among flocks of which one will generally find individuals with marked colour deviations. Wild pigeons (Wood Pigeons and Stock Doves) never have the white rump; the Stock Dove has incomplete wingbars, and the Wood Pigeon has a white stripe on the wing.

Ecology ◈: Cliffs, mainly on the sea coast and along rivers; it flies to open spaces for food. City populations generally stay around buildings, less often on cliffs. ∞: It may be found in large numbers throughout the year at the nesting grounds and in their vicinity; the nests are easily located by the behaviour of the birds.

Bionomy ↔: This is a resident bird, generally nesting in colonies and flying in flocks. ω: The nests are on cliff ledges and in semi-cavities, those of city populations on buildings and in attics; they are simple structures and gradually strengthened by the excrement of the young nestlings. The two white eggs (39.1×29.1 mm) are laid all year round. It has as many as five (or more?) broods and incubates for 18 days. The young are tended by both parents and fledge at the age of 36 days. ◐: Various seeds; city populations also feed on refuse, gathered on the ground.

Conservation This is the ancestor of the domestic pigeon. City populations have a damaging effect on the city environment. Their excrement destroys the surfaces of buildings, and the doves themselves are host to dangerous mites and carriers of diseases caused by salmonella.

1

Stock Dove
Columba oenas

Identification Voice — habitat — appearance — behaviour
∗: Slightly larger than the Collared Dove (33 cm), with a thicker body and short tail. Adults (1) are dark grey-brown with incomplete black wingbars; ♂ = ♀. Juv. birds are duller, browner, and lack the green sheen on the neck.
✦: It leads a fairly secretive life, perches on trees, walks about on the ground, and flies rapidly and expertly. ☉: At the nesting grounds it often utters a short *hoo-oo*. ☏: In woods it may be confused with the Wood Pigeon (p. 267), which, however, is larger, and has a white wing patch, a white patch on either side of the neck and a different voice. Flocks of domestic and city pigeons may be recognised by the fact that they usually include quite differently coloured individuals and that grey birds have a white rump.
Ecology ◈: Old broad-leaved forests, mainly beechwoods, farmland and woodland edge. In the non-breeding season it occurs in open countryside with fields. ∞: At the nesting grounds (Jan.—Aug.) it may be heard the whole day long. In the non-breeding season it may be observed in fields, either by itself or with other pigeons.
Bionomy ↔: It is partly migratory and is found at the nesting grounds in Jan.—Sept. In the non-breeding season it forms small flocks, but single individuals may join flocks of other pigeons. ᴗ: The nest is located in tree cavities and other holes from 1.3 to 15 m above the ground. The two white eggs (38.0×28.6 mm) are laid in Mar.—Sept. It has one to four

broods a year, nests solitarily, and incubates for 17 days. The young are cared for by both parents and fledge at the age of 30 days. ●: Plant seeds and flower buds, gathered on the ground.
Conservation It is a declining species, even though still locally hunted. Protection consists of preserving the nesting sites and actively helping by putting out larger man-made nestboxes.

1

Wood Pigeon
Columba palumbus

Identification Voice — appearance — behaviour
∗: The largest European pigeon (40 cm), about the size of large varieties of domestic pigeons. Adults (1) are grey, with a characteristic white patch on either side of the neck and a white bar on each wing; this is evident mainly in flight, as is the long tail. ♂ = ♀. Juv. birds are duller with less prominent markings, and usually lack the white patch on the neck. ✦: It perches on trees, walks about on the ground, and flies rapidly. When it takes to the air its wings make a loud clapping sound. Flocks fly in irregular formations. ☉: Its call is a hoarse, cooing *ru-ku-koo, ruk-ru-ku-koo.* ∞: It is unmistakable.
Ecology ◈: Woodlands from lowland elevations to the upper forest limit, including small woods and city parks; in the non-breeding season also open countryside with fields. ∞: At the nesting grounds it may be recognised by its regular flights from one spot to another and by its voice. When looking for the nest inspect trees; from below one can often see the sitting birds through the bottom of the nest. Outside the breeding season it is most likely to be encountered in fields.
Bionomy ↔: It is partly migratory, wintering in huge numbers in some areas. It is found at the nesting grounds in Mar.—Oct. ☽: The nest is located on a branch in the top of a tree or in a hedgerow, etc.; it is a small, very flimsy structure of twigs. The two white eggs (40.5 ×29.4 mm) are laid in Mar.—July. It has one to three broods a year, nests solitarily, and incubates for 17 days. The young are cared for by

both parents, 29 days in the nest and a further seven days outside the nest. ◐: Mostly vegetable matter — various seed, often cereal grains, leaves, buds and flowers, gathered on the ground.
Conservation This is an important game bird. Where it occurs in large numbers it may cause local damage to sown crops (peas, cereals, etc.). No specific protective measures are necessary.

267

1

Collared Dove
Streptopelia decaocto

Identification Appearance — voice — behaviour

✳: Smaller than a Wood Pigeon (28 cm), it has a relatively long tail and around the neck a dark collar broken at the front. Adults (1) are pale grey-brown with a narrow neck-band and with a broad white terminal band on the undertail. ♂ = ♀. Juv. birds are duller and lack the dark neck-band. ✦: It perches on trees and walks about on the ground. Its flight is rapid, with regular wingbeats and in a straight line; it generally flies close above the ground in pairs or irregular groups. In winter the birds converge in large numbers to roost together on the same tree. ☉: Often heard, virtually throughout the year, is its loud, deep call, *hu-hoo-hu, hu-hoo-hu.* Also a loud, harsh mewing call, *krreeur.* ☎: It is unmistakable.

Ecology ◈: Built-up areas and their environs, also parks and farmland, from lowland to submontane elevations. ∞: Throughout the year it may be identified by its voice; in built-up areas it is quite conspicuous and not at all shy. The nest, including the sitting birds, may be located easily by looking from the ground.

Bionomy ↔: In general it is a resident bird. In the non-breeding season it usually occurs in pairs or groups. ᴗ: The nest, a small (about 17 cm across), flimsy structure of twigs, is located on the branch of a tree, less often on a building. The two white eggs (30.3×23.4 mm) are laid in Mar.—Oct., in some areas throughout the year. It has as many as six broods a year, and incubates for 16 days. The young are cared for by both parents, 17 days in the nest and

a further seven days outside the nest. ◐: Various seeds; in built-up areas also refuse gathered on the ground.

Conservation It spread from the Balkan Peninsula throughout most of Europe in 1930—1960 and is still expanding its range. Locally it is a game bird. In built-up areas it is sometimes a nuisance because it soils the environment. It does not require any protection.

1

Turtle Dove
Streptopelia turtur

Identification Voice — appearance — size — behaviour

∗: Smaller (27 cm) and less stocky than the Collared Dove. Adults (1) are grey-brown above, pale below, and have a diagonally striped black-and-white patch on either side of the neck; ♂ = ♀. Juv. birds are duller and less contrastingly coloured; the crown is brown, and they lack the striped patch on the neck. ✦: It perches on trees, often on telegraph wires, and walks about on the ground. Its flight is rapid, relatively close to the ground, with regular beats of the backward curved wings; when it flies up, its wings make a clapping sound. ☉: In the nesting period a repeated purring call, *turr-tur-tur* . . . ♋: Very occasionally Europe is visited from Asia by the similar but larger Rufous Turtle Dove (*S. orientalis*), and from Africa and Asia Minor by the smaller Palm Dove (*S. senegalensis*).

Ecology ◈: Farmland from lowland to hilly country with small fields, hedgerows; also parks, gardens, etc. ∞: During the nesting period (Apr.—June) its call may be heard the whole day long. The nest may be located easily by searching thickets and hedgerows; often you may flush a sitting bird. In the non-breeding season it may easily be observed in open countryside in fields.

Bionomy ↔: It is migratory and generally occurs in groups or large flocks. It is found at the nesting grounds in Apr.—Sept. ᴗ: The nest is a small, flimsy structure of twigs which can often be seen through from below; it is placed in bushes or dense small trees, generally not very high up. The two white eggs (30.6×22.6 mm) are laid in Apr.—Aug. It has one to three broods a year, nests solitarily, and incubates for 14 days. The young are cared for by both parents, 20 days in the nest and several more outside the nest. ◑: Seeds of various plants, gathered on the ground.

Conservation It is plentiful in some areas but is declining in others. Its nesting grounds are endangered by the cutting down of hedgerows, which should be prevented.

1

Common Cuckoo
Cuculus canorus

Identification Voice — appearance — behaviour
＊: The size of the Collared Dove (33 cm), it has a slender body, small head, rather long pointed wings and very long tail. Adults (2) are generally grey with fine dark barring below; some ♀♀ have the upperparts brownish and heavily barred and the breast a pale brownish hue, while a small number of birds are reddish-brown instead of grey. Juv. birds (1) always have a white patch on the nape and heavy dark barring on the throat and breast. ✦: It perches on elevated places, e.g. trees, telegraph wires, and flies close above the ground with slow wingbeats, slightly swaying from side to side. ☉: In the nesting period it frequently utters its characteristic cuckoo call; ♀ gives a loud bubbling, laughing *bibibi...* ☜: Europe is occasionally visited by the very similar Oriental Cuckoo (*C. saturatus*) from Asia.
Ecology ◆: Woodlands from lowland elevations to the dwarf pine belt, also cultivated countryside, often by reedbeds. ∞: In the breeding period (Apr.—June) it may be recognised by its far-carrying call, given the whole day long, occasionally even at night; otherwise it may be sighted by chance as it flies from one spot to another. Look for the eggs by examining the nest of its most common hosts in the given area; sometimes the behaviour of ♀ prior to laying eggs attracts one's attention.
Bionomy ↔: It is migratory and is found at the breeding grounds in Apr.—Sept. It occurs singly throughout the year. ৬: The eggs are laid in Apr.—July in the nests of small birds;

the host species differ depending on the given district. The coloration of the eggs resembles that of the host species, but their size is a uniform 22.2×16.7 mm. The incubation period is ˙12 days. The young remain in the nest 17 days and are cared for a further long period outside the nest. ◖: Mainly caterpillars, including hairy (poisonous) ones, as well as adult insects, spiders and worms. Food is gathered on leaves, branches, and occasionally on the ground.
Conservation It is not very numerous, but no special protective measures are necessary.

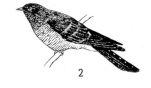

2

1

European Nightjar
Caprimulgus europaeus

Identification Voice — appearance — behaviour

✳: Slightly larger than a Blackbird (27 cm), it has a slender body, large head, short broad bill, large eyes and long, slender, pointed wings that are crescent-shaped in flight. The adult ♂ (1) is patterned dark brown, with white patches on the wings and tail; in ♀ the patches on the wings and tail are yellow-brown or absent. Juv. birds resemble ♀ but are paler, less heavily patterned, and always lack the white patches on the wings and tail. ✦: It is active at night; during the day it rests pressed close to the ground or perched lengthwise on a branch. It flies close above the ground and very rapidly, with abrupt turns in pursuit of insects. ☉: During the nesting period it often gives a muffled, far-carrying, monotonous churring, *rrrrrrrr*. ♋: In southwestern Europe the sibling species the Red-necked Nightjar (*C. ruficollis*).

Ecology ◈: Woodlands and heaths, mainly in drier, warmer districts. In the non-breeding season it may also be found in open countryside. ∞: During the nesting period (Apr.—June) it may be recognised mainly at night by its churring song, otherwise it may be seen only when flushed by chance; look for the nest by walking through suitable sites and flushing a sitting bird.

Bionomy ↔: It is migratory and is found at the nesting grounds in Apr.—Sept., where it occurs singly. ♥: The nest is a shallow depression in the ground, often without a lining. The two white eggs (31.5×22.2 mm) are laid in May—July. It has one to two broods a year, nests solitarily, and incubates for 18 days. The young are cared for by both parents, 16 days in the nest and a further 16 days outside the nest. ◐: Nocturnal insects captured mainly on the wing. It snatches at the insect with its bill and swallows it whole.

Conservation This is a declining species; reasons for its disappearance and methods of protection are unknown. Preservation of its habitats is essential.

1

Common Swift
Apus apus

Identification Voice — appearance — behaviour

✳: Smaller than a Blackbird (16 cm) and with a slender, cigar-shaped body, small head, short tail, and long, slender, pointed wings that are crescent-shaped in flight (2). Adults (1) are dark blackish-brown with a pale patch on the chin; ♂ = ♀. Juv. birds have paler feather tips, a larger patch on the chin, and browner wing feathers and tail. ✦: It rests only beside the nest, where it hangs upright, otherwise it is constantly on the wing, often at great heights. Its flight is speedy, with rapid wingbeats interrupted by brief intervals of gliding flight. It takes to the air from a suspended position. ☉: Its call is a shrill piercing screech, *sreeezeee*, uttered very frequently. ♋: It differs from birds of the swallow family in its dark coloration and manner of flight.

Ecology ◈: Mainly built-up areas, also cliffs, here and there woods, from lowland to subalpine elevations. It captures its food on the wing, often far from its nesting grounds and frequently close above water. ∞: At the nesting grounds it reveals its presence by its calls and its flights from one spot to another throughout the day; look for the nest by examining suitable places. In the non-breeding season birds can be observed flying from one spot to another.

Bionomy ↔: It is migratory and is found at the nesting grounds in Apr.—Aug. ☙: The nest is in a hollow under the eaves and in the walls of houses, in rock clefts and very occasionally in trees. The two to three white eggs (24.8×16.4 mm) are laid in May—July. It has one brood a year, nests mostly in colonies, and incubates for 20 days. The young are cared for by both parents, remaining in the nest for 42 days. ◐: Solely small flying arthropods, caught on the wing by flying with the bill wide open. As a rule these are small species of insects and spiders (less than 8 mm long), but it is capable of capturing even large dragonflies, wasps and bees.

Conservation This is an important synanthropic species. It requires no special protection, but nesting may be encouraged by making hollows on buildings or by putting out man-made nest-boxes.

2

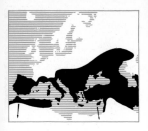

1

European Bee-eater
Merops apiaster

Identification Voice — appearance — behaviour

✳: As large as a Blackbird (28 cm) and with a slender body, rather long, slightly down-curved beak, and long tail with elongated pointed central feathers (2). The adult ♂ (1) is brilliantly coloured blue-green, yellow and chestnut-brown; ♀ has slightly more green on the upperparts and in the brown wing-patch. Juv. birds are duller and their central tail feathers are short. ✦: It perches on elevated places, e. g. on trees, telephone poles and wires. On the wing it often glides, flies in circles and wheels about. ☉: It often utters a repeated liquid twittering, *kruup kruup*. ☂: In flight the silhouette of the wings resembles the Starling's (p. 228). Very occasionally encountered in Europe is the very similar Blue-cheeked Bee-eater (*M. superciliosus*) from north Africa and Asia.

Ecology ◈: Open steppe-like country from lowland to hilly districts. ∞: During the nesting period it may be observed quite frequently in flight or on elevated places and may also be recognised by its voice. Look for the nest in the steep banks of natural watercourses, in the steep sides of ravines, in roadside banks (sometimes even on quite short roads). In the non-breeding season it may be encountered only by chance observation.

Bionomy ↔: It is migratory and is found at the nesting grounds in May—Aug. It occurs in groups. ⚭: It generally nests in colonies in burrows dug in sand or mud banks; the bottom edge of the entrance to the burrow bears characteristic markings made by the bird's feet. The

five to seven white eggs (25.7×21.6 mm) are laid in May—July. It has one brood a year and incubates for 20 days. The young are cared for by both parents, 25 days in the nest and several more outside the nest. ◐: Almost exclusively hymenopteran insects, which the bird catches on the wing.

Conservation It is locally numerous. It is necessary to protect the nesting grounds. Occasionally it may cause damage to bees raised in the vicinity of its nesting grounds.

2

Identification Voice — appearance — habitat — behaviour

✳: Somewhat stouter than a sparrow (16 cm), it has a large head, long, straight, stout bill, short body, tail and legs, and short pointed wings (4). Adults (1) are a glossy blue-green, chestnut-brown and white; the glossy blue back is well visible in flight. The legs are coral-red with black claws. ♂ = ♀, but they differ in the coloration of the bill: in males it is black, in females completely reddish or reddish only at the base. Juv. birds are less glossy, more green, and their breast feathers are edged dark grey. ✦: It perches on branches overhanging water (2), from where it plunges headlong into the water in pursuit of prey (5). It flies rapidly and in a straight line close above the water, occasionally hovering in one spot (3). ☉: In flight it often utters a long shrill whistling note. ⚅: It is unmistakable.

Ecology ◈: Lakes and watercourses, mainly clear slow-flowing streams and rivers with steep banks, from lowland to submontane elevations. When flying from one place to another it may also be encountered on other bodies of water and even away from water. In winter it stays by fast-flowing ice-free sections of watercourses, but also occurs on the sea coast. ∞: Near water it may be located by its voice, by observing flying birds or by examining thickets by the water's surface with binoculars. When looking for the nest, examine possible sites with binoculars.

Bionomy ↔: It is partly migratory and leads a solitary life throughout the year. ෴: The nest is in a burrow excavated by the birds in vertical mud banks (6); the same nesting burrow is often used over and over again. The five to seven white eggs (22.9×18.8 mm) are laid in Apr.—July. It has one to three broods a year, nests solitarily, and incubates for 20 days. The young are cared for by both parents. They remain in the nest for 25 days and several days later fend for themselves. ◗: The birds are tied to water for their food, hunting mainly small fish, also tadpoles and frogs, crustaceans, mol-luscs, aquatic insects and their larvae, occasionally even bits of plants.

Conservation It is not numerous, its numbers exhibiting frequent fluctuations, decreasing markedly particularly after severe winters. It may cause damage at fish farms. It is necessary to protect suitable nesting sites; it will also occupy man-made burrows.

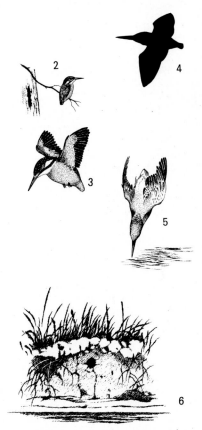

1

European Roller
Coracias garrulus

Identification Appearance — size — behaviour — voice
∗: About the size of the Collared Dove (30 cm) but more robust. Characteristic is the large head with a stout, straight bill. The adults (1) are glossy pale green-blue combined with chestnut and black; ♂ = ♀. Juv. birds are paler and duller, with a brownish breast. ✦: It perches upright on trees, telephone poles and wires, flying to the ground in pursuit of prey. In spring it performs courtship displays at the nesting grounds, flying upward, rolling and wheeling in the air and plummeting to the ground to the accompaniment of loud cries. ☉: It often utters a loud *rrak rrak*. . . . ; young birds in the nest utter loud plaintive cries. ♋: It is unmistakable.
Ecology ◈: Open steppe-like country in lowland and hilly districts. ∞: Its presence at the nesting grounds is revealed mainly by its courtship flights. The nest can be located by observing the birds flying from one spot to another and by examining suitable sites; when the young are being fed (from June), by their far-carrying cries coming from the nesting holes. In the non-breeding season it may be encountered by chance observation.
Bionomy ↔: It is migratory and is found at the nesting grounds in Apr.—Sept. In the non-breeding season it leads a solitary life. ♆: It nests in tree holes (e.g. those made by the Black Woodpecker), less often in ground burrows or in holes in buildings. The three to five white eggs (36.4×29.1 mm) are laid in May—June. It has one brood a year, nests solitarily as well as

in colonies, and incubates for 18 days. The young are cared for by both parents, 27 days in the nest and a further 22 days outside the nest. ◐: Larger insects and small vertebrates. It keeps a lookout for prey from an elevated spot, from where it plunges to the ground to catch it.
Conservation Its numbers are declining steeply, and in some places it has disappeared altogether. The reasons for its decline and methods of protection are not known as yet. Man-made nestboxes may be used as a replacement for tree holes.

1

Hoopoe
Upupa epops

Identification Appearance — voice
✳: The size of the Collared Dove (27 cm), it has a small head, long, slender, downcurved bill, erectile feathered crest, short legs, rather long tail and very broad, rounded wings (2). Adults (1) are pale reddish-brown with black and white barred wings and tail, the pattern being particularly conspicuous in flight. ♂ = ♀; in pairs of birds, some ♀ ♀ may be distinguished by the white markings on the throat and a browner breast. Juv. birds are duller, with the white markings on the wings tinted yellow and a shorter, straighter bill. ✦: It walks about on the ground and flies close above the ground, its flight slightly resembling a bat's. ☉: It quite often utters a low, repeated muffled *poopoopoo*. ♋: It is unmistakable.
Ecology ◈: Mainly parkland and pastureland, light woods, as well as open country with scattered greenery, in lowland and hilly districts. ∞: At the nesting grounds it is instantly and diagnostically recognised by its voice; birds may be observed in open spaces or when flying from one spot to another. Pinpoint the nest by the flights of the birds, mainly when feeding their young, and by examining suitable holes. In the non-breeding season it may be encountered by chance.
Bionomy ↔: It is migratory and is found at the nesting grounds in Apr.—Sept. It leads a solitary life. ꙍ: The nest is in a tree hole not very high up, less often in a ground burrow or in a hole in a building. The five to eight white eggs (26.0×17.9 mm) are laid in Apr.—June. It has one brood a year, nests solitarily, and ♀ in-

cubates for 16 days and is fed by ♂. The young are tended by both parents, 26 days in the nest and several more outside the nest. ◖: Larger insects, occasionally also small vertebrates, captured on the ground.
Conservation Its numbers are on the decline, and in some places it has disappeared altogether. We do not know the reasons for its disappearance nor methods of protecting it. Nesting may be promoted by providing man-made holes.

2

1

Wryneck
Jynx torquilla

Identification Voice — appearance — behaviour

∗: The size of a sparrow (16 cm), it has a slender body, rather long neck, and wedge-shaped head terminating in a straight stout bill. Adults (1) are inconspicuous grey-brown with delicate dark mottling and barring; ♂ = ♀ = juv. ✦: It is very unobtrusive and is rarely seen. It perches on the branches of trees, both crosswise and lengthwise, and hops about on the ground with its tail cocked. It flies in a straight line with regular wingbeats, but only infrequently takes to the air. ☉: It often utters its striking, loud and long-repeated *kveekveekvee...*; young birds in the nest make a hissing sound when disturbed. ☜: It is unmistakable.

Ecology ◁▷: Parkland from lowland to mountain elevations with hollow trees, also gardens and parks. ∞: At the nesting grounds after its arrival there (Mar.—June), it may be recognised by its voice; look for the nest in holes in the area where it is continually present. Otherwise it may be encountered only by chance observation.

Bionomy ↔: It is migratory. It occurs singly and is found at the nesting grounds in Mar.—Sept. ◡: It nests in tree holes, in nestboxes, very occasionally also in ground holes, on buildings, etc. The seven to eleven white eggs (20.7×15.5 mm) are laid in Apr.—July. It has one to two (three) broods a year, nests solitarily, and incubates for 12 days. The young are cared for by both parents, 20 days in the nest and a further ten days outside the nest. ◖: Mainly ants and their pupae, which it scrapes out and collects from nests in trees as well as on the ground; also beetles, spiders etc. Occasionally it will also eat elderberries.

Conservation This is a declining species. We do not know the reasons for its decline nor of any realistic means of protection. The lack of natural cavities may be countered by putting out nestboxes.

1

Green Woodpecker
Picus viridis

Identification Voice — appearance — behaviour
✳: As large as a Jackdaw (30 cm). The large head with a stout straight bill, the rather short wedge-shaped tail and the broad rounded wings are characteristic. Adults are green with a red crown; ♂ (1) has a red moustache mark edged with black, while that of ♀ is all black (2). Juv. birds are duller, with darker underparts barred with black and paler back spotted with white or yellow; these characteristics, however, are evident only until Nov. of the year they hatch.
✦: It climbs on the trunks of trees, often also on buildings, and hops about on the ground, where it breaks up anthills. It flies close above the ground in a strikingly undulating flight (4), interspersing loud wingbeats with intervals of downward gliding flight with wings pressed close to the body. ☉: It often utters a very loud, striking *klukluklu*, resembling laughter. ♋: The Grey-headed Woodpecker (*P. canus*), which has a simpler pattern on the head (3).
Ecology ◈: Woods, mainly broad-leaved ones from lowland to mountain elevations, commons and parkland vegetation, as well as city gardens. ∞: At the nesting grounds it may be located by its calls in Feb.—June, otherwise by observing birds climbing trees and flying from one spot to another. The nest may be discovered by observing the birds, done best when they are excavating a hole, or by checking out holes in areas where they are continually present.
Bionomy ↔: This is a resident and solitary bird. ♡: It nests in tree holes excavated individually

each year. The five to seven white eggs (31.2×23.3 mm) are laid in Apr.—June. It has one brood a year, nests solitarily, and incubates for 16 days. The young are cared for by both parents, 27 days in the nest and a further 21 days outside the nest. ◕: Mainly ants, their larvae and pupae (species that make their nest in the ground or build mounds); in the summer months, to a small extent also various fruits and seeds (e.g. acorns, rowanberries). In the spring months it may peck around a tree trunk down to the inner bark, and lick the oozing drops of sap.
Conservation It is declining in places, but no special protective measures are necessary.

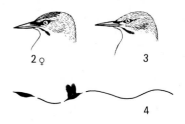

2 ♀

3

4

1

Black Woodpecker
Dryocopus martius

Identification Voice — appearance — behaviour

✳: The largest European woodpecker (50 cm), almost as large as a crow but more slender, with a smaller head topped by a small crest, a stout, straight bill and a narrow neck. Adults are black; ♂ (1, 2) has a red crown, ♀ only a red patch on the nape (3). Juv. birds are duller, with a pale chin and a smaller red expanse on the head or with no red at all. ✦: It climbs on the trunks of trees, vigorously nodding its head; it flies at a low height, leisurely and straight or in shallow undulations. ☉: It often utters a loud *rü rü rü* and a plaintive long-drawn-out *klieh*. In spring it drums vigorously on tree trunks, with a rhythm slower than that of spotted woodpeckers. Young birds in the nest make piping cries. ☻: It is unmistakable.

Ecology ◈: Large older woods from lowland to mountain elevations. ∞: At the nesting grounds it may be identified by its voice and behaviour; the nest may be pinpointed by observing the flights of adult birds, mainly when feeding the young, which utter loud cries, or by checking out holes in old trees in areas where the birds are continually present. In the non-breeding season its presence may be determined by traces of drilling on tree trunks or by chance observations.

Bionomy ↔: It is a resident and solitary bird. ♲: It nests in holes excavated anew each year. The three to five white eggs (34.4×25.4 mm) are laid in Apr.—May. It has one brood a year, nests solitarily, and incubates for 12 days. The young are cared for by both parents, 26 days in the nest and several more outside the nest. ☻: It excavates bark and wood insects, mainly beetles and ants, from tree trunks. Vegetable matter forms a negligible part of its diet, mainly pine seeds, blueberries and elderberries, also sap oozing from trees ringed by other woodpeckers.

Conservation It is not numerous. Damage ascribed to it in forests has not been objectively substantiated. No special protective measures are necessary.

2 ♂   3 ♀

280

1

Great Spotted Woodpecker
Dendrocopos major

Identification Voice — appearance — behaviour

✳: As large as a thrush (23 cm), it has a large head, straight stout bill and characteristic markings (2). Adults are red, black and white; ♂ (1) has a red band on the nape, while ♀ has a black nape. Juv. birds have the entire crown dingy red. ✦: It climbs trees, sometimes hanging from cones. It flies low in undulating flight, the sound of the wingbeats carrying a long distance. ☉: It utters its loud abrupt *chik chik* fairly often. In spring it often drums on trees, rapidly and at length. The young birds in the nest utter loud plaintive cries. ♋: The very similar Syrian Woodpecker (*D. syriacus* — 3), which differs in having a solid white band on the sides of the head and neck; in northern Europe and the mountains of southern and central Europe the White-backed Woodpecker (*D. leucotos* — 4), which has more white in its plumage, and the Three-toed Woodpecker (*Picoides tridactylus* — 5), which has no red in the plumage.

Ecology ◈: All types of woods, larger parks and gardens; in the non-breeding season also areas with scattered trees. ∞: At the nesting grounds it may be identified by its call, in spring also by the drumming and behaviour of the birds; when looking for the nest examine holes in places where the birds are constantly present. In the non-breeding season the birds may be located by their calls, their drumming on trees, and by traces of their activity (feeding places, emptied cones, etc.).

Bionomy ↔: It is mostly a resident bird that leads a solitary life. ♥: The nest is in a tree hole excavated by the bird or else a Black Woodpecker's or Middle Spotted Woodpecker's hole. It also uses the previous year's holes. The five to six white eggs (26.4×19.8 mm) are laid in Apr.—June. It has one brood a year, nests solitarily, and incubates for 12 days. The young are cared for by both parents, 25 days in the nest and a further 14 days outside the nest. ◐: Insects and their larvae, various fruits and seeds. It extracts insects from bark as well as wood, and gathers crawling insects on tree trunks and on the ground.

Conservation It is plentiful. No special protective measures are necessary.

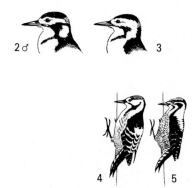

2♂   3

4   5

281

1

Middle
Spotted Woodpecker
Dendrocopos medius

Identification Voice — appearance — behaviour
✳: In size (21 cm) and general appearance it greatly resembles the Great Spotted Woodpecker (p. 281), but has a smaller head and shorter, more slender bill. Adults (1) are black, brownish-pink and white, with a red crown. ♂ = ♀ ; the latter may sometimes be distinguished in pairs by having a duller plumage and a smaller red cap on the head. Juv. birds are duller than adults, and the red crown has black markings. ✦: It climbs tree trunks and branches and hangs suspended from these. It generally flies at a low height in shallow undulations. ☉: It fairly often utters its call, a *kek kek*. In spring ♂ utters an unmistakable loud plaintive *kaikh-kaikh-kaikh*. It drums only occasionally and always very briefly. ☜: It may be confused mainly with juv. Great Spotted Woodpeckers and Syrian Woodpeckers, which, however, have a stouter bill, fewer white patches on the wing and different neck and head markings.
Ecology ◑: Mainly old oak stands in lowland districts. ∞: At the nesting grounds by its distinctive call (Feb.—May). Look for the nest by observing the behaviour of adult birds and examining tree holes. In the non-breeding season the birds can be located by their voice or observed boring holes in search of food.
Bionomy ↔: It is a resident bird and leads a solitary life. ⬗: It nests in tree cavities, which it excavates in soft parts of the tree trunk infested by wood fungi. Sometimes it will use the same nest several years in succession. On rare occasions it will nest in a nestbox. The five to six white eggs (23.8×18.2 mm) are laid in Apr.—May. It has one brood a year, nests solitarily, and incubates for 12 days. The young are cared for by both parents, 20 days in the nest and a further 15 days outside the nest. ◐: Insects and their larvae, plant seeds and fruits. Food is gathered mainly on the surface or in cracks in tree trunks or on the ground; less often is it extracted by boring in rotting wood.
Conservation The species is in decline, apparently as a result of the disappearance of old woodlands, which should be protected.

1

Lesser Spotted Woodpecker
Dendrocopos minor

Identification Voice — appearance — size — behaviour
✳: The smallest European woodpecker (15 cm), merely the size of a sparrow. It has a small head, short bill, broad round wings and short wedge-shaped tail. Adults are contrastingly coloured black and white; ♂ (1) has a red crown, which in ♀ is brownish-white. Juv. birds have the underparts brownish with dark markings, ♂ with the crown feathers tipped red. ✦: It climbs the trunks and branches of trees, hanging from slender terminal branches, and behaves in the same manner also on stouter herbaceous plants. It flies at a relatively low height in undulating flight. ☉: It often utters a loud repeated *kikiki*... In spring it also frequently drums on trees, softly but at length and very rapidly. ♋: It is unmistakable; its voice resembles the Eurasian Kestrel's.

Ecology ◈: Broad-leaved woods and cultivated country at lower elevations, including larger parks and gardens in built-up areas. ∞: At the nesting grounds in Mar.—May it may be identified by the calls and behaviour of the birds; locate the nest by observing the birds. In the non-breeding season it may be heard or observed by chance.

Bionomy ↔: It is a resident and solitary bird. ♺: It nests in tree cavities, which it excavates anew each year in soft wood infested by wood fungi, often on side branches. The four to six white eggs (18.8×14.4 mm) are laid in Apr.—June. It has one brood a year, nests solitarily, and incubates for 12 days. The young are cared for by both parents, 20 days in the nest and 12 days outside the nest. ◑: Insects and their larvae, to a lesser extent also plant seeds. Food is gathered on trees and herbaceous plants.

Conservation This is a rather scarce species. The need to protect it is evident, but ways and means of doing so are not clear.

The figures in brackets indicate the numbers of pages
on which the photographs appear.

J. ANDERLE   (131, 266),
F. BALÁT   (32, 33, 86, 114, 115, 117),
J. BOHDAL   (30, 65, 84, 112, 182, 214, 224),
G. GAGNUCCI, Panda photo   (99, 211, 231),
J. FORMÁNEK   (151, 168, 171, 177, 247, 271, 283),
Š. HARVANČÍK   (78, 92, 136, 181, 190, 206, 239, 242, 245),
L. HAUSER (48, 49, 58, 59, 109, 134, 222, 237, 262),
J. HLÁSEK   (34, 75, 76, 79, 80, 83, 105, 107, 122, 123, 159, 175, 198, 202, 217,
    223, 234, 254, 267, 272, 273),
L. HLÁSEK   (35, 50, 54, 60, 64, 72, 82, 85, 87, 89, 90, 100, 130, 132, 135, 143,
    150, 156, 157, 158, 176, 185, 187, 192, 193, 199, 200, 201, 208, 212, 225, 230,
    235, 246, 249, 261, 265, 278, 279),
P. MACHÁČEK   (27, 28, 31, 36, 38, 42, 44, 45, 46, 47, 77, 88, 93, 95, 96, 98,
    101, 103, 106, 111, 113, 126, 152, 160, 170, 186, 189, 197, 203, 210, 213, 215,
    226, 270, 274, 277),
P. PAVLÍK   (40, 62, 63, 66, 67, 69, 70, 74, 110, 124, 128, 129, 133, 137, 139,
    140, 141, 142, 144, 145, 146, 147, 153, 154, 155, 162, 163, 164, 165, 166, 167,
    169, 172, 173, 174, 178, 180, 184, 188, 191, 195, 196, 204, 205, 207, 209, 216,
    219, 220, 227, 228, 229, 232, 233, 236, 238, 240, 241, 243, 244, 248, 256, 257,
    258, 260, 268, 269, 276, 280, 281, 282),
A. PETRETTI, Panda photo   (104, 116),
P. PODPĚRA   (108, 194, 164),
T. PODPĚRA (138),
H. SCHEUFLER   (81, 91),
E. STUDNIČKA   (52, 55, 56, 68, 94, 120, 127, 218, 253, 255),
J. ŠEVČÍK   (26, 39, 41, 57, 61, 71, 97, 102),
M. ZELINKA   (179),
J. ZUMR   (73, 252, 259).

Bibliography

Austin, O. L. Jr., and Singer, A.: *Birds of the World*. London, New York, Sydney, Toronto, 2nd ed. 1970.

Bergmann, H.—H., and Helb, H.—W.: *Die Stimmen der Vögel Europas*. München 1982.

Bezzel, E.: *Kompendium der Vögel Mitteleuropas: Nonpasseriformes — Nichtsingvögel*. Wiesbaden 1985.

Bruun, B. et al.: *The Hamlyn Guide to Birds of Britain and Europe*. London, New York, Sydney, Toronto 1986.

Cady, M., and Hume, R.: *The Complete Book of British Birds*. Basingstoke and Sandy 1988.

Campbell, B., and Lack, E. (Eds): *A Dictionary of Birds*. Calton 1985.

Chandler, R. J.: *The Macmillan Field Guide to North Atlantic Shorebirds*. London 1989.

Cramp, S. (Chief-editor): *Handbook of the Birds of Europe, the Middle East and North Africa (The Birds of the Western Palearctic)*. Vol. I.—V., Oxford, London, New York 1977.

Delin, H., and Svensson, L.: *Photographic Guide to the Birds of Britain and Europe*. London 1988.

Ferguson-Lees, J., Willis, I., and Sharrock, J. T. R.: *The Shell Guide to the Birds of Britain and Ireland*. London 1983.

Glutz von Blotzheim, U., Bauer, K., et al.: *Handbuch der Vögel Mitteleuropas*. Bd I.—XI., Wiesbaden 1966.

Harris, A., Tucker, L., and Vinicombe, K.: *The Macmillan Field Guide to Bird Identification*. London 1989.

Harrison, C.: *An Atlas of the Birds of the Western Palearctic*. London 1982.

Harrison, C. O. J.: *A Field Guide to the Nests, Eggs and Nestlings of British and European Birds*. London 1985.

Holden, P., and Sharrock, J. T. R.: *The RSPB Book of British Birds*. London 1982.

Howard, R., and Moore, A.: *A Complete Checklist of the Birds of the World*. Oxford rev. ed. 1984.

Hume, R., Wallace, I., et al.: *Birds by Character*. London 1990.

Palmer, S., and Boswall, J.: *The Peterson Field Guide to the Bird Songs of Britain and Europe*. 15 LP records, 16 cassettes.

Parslow, J. L. F., and Everett, M. J.: *Birds in Need of Special Protection in Europe*. Strasbourg 1981.

Peterson, R. T., Mountfort, G., and Hollom, P. A. D.: *A Field Guide to the Birds of Britain and Europe*. London, 4th ed. 1984.

Svensson, L.: *Identification Guide to European Passerines*. Stockholm (3rd ed.) 1984.

Index of common names

Index of Latin names